BECOME A MODERN SHAPESHIFTER

In more ancient times, there were individuals with a capability of living between the physical and the spiritual planes. They could adapt themselves and change their energies according to their life circumstances. They could shape and mold their environments, becoming whatever they dreamed. They were the *shapeshifters* of myth and lore. They lived the dreamtime while awake or asleep.

What humanity is just again rediscovering is that what we dream *can* become real. Learning to walk the thread of life between the worlds—to become a shapeshifter—is available to all. The techniques may have been lost, but they were not destroyed.

Nothing is so universally fascinating as our dreams. They shift and dance, amaze and frighten. They are an important part of our life, and yet there has always been the assumption that this life function is beyond our control. NOTHING IS FURTHER FROM THE TRUTH.

We all can learn to shift the energies of our consciousness, the circumstances of our lives, and we all have the potential to stimulate dream awareness for greater insight and fulfillment. Through the use of our ancient myths and tales, we can initiate a process of dream alchemy. We can control the dream state and its energies so that we can be put in touch with realities and energies that can open us to greater productivity during our waking hours.

When we control the dream state, we unveil our own inner potential, clear out the debris we have accumulated within our subconscious. We can assist and inspire ourselves and others, and we can visit all spots upon the earth. We can work with time to correct the "karma" of the past and set new patterns for the future. We can reshape our lives to align our circumstances with our greatest visions. We can begin the process of weaving a fabric of life that frees us from our greatest "demons" and unveils our greatest strengths. We open ourselves to all doorways, all time and all dreams.

About the Author

Ted Andrews is a full-time author, student and teacher in the metaphysical and spiritual fields. He conducts seminars, symposiums, workshops and lectures throughout the country on many facets of ancient mysticism. Ted worked with past-life analysis, auric interpretation, numerology, the tarot and the Qabala as methods of developing and enhancing inner potential. He is a clairvoyant and a certified spiritualist medium.

Ted is also active in the healing field. He is certified in basic hypnosis and acupressure and is involved in the study and use of herbs as an alternative path. He combines his musical training with more than twenty years of concentrated metaphysical study in the application of "Directed Esoteric Sound" in the healing process. He uses this with other holistic methods of healing, such as "etheric touch," aura and chakra balancing, and crystal stone and gem techniques, in creating individual healing therapies and higher states of consciousness.

He is a contributing author to various metaphysical magazines with articles published on such subjects as "Occult Christianity," "Working With Our Angelic Brethren," and "Metaphysical Mirrors in Our Lives."

To Write to the Author

We cannot guarantee that every letter written to the author can be answered, but all will be forwarded. Both the author and the publisher appreciate hearing from readers, learning of your enjoyment and benefit from this book. Llewellyn also publishes a bi-monthly news magazine with news and reviews of practical esoteric studies and articles helpful to the student, and some readers' questions and comments to the author may be answered through this magazine's columns if permission to do so is included in the original letter. The author sometimes participates in seminars and workshops, and dates and places are announced in *The Llewellyn New Times*. To write to the author, or to ask a question, write to:

Ted Andrews
c/o THE LLEWELLYN NEW TIMES
P.O. BOX 64383-017, St. Paul, MN 55164-0383, U.S.A.
Please enclose a self-addressed, stamped envelope for reply, or $1.00 to cover costs.

The Inner Guide Series

DREAM ALCHEMY:

Shaping Our Dreams to Transform Our Lives

Ted Andrews

1991
Llewellyn Publications
St. Paul, Minnesota 55164-0383 USA

First Edition
First Printing

Cover painting ©1991 Liz Dodson
  in cooperation with Spirit Art, Minneapolis, MN

Library of Congress Cataloging-in-Publications Data
Andrews, Ted, 1952-
    Dream alchemy : shaping our dreams to transform our lives /
Ted Andrews. — 1st ed.
      p. cm. — (Llewellyn's Inner guide series)
    Includes bibliographical references.
    ISBN 0-87542-017-6 : $12.95
    1. Dreams. I. Title. II. Series: Llewellyn Inner Guide Series
BF1078.A59   1991
135'.3—dc20   91-19444
                                                            CIP

Llewellyn Publications
A Division of Llewellyn Worldwide, Ltd.
P.O. Box 64383, St. Paul, MN 55164-0383

About Llewellyn's Inner Guide Series

Each of us faces in two directions, like the alchemists' double-headed Phoenix risen from ashes and born again.

In one direction, we face the Outer World—and know that should we ignore this world we suffer and die; in the other direction we face the Inner World—which all too commonly we ignore to our peril!

It is to this Inner World we now turn—without ignoring the Outer one—to avoid the perils facing all humankind. To meet the challenges of today, we need new Awareness, and new sources of Knowledge and Power—and these may be found only within the Ultimate Source from which all have their being, and that way lies within.

The Western Esoteric Tradition—in its Mystery Schools, Magical Orders, and secret Lodges—has taught many techniques for Inner Awareness and growth to those who have sought out such wisdom. Their guidance has been there, accessible to the few who could be provided for by the Lodge system, filling the needs of the times.

Now the time has come to expand access to these esoteric techniques beyond the limitations of the Lodge, and to publish them in modern form for the benefit of the many. *Just as humankind stands at the edge of Outer Space, so must we—simultaneously—explore the paths and Worlds of Inner Space.*

Each book in the Inner Guide series, as in Llewellyn's Practical Guide series, is self-contained and complete in presentation—yet each is also like a building-block that can be placed anywhere in the personal structure that is your evolving self. Practical Guides build your inner talents for application in the outer world; Inner Guides direct your inward growth—yet, they too, have measurable effect in the outer world, for both benefit the Whole Person.

—*Carl Llewellyn Weschcke*

Other Books by Ted Andrews
Simplified Magic, 1989
Imagick, 1989
The Sacred Power in Your Name, 1990
How to See and Read the Aura, 1991

Forthcoming
Sacred Sounds: Transformation Through Music and Words
How to Uncover Your Past Lives
How to Meet and Work with Spirit Guides
The Healer's Manual

DEDICATION

To Nettie, Paul, Christian, and Gretel—
To their dreams of a thousand dogs and
To all of the dreams they have yet to unfold.

TABLE OF CONTENTS

INTRODUCTION

Modern Shapeshifting
and Dream Alchemy

Nothing is so universally fascinating as dreams. Dreams shift and dance. They mold themselves into scenarios of wonder and terror. They delight and amaze, amuse and frighten. They are never the same and yet always the same in the way they manifest themselves within our lives. I once heard a quote attributed to Cicero: "Nihil tam prepostere, tam monstuose cogitari potest quod non possimus somnare."* ("We can dream about anything, no matter how preposterous or unnatural it may be.")

Dreams are a part of our life. And as with all life functions, they serve a purpose. Discerning that purpose and controlling that function is the purpose of this book.

In more ancient times there were certain individuals with a capability of living between the physical and the spiritual. They could adapt themselves and change their energies according to their life circumstances. They could shape and mold the life environment, creating whatever they desired and becoming whatever they dreamed. These were the shapeshifters. They lived the dreamtime while awake or asleep. There were no limits to where they could go or who they could be. These were the alchemists, shamans, magicians and wise ones of our myths, tales and legends.

Learning to shift the dream to reality and the reality into dream—to walk the thread of life between the worlds—is to become the dreamwalker. Much of the ancient knowledge of techniques for doing this has been lost, but they have not been destroyed. They can be found again by those willing to put forth the effort and follow the

---

*Moses Hadas, *Scipio's Dream*, (New York: Modern Library, 1955).

journey. There are guides, reflections, and ways to unfold this knowledge within ourselves.

WHO IS A SHAPESHIFTER?

Shapeshifting is natural to all of humanity. Everyday on some level, we shift our energies to meet daily trials, responsibilities and obligations with great success. We learn early in life when and how to smile, when to be serious or studious, according to the occasion. Shapeshifting is not just transforming ourselves into some beast, as often told in ancient tales (tales more symbolic than actual). It is a matter of controlling and utilizing one's highest energy and potential to meet whatever situation life requires. It is a process of becoming active, of controlling what manifests rather than being passive and allowing to manifest whatever may come.

A shapeshifter is one who can . . .
— relate to all people and adjust behaviors to work and live as conditions may warrant.
— be gentle according to need and yet be capable of expressing great strength.
— discipline himself or herself to achieve a goal.
— adapt to change, pleasant or otherwise.
— turn a foul mood into a pleasant one.
— take limitations, self-imposed or otherwise, and use them as part of a growth process.
— find the creative possibilities within limitation and thus overcome limitation.
— overcome fear.
— put aside hurt and anger to achieve a result.
— transform the pains and hindrances of life—past and present.

It is this kind of shapeshifting which we can develop to a fine degree. It is something we can all accomplish. It is the spiritual lesson behind all dreams, regardless of content or message. We have taken physical form to shift the energies and consciousness of the past into new and more creative expressions. It is our dreams which provide the reminders and means of facilitating this shifting of energy on all levels.

Learning to employ ancient and modern techniques to facilitate this process in all areas of our life is part of the purpose of this text. We can learn to shift the energies of consciousness, to shift the past and present circumstances of our lives. We can learn to do this in a controlled, gentle manner. We can learn to shift into higher awareness when reviewing past experiences. And we can reshape energies to eliminate karma or to manifest new opportunities. It all lies within our bounds.

We all have the potential to become a dream walker, one who can stimulate the dream awareness for greater insight, fulfillment, love and abundance. The dream life is essential to our growth. It is not a replacement for our waking life, rather it strengthens and illuminates it for our benefit.

Our nocturnal life puts us in touch with realities and energies that can open us to greater productivity during our waking hours. We can become as useful and active within our sleep as we are when awake. We each have the potential of becoming our own invisible helper.

When we learn to shapeshift and control the energies of the dream state, our lives are rewarded. There are many ways to use our formally dormant time. We can use the hours of sleep to help those who suffer or sorrow. We can learn to extend help and encouragement to both the living and the dead. We can give and receive higher instruction. We can assist, inspire and advise those who would be unlikely to listen to us while awake. We can open ourselves to creative inspiration. We can visit all spots upon the planet. All art and music is at our disposal.We can work with time to correct the karma of the past and set new patterns for the future. We can re-manifest situations that were handled improperly so they may be straightened out. The potentials are unlimited.

Dream alchemy is the process of learning to control and direct the dream state and all of its energies so that we can better come to know ourselves on all levels. It is using dream energy to initiate the process of transformation.

In ancient societies, certain laws were taught to the spiritual student. When learned, these laws enabled the individual to control various aspects of energy in the natural and supernatural worlds. The laws and principles were universal, but every society expressed them in the way best understood by those living in that particular time and environment. One of these which bears strongly upon dream alchemy is the ancient Hermetic Principle of Correspondence: "As above, so below; as below, so above."

This principle teaches us that all things are connected. Everything upon the Earth is reflected in the Heavens, and everything in the Heavens is reflected upon the Earth. What we do on one level will affect us on all levels. Nothing is disconnected. Thus our sleeping life and our waking life are linked. They reflect and influence each other.

Working with this principle is what enables us to uncover the hidden side of things. It enables us to make correlations. These may be the correlations of hidden phenomena to the natural world or it may be the hidden motives, emotions or mental and spiritual energies influencing our physical lives. Stimulating greater dream activity and awareness, and then learning to control and mold those energies according to certain patterns, opens us to the hidden side of things.

Formal initiation practices are no longer necessary for awakening greater spiritual expression. Spiritual unfoldment does not have to involve severe initiation trials. We can open ourselves to higher learning and perception through the dreams which come naturally and gently to us every night.

For those just opening to the psychic and spiritual realms, dreams are one of the safest and easiest ways of beginning. No tools are necessary. There are no expenses. It is safe, and it involves only limited waking time to elicit results. The only thing required in bridging our consciousness to higher realms is a better understanding of the dream process and a little persistence.

As we learn to work with and control our dream time energies, we also initiate control over our waking life situations as well. The dreams do not eliminate the obstacles, but they can be used to reveal our obstacles as a means to a higher end. What we do on one level affects us on all others. What we do in the dream time will reflect and affect what we do in the waking time.

Commitment to dream alchemy is a commitment to becoming the modern spiritual disciple. We are learning to alter, control and manipulate our waking and sleeping energies for growth. We are learning to become the spiritual seer and sage—the Merlin of our life. "Even during his lifetime Merlin was largely ahistorical and unrevealed. He is even unrevealed in the manuscripts that recount his life story. He was always largely unknown to the greater public, except as 'Merlin.' When he was summoned by kings or needed desperately to recruit other allies, he came silently, disguised as a poor shepherd, as a woodcutter or as a peasant. Even the sovereigns failed to recognize him under his various disguises. He practiced this concealment habitually and for a long period of time."*

Like this description of Merlin, our dreams come silently and under many guises. We can learn to transmute our dream energies to create a new "you." There are many ways in which the transmutational and transformational process can be initiated. Dream alchemy is but one, and it is natural to us all.

We can become the shapeshifters of our lives, shifting the shape of them into alignment with our greatest dreams and visions. We can recreate and re-manifest what has been relegated to fiction and myth. Our lives can become like that of all the sages throughout history. We can walk in all environs visible and invisible. We can bridge the physical to the spiritual and back again. We can weave a fabric of life that becomes a carpet of continually shifting fibers of light and radiance, a carpet upon which we can walk through all doorways, all times and all dreams.

---

* Norma Lorre Goodrich, *Merlin*, (New York: Franklyn Watts, 1987), p. 9.

PART ONE:

The Mysteries of Sleep and Dreams

"Do we dream because we fear going to sleep and never waking up or do we dream to prove there is no death?"

—Anonymous

"Dreams more than anything entice us toward hope. And when our hearts spontaneously present hope to us, as happens within our sleeping state, then we have in the promise of our dreams a pledge from the divinity!"

—Synesius

CHAPTER ONE

A Different Look at Dream Processes

Dreams play a vital role in our day to day life. They are more than a stress-release mechanism. Dreams put us in touch with other realities and planes of life not consciously acknowledged.

We are more than just physical beings. We are comprised of other, more subtle bands of energy. Whether we call these subtle bodies our emotional, mental and spiritual selves does not really matter. We must learn to recognize that we operate on more than just the purely physical level. These more subtle aspects of our selves interpenetrate and influence us while in the physical and will do so throughout our entire incarnation. (Refer to "The Incarnation Process" diagram in this chapter.) These subtle aspects of our consciousness and energy place us in contact with other dimensions and planes. They give us more mobility and control, more than what we often believe is possible. Learning to recognize the subtle interplays between the different aspects of ourselves and learning to control and direct them is what all dream work is about.

Occultism teaches us that control of the environment begins with control of the self, and yet there is an aspect of all of our lives that we do not try to control because we believe it can't be controlled. That aspect is our dreams! We believe we can't change what we are dreaming. We believe we can't change our awareness while in the dream. We believe we can't program dreams for insight, inspiration or manifestation. We believe it is simply a phenomer the night that operates according to some strange, unk Anything which plays a vital function in our lives ca Dreams play a vital function, but we have come to a part of an autonomic process that we cannot control. W

3

THE INCARNATION PROCESS

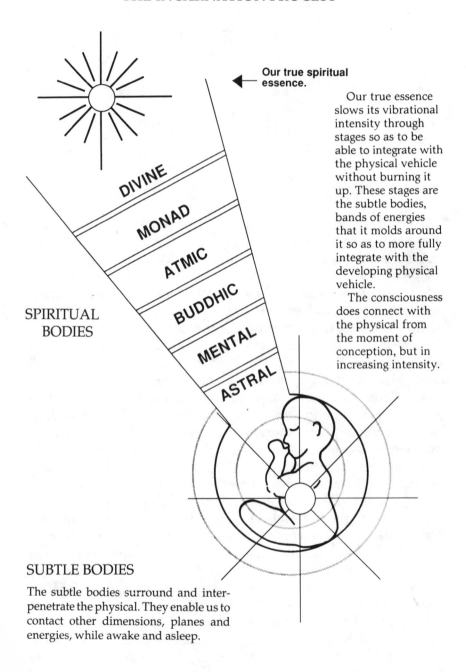

Our true spiritual essence.

Our true essence slows its vibrational intensity through stages so as to be able to integrate with the physical vehicle without burning it up. These stages are the subtle bodies, bands of energies that it molds around it so as to more fully integrate with the developing physical vehicle.

The consciousness does connect with the physical from the moment of conception, but in increasing intensity.

DIVINE

MONAD

ATMIC

BUDDHIC

MENTAL

ASTRAL

SPIRITUAL
BODIES

SUBTLE BODIES

The subtle bodies surround and inter-penetrate the physical. They enable us to contact other dimensions, planes and energies, while awake and asleep.

are simply at the mercy of whatever that process wishes to present to us each night. Nothing could be further from the truth.

You can influence your dreams to empower yourself. This book is designed to help you do that. By following the suggestions outlined in this book, you will learn:

1. How to alter sleep conditions.

2. How to stimulate greater dream activity.

3. How to understand and use mythic symbols and images to shape dreams and meditations in order to provide information along lines you more consciously choose.

4. How you can use the dream state to open more fully and consciously to the subtle, archetypal energies and dimensions influencing you.

5. How to use dream work as a dynamic process of self-understanding and self-transformation.

WHAT ARE DREAMS?

Dreams are a reality separate from our waking consciousness. The images shift and change, scenarios altering in seemingly disconnected manners. They are farcical and they are terrifying. They are ridiculous and serious. They are emotional and they are spiritual. They are to most people incomprehensible.

Dreams have been defined in many ways by many people. They have been called manifestations of images and sounds. They have been likened to a mirror of our life—conscious and unconscious. They have been called creations of the night. They mystify and perplex, but they unite us all, for it is the one experience we all share—whether rich or poor, mighty or weak, male or female, earthy or spiritual. We all dream. If for no other reason than its universality, dream work should be a part of our overall educational process.

Every night when we fall asleep, certain processes take place. It is important to understand them, so we can more easily control and direct them. The subtle bodies work with the physical functions and energies. The astral (one of the subtle bodies) is most active during altered states of consciousness—especially sleep. When we lie down to sleep, the subtle bodies exteriorize themselves from the physical. This exteriorizing serves several purposes. It enables the energy debris and tension accumulated during the day to be shaken

THE EXTERIORIZING OF THE SUBTLE BODIES

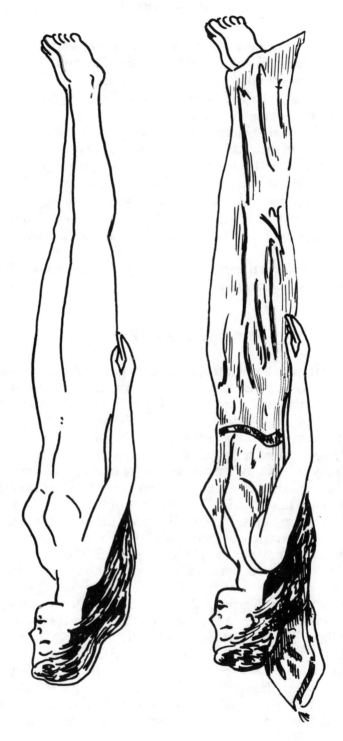

By going outside the physical body, the subtle bodies are able to more easily shake off the debris of emotional and mental energies accumulated throughout the day. This facilitates the rest and recuperation of the physical body. Part of this shaking off is reflected in our dream's scenarios.

free from the energy fibers of your essence. It enables the physical body to relax and re-energize itself. It provides opportunities to connect with teachings and activities on other dimensions. Without the encumbrance of the physical body, the subtle bodies can draw energy directly from the universe. Then upon awakening, when the subtle bodies reintegrate with the physical, the physical body is re-energized.

One of the problems of modern society involves the use of alarm clocks. The alarm clock may sound before the subtle bodies have reintegrated in a fully balanced manner. It jars this integration of energies. As a result, an individual may spend the entire morning drinking cups of coffee and trying to get his/her "act together." It may take until mid-morning or longer before the subtle shuffles itself into proper alignment. Through the techniques within this book, this can eventually be avoided. As you learn to control the dream state, you will also be learning to control the awakening as well.

As this separation occurs during sleep, the ego also separates itself from the physical, working through the subtle bodies for various purposes. These purposes can be determined and controlled. Even though the ego withdraws from the physical, it maintains close contact with it. This is accomplished through a band of energy known as the etheric.

The etheric is the bridge; it connects the astral and other subtle bodies to the physical. It is like a web of energy that protects the physical body. It prevents undue and premature influence from the more subtle planes of life and from the beings and energies operating through them. It also serves to ground our consciousness to the physical, for this is where we have come to grow, learn and express our creative spiritual energies. It is often this band of energy which can prevent clear recollection of everything that goes on during the sleep state.

Learning to exercise and strengthen the subtle bodies so that we can expand our consciousness is one of the functions of dream work. Exercises in meditation and visualization also serve to develop the ability to extend the consciousness beyond physical life dimensions.

It is like learning to do anything. There are always preparatory exercises. These exercises stretch and strengthen our muscles to prevent injuries and imbalances. We do not attempt intricate gymnastic moves without learning the basics or without loosening and stretching the muscles before performance. It is the same with dream alchemy. There are exercises to loosen and stretch our energies and develop the ability to extend the consciousness to those more subtle realms with greater control and awareness.

When we attempt to shape our dreams, we do so for a variety of reasons. It is a dynamic prelude to conscious astral projection, the use of our subtle bodies as separate vehicles of consciousness to explore the more subtle dimensions surrounding us. Dream alchemy—especially mythic dream work as outlined in Part Two—is a powerful means of strengthening these energies.

As we work with the process outlined within this book, we are asserting control over a previously uncontrolled aspect of our lives. This will affect other areas of our lives. What we do on one level affects us on all levels. As we learn to shape and control our sleep and dream processes, we initiate opportunity to shape and change our waking life processes as well. "As above, so below; as below, so above."

CHAPTER TWO

Understanding Our
Dream Archetypes

Dreams are multidimensional. No matter how much we try to control and direct them, they will always reflect energies that deal with all aspects of ourselves. They will not limit themselves to our singular purposes. They are like gifts within gifts.

We can develop lucid consciousness within the dream scenario, but there will always be a free variable. The scenario will reflect more than what we may have set in motion. The images, sounds and symbols will reflect our individual purposes, but they will also reflect what is going on in our life on physical, emotional, mental and spiritual levels. It is such a dynamic, creative process that it can follow the program we have shaped for it, and it will still incorporate information and perspectives that we can apply to other aspects of our life as well.

Anyone wishing to make the most of dream alchemy must learn to work with symbology. It is the language of the unconscious mind. Symbols are the only way the unconscious mind has to communicate with the conscious aspect of ourselves. If we intend to step out upon the path of higher and controlled evolution, we must become aware of the power and significance of symbols within all aspects of our consciousness.

To understand symbols is to understand ourselves. They provide the clues to our deep-rooted, instinctive actions and capabilities. They help us to understand what the basis is for our beliefs, superstitions and fears. They are the keys to opening levels of being we have either ignored or of which we have been ignorant. Symbols form the bridge that enables us to cross from the rational to the progressively intuitive levels of being. (Refer to the diagram "Forming the Rainbow Bridge," in this chapter.)

9

FORMING THE RAINBOW BRIDGE

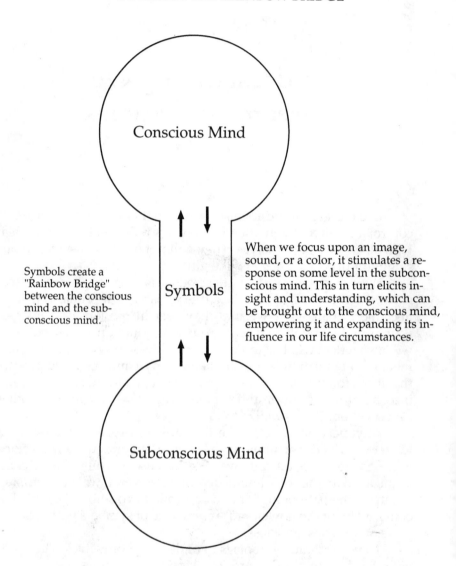

Symbols create a "Rainbow Bridge" between the conscious mind and the subconscious mind.

Symbols

When we focus upon an image, sound, or a color, it stimulates a response on some level in the subconscious mind. This in turn elicits insight and understanding, which can be brought out to the conscious mind, empowering it and expanding its influence in our life circumstances.

Symbols form the bridge between the subconscious mind and the conscious mind. The symbol reflects what is the true reality within the individual. By learning to interpret it more consciously, we form a universal bridge between both aspects of our selves. When both work together we have access to all realms and all times and we expand our ability to impact more effectively upon our world.

Dreams help us to solve problems and to quicken us to new potentials. Because of this, the imagery is the key to understanding and actualizing the messages we receive through them. This is especially important if we remember that every dream reflects energies from all levels of our being—body, mind and soul. Unless we understand the language, we cannot receive the message.

All symbols can be broken down into three basic categories:

1. *Conventional*: These are images and symbols conventional in their significance to all. They hold the same basic reference for everyone. If we see the image of the American flag, it brings to mind for most of us references to patriotism and America. It has a significance basic and common to most people.

2. *Personal*: Personal images and symbols have a significance peculiar to yourself. An acorn to many people may be "the seed from which comes the mighty oak," but there might be someone who associates pain with the acorn. Maybe as a child an acorn fell from a tree and hit them on the head.

We make all symbols personal. No matter whether it is a conventional or an archetypal symbol, we each add our own peculiar significance and meaning to it. When we use symbols and images in magic, meditation, and dream alchemy to invoke certain energies into our life, the energy invoked will be similar to that invoked by others using that same symbol or image. The symbol will translate itself and manifest in a manner uniquely appropriate to you and your life circumstances.

3. *Archetypal*: Archetypal symbols and images are universal. They are the primal energy pattern, translated through secondary images. They are shared by all people and ultimately affect us all in the same manner. Carl Jung referred to them as part of the "collective unconscious." They are the energies behind all other images and symbols. They are the source of energy and power behind the images and symbols we employ.

All symbols are derived from an archetypal source and thus will lead us back to that source at some point. In dream alchemy, the images and symbols reflect certain archetypal energies that are most active within our life. In the mythic dream work techniques of Part Two, we use the symbols and images of myths to release specific manifestations of those archetypal forces into our life.

Symbols with universal meanings do exist, but we will place our own particular twist upon the symbols we use. Symbols—whether conventional, personal or archetypal—touch our own objective and subjective realities. They are the means by which our subconscious mind can bring forth information that might not otherwise make it to the conscious, rational mind.

Sometimes the subconscious presents information we'd rather not face. As we go through life, we tend to form our own realities. We allow our energies to adjust to those realities or to become complacent about them. This complacency, manifesting through our convictions and opinions, prevents us from thinking and developing fully. When this happens, the subconscious mind responds with a new symbol or a strong dream (often in the form of a nightmare) to shake that complacency.

For this reason, the meaning of symbols will change as you go through life. As a child, a snake may signify something to be afraid of, but as we evolve and expand our knowledge, we realize that it is more than just a personal symbol of our fears. It is a universal symbol of higher knowledge and initiation. We move from a superficial significance to a more archetypal experience of the symbol. (Refer to the diagram "Touching the Archetypes," in this chapter.)

UNDERSTANDING OUR SYMBOLOGY

All symbols have an exoteric and an esoteric aspect to them. Learning to understand and work with them is the key to using our dream communications to the fullest. Dream symbols represent more than that which is first apparent, but we must always start with the obvious and work to the not-so-obvious.

A spiritually trained individual will be able to interpret dreams more fully and accurately than one who depends upon reason alone. We can come to understand the messages of our dreams as much by intuition and empathy as by analysis.

Symbols and images within dreams take forms which portray both obvious and abstract qualities. We must learn to see and recognize what is suggested by the imagery on all levels of our life. A symbol will usually mean at the very least what we think it means. A dream symbol or image is extremely chameleonlike, assuming a manner that encompasses the moods and attitudes of the individual. Thus we must learn to move beyond the obvious. We must

TOUCHING THE ARCHETYPES

Superficial Level of the Image, Symbol or Dream Scenario

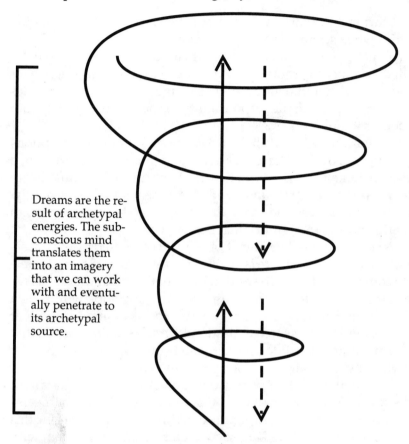

Dreams are the result of archetypal energies. The subconscious mind translates them into an imagery that we can work with and eventually penetrate to its archetypal source.

Archetypal Source
of Dream or Meditation Imagery

All symbols and images are connected to some archetypal energy in the universe. When we meditate upon them, we release those energies into our lives in some area. The dream images show us where archetypal energies are playing so that we can give them greater focus and attention. The dream images and scenarios may reflect a variety of archetypal energies that are most active within your life at that moment or that need to be more focused upon at that moment. The images will be drawn from many sources, so as to move the individual beyond a superficial observation or acknowledgement of the dream activity. They are invitations to expand one's perception and cognition.

overcome superficiality in dealing with symbology. (This superficiality, the treating of our dreams and dream imagery with little significance, is caused by indifference to the importance of the dream state.)

Learning to work with symbology enhances our reasoning abilities while stimulating greater originality at the same time. We learn to use them to understand and to induce experiences. We use them to trigger new thoughts and awarenesses, and through symbology we open to the hidden side of things. A symbol both hides and reveals—placing the responsibility for our growth and its consequences in our own laps!

In working with symbols, we start with our own perceptions and insights. To awaken from a dream and immediately reach for a dream dictionary serves little beneficial purpose. We must begin with what that imagery and symbology means to us personally. Once we have determined that, then we can go to other sources to enhance and expand our original perceptions.

When confronted by a symbol, we are confronted by the uncertainties of life because there is never 100% assurance of correct interpretation. We are forced to see that life is not as cut and dried as we like it to be. Working with dream alchemy develops within us a greater flexibility of response to life. It helps us to understand that we must continually search and extend ourselves. It teaches us that we can use others as guides, but ultimately the responsibility is ours. Growth only comes through our persistent efforts.

In all of the ancient mystery traditions, symbology was taught and studied. The masters would weave their teachings with symbolism, thus hiding the ancient secrets from the profane. In this manner, the secrets were kept sacred. Our dreams are woven with symbolism, and often this symbolism seems as incomprehensible as the ancient secrets. But, if we intend to enhance our own spiritual growth and knowledge, we must come to understand our own symbology. Dream work is the easiest method of doing so. Our subconscious mind chooses symbols and images that it knows we can understand and use if we put forth the effort. We are *never* given a dream that we cannot interpret!

The human mind makes associations with symbols and images and their corresponding realities in three different ways. The first is through similarity. The image or symbol is similar to something recognizable. The symbol and some aspect of the individual's life always have something in common. The second way is through contiguity. This is a free association between the image/symbol and that which it represents. If we dream of bread, for example, we might also associate butter and jelly with it. This is an important part of the interpreting process. The third manner is through opposition. Sometimes we are resistant to straightforward messages in the dreams. We may be complacent or denying aspects of our life. In order to get a message across, the back door is utilized. A dream sequence will unfold that is opposite to what it appears to be. It is as if the subconscious mind is using reverse psychology to get us to pay attention.

Recognizing whether your symbols and dream scenarios are ones of similarity, contiguity or opposition comes only with time and practice. As you work with your dreams, you will discover the method that your subconscious mind uses. Just as no two people speak in the same manner, neither do any two subconscious minds. Studying the symbols you use in your day-to-day life will open you to greater insight to the symbology within your dreams. What is the significance behind the symbols in your church? Examine your surroundings, your decor and furnishings. What do they say about you? Look at your clothes, trinkets, jewelry, etc. What are they symbolizing about you and your attitudes? Read the ancient myths and scriptures with an eye for the symbolism within them. Look at the architecture of our culture. What does that reflect?

Symbols are the bridges between thinking and being. They provide messages about the world of reality around us. Because of this, most symbols speak figuratively and not literally. The symbology of your dreams will be couched in imagery that you can understand. In order to communicate messages to your conscious mind, the subconscious will draw upon all aspects of your life. Childhood memories, the day's activities, people from your past and present, religious and social attitudes and anything with which you are familiar or to which you have been exposed may be used to communicate with you. Symbols are the language that the higher self speaks in. The subconscious mind translates those symbols into imagery and scenarios that you can work with and understand. The interpretations will be individualistic, and they will change as you progress through life. Spontaneous interpretation is important, but do not stop there.

GUIDELINES TO DREAM SYMBOL INTERPRETATIONS

All dreams work to accomplish one of two things: to solve the problems of the dreamer's conscious, waking life and to quicken the dreamer to new potentials and creativity. Because dreams come from all levels of our being, understanding the imagery and type of dream is the key to understanding and actualizing the message you receive during sleep. Some dreams are seemingly meaningless. Often these are psychic exercises for the subtle bodies. They serve to shake off that energy debris of the day and to stretch and strengthen the astral muscles. Even among those dreams which are exercises, there will always be some other message or meaning that can be ascertained.

Remember that the symbol could be literally representing what it appears to be, as well as having other references. The images and symbols of the dream scenario may also represent aspects of your personality. Begin with first impressions and then move on. Don't stop with the obvious. Dreams are representations, not reproductions. The dream images *always* represent more than themselves, and so the more we work with them, the more we will understand.

Symbols express that for which we have no words. By being willing to work with them, we utilize both hemispheres of the brain and more fully tap the subconscious mind, which in turn opens the doors to our intuitive selves. Dreams do not come to tell us what we already very consciously perceive.

Look at the dream images and symbols as pieces of a puzzle that can put together only by finding out what they mean to you. How do you relate to the dream? Begin by looking at how the dream could be reflecting something going on in your waking life. Then move to the more subtle. Free associate with the dream images. What is the first thing that you would normally think about in connection to that symbol or image, activity or person appearing in your dream scenario? Even though other individuals appear in your dream, they may be doing more than representing themselves. They may also also represent qualities or characteristics. For example, you may dream of your grandfather, a man who was very kind to you. The quality of kindness is associated with your grandfather, so dreaming of him could symbolize kindness as well.

Examine the emotions within the dream scenario. What is the

predominant emotion associated with the dream? When you awaken, does a particular feeling remain? Are you frightened, frustrated, happy, excited? Dreams often exaggerate emotions, qualities and situations to get a particular message across to an individual. This does not mean that you have that quality or will experience that situation to the intensity experienced within the dream. When this occurs, we are often being given a strong thump on the head to pay attention. This is what nightmares do. They are dynamic calls for attention. They show us our greatest fears, fears that must be confronted.

Dreams often can come in a series. The various dreams in a single night or a single week may simply be different in their form but not in the underlying message. The subconscious mind may be communicating the same message to you in different ways to make sure that you do receive the message. Look for relationships and symbols that reoccur and notice the similarities. Ask yourself what they have in common.

Do not lose touch with your common sense in dream work. Many dreams may seem on the surface to portend future events or dramatic situations. Do not jump to conclusions. With practice, you will be able to discern if a dream is one of precognition (reflecting future events). Remember that it may be the emotion generated that is key, and the scenario that generated it is simply a tool to make sure the message is received. Proper dream interpretation leads toward greater understanding of yourself. It involves developing the ability to actualize the new insight into your day-to-day life circumstances.

RECOGNIZING THE ARCHETYPES IN YOUR DREAMS

The archetype is the primordial source or energy, translated through symbols and images into our dreams. Just as the moon reflects the light of the sun, so the images and symbols of our dreams reflect the archetypal energies at play in our lives. In and of themselves, they are not sources of light, but their ability to reflect enables us to see more clearly. The subconscious mind takes this abstract, archetypal energy operating within our life and translates it into dream symbols and imagery. When we work with that imagery, it leads us back to the primal source. We begin to see what archetypal forces are most predominant within our lives. As we work with our dream imagery and symbols, we will be able to apply more universal meaning to it.

Part of the process of dream alchemy is learning to manipulate symbols and images to elicit specific effects in our dream states. It involves learning to connect and communicate with those more dynamic archetypal forces.We must recognize that symbols and images touch both objective and subjective realities of the individual. They are the means by which the subconscious can bring forth information to the rational mind. It is also the means by which the rational mind can link with deeper levels of the subconscious which is the mediator and translator of the archetypal forces of our life.

Carl Jung categorized the archetypal energies into seven basic types. These seven types manifest and reflect themselves in our lives through a variety of symbols and images.

1. ARCHETYPE OF THE SELF
Common Symbols: Homes and houses, books, temples, eggs, seeds,
lit candles, births, weddings, gifts, cars.

This is the energy of the true self, that which lies behind our personas and delusions in everyday life. It deals with our ego and individuality, our creative abilities and the gifts/potentials that lie within. It is the source of our own innate power. Many dreams reflect a lack of use, misuse and even abuse of our creative energies. The symbology and imagery translated from this archetype is designed to inspire and awaken the higher self within us. In many ways, all dreams can be seen as originating from and reflecting this archetypal force. All dreams do help us to grow to our potentials. When the symbology and imagery of the dream most dynamically reflects energies of the self, this can be a call to do more work and to prepare for more growth in your outer life.

2. ARCHETYPE OF THE FEMININE
Common Symbols: Throne, moon, tapestries, veils, water, beds, spiders, cave, womb, gates, doorways, fertility, the night, and all female persons.

We are all a combination of feminine and masculine energies. This is often expressed in many ways: yin and yang, magnetic and electric, negative and positive, receptive and assertive, intuitive and rational, etc. The feminine energy in life is what creates relationships. It is the creative force for the beauty and flow of life. It is the force of the intuition, receptive and accepting. It can nurture and it can suffocate. It is intuitive and non-logical. The archetypal feminine has had many symbolic associations in myth, legends and dreams. The dream state itself is a function of the feminine energies active within our life.

If we have difficulty remembering dreams or feel we don't dream, it is likely that we are not acknowledging or honoring some aspect of our feminine energies properly. The feminine energy reflects itself through mystery. It is the gate or doorway through which we enter or exit into the mysteries of life. If we find through our dream work that the feminine energies are inactive or unbalanced, we can use dream alchemy to balance its expression and flow within our lives. The mythic dream work techniques in Part Two are effective for this or for any of the archetypal forces

3. ARCHETYPE OF THE MASCULINE

Common Symbols: Phallus, sword, the sun, daytime, towers, scepter, the sexual seed, acts of penetration.

The archetypal masculine force of the universe is also reflected in our lives and through our dreams. In life, the masculine deals with fathering. It is the force of making, building, directing and organizing. It is the rational aspect of our nature. It is the assertive force. It is the penetrating energy. It is the masculine force which initiates activity or urges us to initiate. The archetypal masculine within our life may reveal itself through dreams that show us accomplishing or failing to accomplish. It may reflect itself in dream scenarios where we are decisive and discriminating. If we have dreams that reveal an indecisiveness, it can reflect a weakness in the expression of our masculine forces. In dream scenarios the strength of our masculine energies is revealed through our ability or inability to decide, act, or accomplish. This provides clues as to what and how to actualize our masculine forces in our conscious, waking life. It can reveal a need to soften our expression of the masculine or to express it more assertively, depending upon the circumstances of the dream scenario itself.

4. THE ARCHETYPE OF THE HERO

Common Symbols: Battles, struggles, teachers, opening to new surprises, youth, shields, healing and health, fighting and confronting.

This universal energy is a predominant part of much dream activity. We are the heroes—the protagonists—of our lives. We are the ones who must face the difficulties and surmount them in life and dream scenarios. In myths and legends, the individual conquers and is victorious. In dreams we see what we must conquer or surmount within our physical life. This may be an obstacle of the work environment or an emotion that is hindering our growth. Dreaming of confronting something (or someone) is an indication of the hero's energy being activated.

The energy of this archetype provides insight into that which can be used to heal us on any level. Dreams which show us confronting, fighting, and trying to surmount something or someone are calls to draw upon the archetypal hero energy of the universe and to do so with success. We must remember that we are meant to win in life. We are meant to conquer our obstacles, although we often allow ourselves to be programmed for the opposite. Dreams which show us confronting and fighting tell us it is time to confront something within our waking life. It doesn't mean we must fight, as there are many ways to confront and overcome obstacles. Many do not know how to succeed in this, and this is one of the great benefits of mythic dream work. We will learn to use myths and legends with hero symbols to shape dreams that provide insight in how to win.

5. ARCHETYPE OF THE ADVERSARY

Common Symbols: Monsters, demons, beasts, tyrants, walls, fears, anything confronted, and obstacles to success.

The monsters and beasts of our nightmares reflect the adversaries in our lives. These dreams are calls to inform us that we are not confronting our adversaries or are doing so inappropriately. We may dream of fighting (reflecting an activation of the archetypal hero energy), but the fighting may be ineffectual within the dream. This tells us that we are handling and confronting our adversaries in an incorrect manner, and we must find a more effective means of eliminating them.

The archetype of the adversary is the agent of change. It forces us to confront. The adversary destroys and wounds what is. It manifests the unexpected. It tears down the old, so that the new can rise. It uses fear, anger and strong emotions to force confrontations, to force a drawing upon of the heroic energies of the soul.

Much of the adversarial energy playing in our life is subtle. It is the limitations we have imposed upon ourselves or allowed others to impose upon us. At some point we must break down those limitations.

To many people, this adversarial energy seems evil. However, it is by confronting our adversaries in all of their guises that we enable the brilliance of the soul to shine forth. Negative attitudes and emotions do hinder and limit, and thus they are often considered evil. An old saying tells us that "evil prospers when good people do nothing." This is why our nightmares arise. They show us adversaries that are prospering in our life. They are showing us what we most need to confront.

Through dream alchemy, we can learn to use the symbols and images found in myths and tales to reveal our hidden adversaries. We can also learn to control our dreams so that we can conquer the adversaries as well. As we conquer them in the dream time, the opportunity to do so in our waking time will also manifest.

6. ARCHETYPE OF DEATH AND REBIRTH

Common Symbols: All rites of initiation, births, baptisms, weddings, deaths, scythes, altars, clocks, dances, songs and prayers, transitions, crossing over (roads, rivers, etc.).

Everything is in a state of transition. At certain times in our life transition is more prominent. Our dreams reflect this archetypal influence within our lives and they give us insight into it. This is the particular function of the force we call the archetype of death and rebirth. It deals with the energy that brings the end of one aspect and the beginning of another. We die to be born and are born to die. Dreams of change, crises, and sacrifice all reflect these archetypal energies at play within our life.

In order to handle transitions, we must first recognize them. There are certain times when big changes are much more likely to occur. This is often revealed through our dreams. We can use the techniques of dream alchemy and mythic dream work to enhance these revelations. This will be covered in greater detail in Part Three, "Working With Dream Cycles."

7. ARCHETYPE OF THE JOURNEY

Common Symbols: Trees, pilgrimages, staffs, buildings, mountains, streams and rivers, winding roads, climbing or ascents, and traveling in any mode of transportation.

Just as all dreams reflect the universal energies of the self, so it is that some dreams reflect our personal journeys. Our whole life is a journey of growth and evolution. Everything we encounter affects the ease or dis-ease of that journey. Life is continual movement and development. This continual development involves aging, building upon what has come before, opening to new directions, and even the inability to see where we are. Our journeys can be clear or we can become lost, wandering aimlessly. This is reflected within our dreams.

Through the dream alchemy techniques presented throughout the rest of this book, we can shape our dream activity to elicit greater information about the course of our present journey in life. If we can recognize that the course is misdirected, we can institute energies of transition (archetype of death and rebirth) through mythic dream work to reveal the necessary course changes.

The seven archetypal energies are neutral. At their highest and purest, they can only be experienced in a positive manner. As we go through our own unfoldment process, however, they may be reflected in our dreams as either positive or negative.

There are many different archetypal forces, but the seven listed in this chapter are the most influential within the dream state. Each has its own specific strengths and qualities through which we can identify them. In post-dream evaluations, it is always good to place the images of your dream scenario into one of these seven categories. Learn to recognize the predominant archetypal force active within the dream. You will discover as you categorize your dreams according to the archetypal force that more than one will be recognizable within the dream sequence. This reminds us that we are multidimensional and thus operate from many levels simultaneously.

Take the major images, individuals and sequences and list them in a dream journal. Use the guidelines for this in chapter three or the sample worksheets listed in Appendix A. List them in the order that is most memorable or which stimulated the strongest emotional response, as those images will be of greater importance. This lets you know which archetypal energy is the predominant one.

Review the seven archetypes, and list one of them for each major image or person within the dream. If you have a female character, this obviously reflects some aspect of the feminine archetype. You will often find that more than one archetype can be applied to a particular dream image. For example, a male with whom you are fighting would not only reflect the masculine archetypal force but also the adversarial archetypal force that is active within your life. Your confrontation with this individual can reflect the subconscious wanting you to express the heroic archetype more productively. Examining the various combinations helps us to pinpoint more closely the part of our life reflected by the dream.

Once you have identified the major archetypes, some evaluation is necessary. *This is the time to question,* keeping in mind that dreams often raise questions rather than answer them. They show us the area needing attention. Is this archetypal energy one that you are being encouraged to express more fully within your life? Is this dream revealing an archetypal energy that you have not utilized to your fullest? Is this dream showing you where you have been successful with these energies in the past and thus need to bring them out again? Are these archetypal energies helping you to focus on the need to resolve some current situations? (When we see ourselves confronting an adversary, and our attempts are unsuccessful, this indicates a call for you to take another course of action in resolving the situation.)

Trust your first impressions in determining the archetype. There are no absolutely wrong answers or correspondences. Your dream will apply in some degree to that which you believe it does, but it is not limited to that. The association between the dream, its archetype and its role within your waking life could not have been made had there not been at least some basis for it.

CHAPTER THREE

Creating the Dream
Journal

Keeping a dream journal is the most important part of all dream work. By keeping a dream journal, we are telling the subconscious that we are committed to expanding perceptions through dreams. Recording the dreams also serves as a means of grounding the dream experience so that we can more fully actualize it. Dreams are ethereal and ephemeral. Their significance can easily elude us. By recording them, we take them out of that ethereal realm and crystallize them into the physical. Recording them and looking at them in black and white elicits many significances of the dream which otherwise may be lost.

When you record your dream, you are offering a "thank you" to your higher self. It is a positive acknowledgment of the gift. Every dream is a gift! This gift needs to be actualized. It needs to be made a part of your life. Recording it is the first step. It is the receiving of the gift. Next comes the unwrapping (interpretation) and then the applying of the gift to your life.

Record all the dreams that you have in a single night. No matter how ridiculous or frightening, they are all significant. The more ridiculous and frightening, the more urgent and important they are. The higher consciousness is going out of its way to get a message across. Most of the time we awaken ourselves out of our nightmares. This waking is an inability to face what the subconscious is showing you. It shows us what we most fear. The feelings are amplified to make sure that we pay attention.

It is actually best to keep two dream books. One you should place beside your bed to record the dream the moment you awaken from it. Don't worry about turning on the light. Don't get up and use the bathroom first. It takes approximately ten seconds to break that connection with the dream state. Simply reach over and scribble down the main details in the dark. It is good to remain in the same physical position in which you awakened. In the morning you can go back and decipher your writing. You will have recorded enough of the details, so that the memory of the full dream will be triggered when you rewrite it in the second dream book. Some find it easier to keep a small recorder next to the bed and record the dream that way. This is also effective, although if you share your bed, it can disturb the sleep of others.

In the morning set aside a special time to examine the dream more closely, filling in the details. This should be a time that is special for you. Your dreams are your special communications. They deserve certain respect and reverence. As you fill in the details of the previous night's dream, ask yourself questions concerning its significance. Much insight comes while recording it in your journal.

Recording our dreams and our responses to them serves many benefits. The recordings can be used in creative work and for inspiration. It helps us to consciously bridge levels of our mind that register and evoke impressions with those levels that formulate them. Recording dreams helps to ground the archetypal energies into greater recognition. It helps us to see the quality of our dreams and it challenges us to improve it. It helps us to absorb the higher archetypal energies that are active within our life and then to use it for instituting changes. By keeping a dream journal, our power of communication (verbal and written) improves because the conscious mind is being aligned with our abstract mind. Most importantly, we develop the ability to interpret, create and ultimately manipulate symbols so that the archetypal energies behind our dreams can affect our lives as gently or as dynamically as we choose.

There are many ways of setting up and using a dream journal. Use your own creativity in establishing your Dream Alchemy Journal. Keep in mind that the more care you take in your journal work, the stronger will be the lines of communication with the dream state. The worksheets in Appendix A and the guidelines that follow are suggestions only. Organize your own journal.

In the front of your journal, write some kind of dedication. Dedicate the etheric and auric value of the journal to helping you understand your life and expand your consciousness. You may wish to also include a spiritual verse that asks for higher inspiration and understanding. Have a place to record the day and date of the dream and the dream itself (as best remembered). Your memory of the dreams will improve the more you work to record them. The recording strengthens the connections between waking and sleeping consciousness. The dreams will become clearer, more vibrant and memorable.

While recording your dream, question yourself. Does this relate to something that has happened to you recently? Does it seem to reflect more of what is yet to happen? Does it seem to relate to immediate problems, worries or concerns? Jot down ANY possibilities that come to mind. Dreams reflect what is going on in your life on all levels simultaneously. If an aspect of your life is brought to mind while recording the dream, the possibility is great that it relates to the dream in some manner.

We do not want to merely interpret the dreams. We want to relate it to our lives. Once the dream is recorded, utilize any of the following to help you relate to it.

1. Trust your first impressions, but don't stop with the obvious. The events, images and symbols within the dream represent aspects and energies of your life, presented in a manner so you can see them from a new perspective.

2. Take the major images and events and relate to them specifically. Dream dictionaries may help, but it is more important for you to work out the personal significance of the imagery. What does this image, person or kind of event represent for you? For example, three different individuals may dream of elephants. To the first person it may represent joy and fun times because of an association with the circus. To the second person it may represent conservatism and political influence because of its association with the Republican Party. To the third, it may represent hard work and good memory. Begin with whatever the image has always meant to you personally. Later we can build upon this to discover more subtle significance. Begin with the familiar and move to the un-familiar.

3. Free associate with the images. This is a process made popular through psychological evaluation. A word is given, and the individual responds with the first thing that comes to mind. Do this with the images, people and major scenes of the dream. Don't worry about being led off on a tangent. Dream images are multidimensional.

4. Create a dream report. This is similar to book reports we did in school. Here's how:

- Give your dream a title. Don't make it fancy. Just have it relate to what the dream is about.
- What is the major theme or issue of the dream. (What was its primary activity?) State this theme in a single sentence.
- What are the effects of this dream on you? What is the major emotion associated with it? What were you feeling while in it? What were you feeling when you awakened from it? Was there elation and success? Was there fear? Even if you don't remember the dream content, the waking mood can reveal much about the message of the dream itself.
- What question(s) does the dream leave unanswered? This is especially important. If we can figure out what was not resolved while in the dream, it will provide insight into what   is not resolved while awake.

Leave a space in your journal for a periodic review. Usually a half page is adequate. Every so often, go back and look over the dreams and see what has unfolded in your life since the dream. Are there any correlations? Did the dreams in any way reflect major issues and events that you have encountered since then? This is an excellent way of checking your increased ability to understand the dream messages and to recognize the role they play in your life.

CHAPTER FOUR

Increasing And Influencing Dream Activity

Stimulating greater dream activity is the prelude to shaping and controlling the dream state. One of the most powerful means of stimulating greater dream activity is simply by paying more attention to it. If we give our dreams no relevance or if we look upon them as silly and frivolous, it becomes increasingly difficult to remember them and work with them. The purpose of increasing dream activity is so we can remember them and utilize them more effectively in enhancing our lives.

There's an old saying "a dream unexplained is like a letter unopened." Dreams are communications to us, for us and about us. We would not let a letter from a distant friend set on our table, unopened and unread. Dreams are gift communications.

Many complain that they just cannot remember their dreams, or they believe they don't dream at all. What we must realize is that we have to put forth some conscious effort in the dream process. If someone speaks to us and we never acknowledge that person's presence or that what is being said is worth listening to, eventually that person will quit speaking to you except in extreme cases. Our dreams are the same way. If we do not pay attention to them, eventually the communications cease, except in extreme situations which are our nightmares. When we work with the techniques and tools that follow, we are passing on a message to other levels of our consciousness. We are sending the message that we wish to reopen communication.

Initially, the results may not be as dramatic as you would like, but this can be a testing of your willingness to re-establish the subtle communication lines. The more you do while awake to prepare for sleep, the stronger the message becomes. Likewise, the more you work with your dreams while awake, the stronger your waking intuition will become. If you work with the techniques in this chapter alone, within one month a tremendous difference will be experienced. Your dreams will become more colorful, vibrant, informative and memorable.

TECHNIQUE ONE: DREAM TANTRA

One of the most powerful means of stimulating greater dream activity is the use of dream tantra. The purpose of dream tantra is to develop a continual consciousness, an unbroken continuity through both waking and dreaming states. Although most people associate tantra with forms of sexuality, it corresponds to a wider spectrum of spiritual activities. Tantra comes from the Sanskrit "tanuti," meaning "to weave." It is a spiritual method originating in Hinduism, combining the use of ritual, discipline, and meditation. It draws upon all of the metaphysical sciences to expand awareness in all states of consciousness. It employs the feminine energies of power and creativity to unite and explore the universal and spiritual through the physical. Because of this, it is a term very applicable to mythic dream work. We will use dream tantra (dream rituals, disciplines, and meditations) to direct the "weaving" of our dreams.

When we are working with dream alchemy, we are developing will and control of will over the dream state. There is an energy center in the body that corresponds to control of the will and it can be stimulated through specific techniques to increase dream activity. It is called the throat chakra. The throat chakra is one of the energy centers in the body controlling our force of will, in conjunction with the unconscious mind. Here's the dream tantra technique to activate the throat chakra:

Visualize a ball of red light in the throat area of the body. Red is stimulating and activating. Using it is like turning on a light switch. In the middle of this ball of crystalline light, visualize the ancient Sanskrit symbol of the Om in bright scarlet. The Om in Eastern philosophy is the sound from which all sound came forth in the universe. It is the creative word. This symbol, when used with this visualization, awakens and activates the energies of the unconscious mind.

The Symbol of the Om

31

For this exercise, it is important to lie on the right side of the body, while continuing to visualize the Om symbol in the throat center as you go to sleep. Since our masculine or sun energies are associated with the right side of the body, by lying on the right side, we are telling the subconscious to keep the masculine energies subordinate while we activate the feminine. In this position, the left side, (associated with the feminine or moon energies), becomes dominant. Using this position with this visualization activates the feminine psychic channel. This in turn facilitates creative dreaming.

You can also use the symbol of the trident instead of the symbol of the Om. In Eastern philosophy, the tridentit was the symbol of Shiva, the ultimate yogi. It also is symbolic of the junction of nerves found at each psychic center.

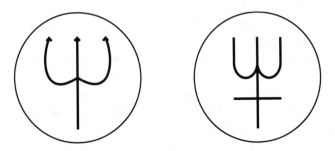

Two Variations of the Trident Symbol.

The trident is also a glyph used to represent the influence of the planet Neptune in the astrological chart. Neptune rules the unconscious and dream states. This symbol or the symbol of the Om helps to stimulate the ability to retain consciousness during dreaming. This lucid dreaming ability is important in dream alchemy, and so many of the techniques in this book are designed to develop lucid dreaming.

When we become aware *that* we are dreaming *while* we are dreaming, we can change ourselves and the dream. This ultimately opens us to dream magically, and with an awareness of our true nature of existence. In Part Two, we will be using lucid dreaming and combining it with the use of myths, tales, and legends to shape our dream scenarios.

Part of the mythic dream work process involves using symbols to create an astral doorway. An excellent preliminary exercise is to practice visualizing the symbol in a ball of red light within the throat chakra. Then visualize it emanating out from the throat to form a second ball of red light, large enough for you to walk through. See it as a door through which you can enter into dreamland. This visualization will be developed in the Part Two, but it is an important facet of dream control and direction.

TECHNIQUE TWO: DREAM HERBS

One of the most ancient and effective techniques for increasing and influencing dream activity is through the use of herbs. Dream pillows and sachets can be made by choosing herbs and fragrances that affect sleep and dreaming and then wrapping them in a square of cotton muslin. Placing these sachets under or inside the bed pillow (or next to the bed) enables them to work effectively and gently while you sleep. The use of herbs in dream baths, as described in chapter five, is also effective. Drinking certain herbal teas also enhances dream states.

At this point, we are working primarily with physical things to stimulate greater dream activity. Through these outer activities, we work to restore communication with those levels of consciousness which speak to us through dreams. The more physical activities we use to prepare for sleep, the stronger the message is sent to the subconscious that we are open to communication again. Using herbs is one way to open to that communication. Here's a list of herbs to help influence dreams:

Agrimony

This is an excellent herb to use when there is an inability to fall asleep due to emotional problems. It is calming. It is also effective as a flower essence.

Anise

This herb elicits a protective energy, particularly against disturbing dreams. It has a unique ability to keep one safe in dreams. It is stabilizing to the astral body. When we are asleep we often travel in our astral body, so this protective herb is particularly beneficial.

Ash Leaves

The ash is a tree that wands are often made from. The leaves of the ash tree, when included in dream pillows, stimulate prophetic dreams.

Bay Leaves

This is a stimulating herb and fragrance. It is soothing to the respiration and to the heart chakra of the body. It can be used to stimulate dreams of inspiration. It can be used to stimulate dreams that reveal what is blocking the manifestation of love within our lives. Many times negative past events create a closing down of the full expression of love. This herb and fragrance stimulates dreams that can reveal those blockages, bringing out the events and emotions that are congesting your full and true expression of love.

Celandine (lesser)

This herb makes a good wash, bath or drink in conjunction with dream alchemy. It is beneficial to use in the ritual dream bath described in the "Rite of Dream Passage" of chapter five. It is a very psychic herb. It enhances and stimulates dream activity, restoring a delight in opening and working with dreams.

Cinquefoil

This herb can be used in dream rituals and baths to open to greater awareness of our perfect partner in life. If male, it can stimulate dreams involving a female or the qualities of a female most beneficial to you. If you are a female, it may stimulate dreams involving the ideal male or the ideal male qualities for you.

Dragon's Blood

Dragon's blood as an herb has a long tradition associated with the art of shapeshifting. According to the tradition, this herb enables one to assume various shapes and guises, and facilitates traveling both astrally and physically. It can be an excellent aid in mythic dream work, but the herb must be infused (through meditation) with the purpose of the individual.

Ferns

This plant has a tradition of invisibility associated with it. The seeds, as part of a dream pillow, enable the individual to go about the business of dream alchemy undisturbed by physical and non-physical energies.

Hops

Hops are effective in herbal sachets and pillows for dreams. They are also effective when prepared as a drink prior to sleep. Calming and soothing, they help to restore or instill a peaceful sleep.

Mugwort

Mugwort is a powerful herb for use in dream alchemy. It is also effective as a flower essence. It is known as a visionary herb, and opens one to dreams of the future, and thus it is effective to use with experiments in mythic dream work. It can stimulate dreams which open you to mystical experiences and inner enlightenment.

Peppermint

All herbs of the mint family are known as the friends of life. They have beneficial effects. While spearmint may have the physical effect of being more calming than peppermint, peppermint is more effective with dream alchemy. When taken as a tea in the evening before sleep, it stimulates more interesting dreams with a leaning toward the prophetic. The leaves make a powerful addition to sleep sachets and dream pillows.

Vervain

Vervain, along with mugwort, is one of the best herbs for the mythic dream work techniques described later. It is a visionary herb and it is especially effective when utilized in dream quests or as a prelude to dream quest processes.

TECHNIQUE THREE:
USING HERBS TO INFLUENCE NIGHTMARES

Everyone has nightmares on occasion. In most cases, we force ourselves to wake up out of them. This is so we do not have to confront what is in them. Most adults need to recognize that nightmares are important messages. The more frightening they are, the more urgent and important the message is. Nightmares show us our greatest fears.

There are herbal remedies to ease nightmares and to facilitate our exploring them. It is never easy to face some aspects of our life, but unless we do so, we may be forcing our psyche to get in touch with us in other ways, such as through crisis or illness.

In the case of children, nightmares can be a problem. Children are very sensitive to the environment of their homes. There is an unrecognized psychic link to the energies of both parents. Even in cases where effort is made to hide any disharmony from the children, it will still be sensed on some level. Often this is reflected through the dreams of children. Being open to talk about your dreams and those of your children is beneficial to all.

A child's nightmares may also reflect fears that the child has brought with him or her into this incarnation from previous ones. In cases such as these, it is important to take measures to ease the nightmares and help the child to understand them as much as possible. If they are not dealt with, the child can develop a fear of sleep. This will create even more problems.

Sleep sachets, dream pillows and dream fragrances are extremely effective with children. They ease the emotions and help them to enjoy peaceful sleep. They also enable the children to speak more openly about their dream experiences. This creates opportunities to correct the cause of the nightmares.

The following is a list of herbs known to be helpful when dealing with nightmares.

Anise

A sachet of anise will help prevent nightmares. It helps the individual to feel safe and secure. It is calming to emotions.

Cedar

Cedar has a fragrance that is cleansing to the environment. It purifies and stabilizes the aura of the individual. It balances emotional and mental energies. It is a strong remedy for bad dreams.

Huckleberry

When used as an incense before going to sleep, it calms and balances the aura. It also assists in having dreams which can come true, especially those which are precognitive.

Mistletoe

This is an herb which helps restore peaceful sleep and transmutes nightmares into beautiful dream experiences. It can be included in dream and sleep sachets, or it can be used separately by placing it within the pillow or over the headboard.

Morning Glory

This is a powerful herb for correcting and stopping all nightmare activity, especially in children. Simply place it under the pillow of the child, and it will restore peaceful sleep.

Purslane

This is another herb which can be burned as an incense prior to going to sleep. It can also be used in a dream pillow. It provides protection against bad dreams.

Rose

Rose is a powerful fragrance and flower for use in restoring refreshing sleep, especially after a series of nightmares. It balances the heart and the emotions. It stimulates refreshing dreams to heal and soothe the causes and conditions of disturbed sleep.

Rosemary

Rosemary is an ancient English herb, and it is still associated with elves, fairies and other friendly spirits. When used for sleep and dream purposes, it is effective as an oil or as part of a dream sachet. You can also place a sprig under the pillow itself. It stimulates inner peace, driving away nightmares and restoring good sleep. It can be placed beneath the bed to protect one from frightening and evil dreams from deep within the subconscious. It draws those of the fairy kingdom to watch over children and guard them at night.

Thyme

This herb is balancing to the emotional state of the individual. It enables you to sleep more peacefully. It can also be used to help children whose nightmares may be the result of fears brought over from their previous lives. It also has benefits in working with mythic dream techniques described in Part Two.

TECHNIQUE FOUR: DREAM FRAGRANCES

Fragrance is one of the most effective means of altering sleep states and dream consciousness. Aromatherapy is growing in acceptance and popularity in all of its forms: herbal scents, essential oils, incense, potpourri, etc. Every fragrance alters the vibrational rate of the environment and the individual according to its properties. Fragrances most strongly affect the etheric, astral and mental bands of energy. This is why they are so effective in dream alchemy. They penetrate the consciousness on those levels during sleep.

Essential oils have most often been used for two purposes: therapeutic, as an aid in restoring health; and metaphysical, for spiritual upliftment and perception. In dream alchemy, fragrances aid the normal sleep and dream processes by assisting in freeing the body from lower influences and in opening to higher influences.

There are a number of ways of using the oils and fragrances. They can be used in a bath, prior to retiring for the night. One half capful (or less) of essential oil per bath is all that is required. This will be explored further in the next chapter on "Rite of Dream Passage." You can also anoint yourself with essential oils before retiring. The oils can be used in vaporizers, or you can place a drop or two within a bowl of water, setting it next to the bed as you go to sleep. With incense and potpourris, you can burn them as you go to sleep, allowing the fragrance to carry you off into dream time. The best part of working with the oils and fragrances is that it enables you to experiment and play with the process to find what works for you. Use the following list to help you discover more.

Apple Blossom
This is extremely effective in the mythic dream work techniques described in Part Two. The fragrance of apple blossom has an ancient mythology surrounding it. It helps connect you with the energies and symbols within myths. It is good for promoting energies of love and for connecting into the nature kingdoms. It has ties to the energies of the unicorn which lives beneath the apple tree.

Chamomile
This is a powerfully effective fragrance for children who have difficulty sleeping or who are colicky at night. It stabilizes the aura, and it awakens a sense of security while sleeping. (It is a member of

the ragweed family, and those with allergies should be cautious of its use.)

Eucalyptus

This is one of the most versatile and powerful oils for dream-work activity. It balances the emotions and calms disturbed states of mind. It facilitates the healing and easing of grief and hostility through sleep. It was used in the ancient mystery schools to balance the awakened siddhis (psychic energies) of the students while they slept. It eliminates nightmares and can be used to facilitate consciousness while dreaming.

Frankincense

This fragrance is cleansing and protective. It eliminates negativity within the sleep environment and restores peace to dream states. It can open the individual to high inspiration and spiritual insight through the dreams.

Jasmine

This fragrance is calming to the heart and to the emotions. It can be used to stimulate prophetic dream sequences. It is an excellent fragrance for learning to transform our energies in a variety of ways.

Lavender

This is a very powerful sleep fragrance. Lavender was always considered a magical herb. It eliminates emotional and mental stress, and it can be used to treat insomnia. It can also open you to visionary states while dreaming. It is excellent when used in a bath prior to retiring or as part of any ritual of dream passage.

Myrrh

Myrrh is a powerful healing and cleansing oil. It soothes the emotions and the astral body, making for more peaceful rest. It can stimulate dreams of emotions that are creating blocks within your life. It may stimulate dream activity in which past events are replayed, events whose repercussions are still impacting you.

Rose

(Refer to the previous section on nightmares.)

Rosemary
 (Refer to the previous section on nightmares.)

Sage
 Sage is a fragrance that can open you to spiritual illumination in the dream state. It stimulates awareness of inner tension and helps to release it through the sleep process. This is one of those herbs which can open us to all times in mythic dream work. It helps us to integrate and synthesize all times and experiences and all symbols into our present life awareness. It can awaken through dream alchemy a true sense of our immortality.

Tuberose
 This fragrance has been referred to as the "Mistress of the Night." It brings serenity and peace of mind. It can be used to increase dream sensitivity—especially in areas of relationships. It helps turn our daily dreams toward the spiritual light.

Wisteria
 This fragrance has been used by occultists, metaphysicians and healers to attract high vibrations in all situations. It is activating of more colorful dreams. It is also known as the "poet's ecstasy" as it stimulates creative expression and inspiration, especially when used with dream alchemy. It can be used effectively with the mythic dream work techniques. It assists the individual in developing lucid dreaming that leads to conscious astral projections.

TECHNIQUE FIVE:
FLOWER ESSENCES AND DREAMS

Flower essences are elixirs made from the flowers of various plants, herbs and trees. They contain the etheric energy pattern of the flower. Each flower and each essence has its own unique vibrational characteristic. They can be used before sleep to stimulate dreams that will reveal information about characteristics we may need to change or those we may need to enhance. The bibliography lists several sources of information on these wonderful remedies. Those listed below are specifically effective in altering and shaping sleep and dream states.

Amaranthus
This essence is excellent for excessively radical dreams and nightmares. It calms disruptive dreams that stem from biological sources. It also can activate visionary dreams as well.

Aspen
This is an excellent remedy for sleep-walking due to anxieties. This is a good flower remedy for children who have developed a fear of dreams and the dark. It assists them in moving past the fear level of the astral to connect with higher energies. This is usually symptomized by such activities as needing a door open or a light on.

Blackberry
This is a remedy for the fear of going to sleep. If used in conjunction with meditation and creative visualization, it can stimulate problem-solving through the dreams. Higher teachings will be revealed through the dreams, and creativity will be more easily transferred and manifested within the physical.

Celandine (lesser)
This flower remedy has many of its herbal qualities. It stimulates dreams which transfer information, and it facilitates the activation of lucid dreaming, along with instructions from spiritual guides while dreaming.

Chaparral
This remedy stimulates deeper states of consciousness, and it

helps us in understanding the archetypal symbols within our dreams. This is very effective in the mythic dream work techniques to follow. It facilitates using dreams to uncover information from our past, and it will stimulate an emotional cleansing of the subconscious during the dreams.

Clematis

This remedy is for the "day dreamy" kind of person. It is a good remedy for when there is a loss of sleep. It awakens the creative potential and facilitates greater control of the fertile imagination.

Comfrey

Comfrey balances the nervous system so that sleep is more restful. It balances the right and left hemisphere functions during sleep, and it is an excellent remedy to take prior to retiring and upon awakening, as it assists in remembering dream content.

Corn

Corn is another remedy for when we become overly "day dreamy." It helps prevent us from becoming lost in our dreams. While you are asleep, it works to cleanse the astral body so that upon awakening the astral body will reintegrate more easily with the physical body.

Forget-Me-Not

This is an excellent remedy for times of disturbed sleep. It stimulates the pineal gland and facilitates the release of tensions through dreams. It stimulates visions and helps us to use the dream state to connect with spiritual guides or those who are living beyond the physical.

Honeysuckle

This is a remedy for when we are troubled by thoughts, emotions and dreams of the past. It enables us to put them into perspective, so we can move beyond them.

Iris

Iris essence will stimulate creative inspiration in dreams, expanding avenues for artistic expression. It facilitates attracting ideas from higher realms into our dreams and putting them into waking consciousness for greater expression.

Live Forever

Live Forever acts upon the dream state in a manner that helps coordinate our spirit guides and their information so that the illumination can pass through the dreams into our conscious mind. It helps align the dream consciousness with waking consciousness.

Marigold

This is a remedy that generally heightens psychic sensitivities and clairaudience through the dream state. It opens the inner ears in sleep, so that they function more strongly when awake.

Morning Glory

This remedy helps one who is having difficulty with disturbed and restless sleep. Refer to the herbal qualities listed in the technique on correcting nightmares.

Mugwort

Mugwort is powerfully effective for dream work of any kind. It increases awareness during dreams, especially of spiritual thresholds we may be encountering within our life. It stimulates lucid dreaming, increases psychic sensitivity. It initiates clarity of the dream experience and its purpose to our waking life.

Pennyroyal

Pennyroyal essence is cleansing to the auric field and to the astral body. It helps provide psychic protection during sleep and while awake. It strengthens our subtle energies so that we can get beyond negative awarenesses to positive and enlightening experiences. It helps prevent the energies and thought forms of the day from intruding upon the dream state.

Saint John's Wort

This is one of the most beneficial dream essences. It releases hidden fears into our dreams so that we can confront them and eliminate them on that level, rather than in the physical. It stimulates past life revelations through dreams. It helps in developing lucid dreaming that can lead to conscious astral projection, especially beyond the lower astral plane. It eases cluttered dream states and nightmares. It eases and prevents the overly expanded dream consciousness which can cause an inability to reintegrate properly into body consciousness after sleep. It helps eliminate fear of out-of-body experiences. It strengthens the inner light as we expand our perceptions beyond the physical.

Spruce

Spruce is an essence that helps to detoxify the body during sleep. It is beneficial in overcoming disorientation and lack of direction. It stimulates dreams that give greater focus.

Star Tulip

Star Tulip is a remedy for greater dream recall. It stimulates greater awareness of the more subtle realms to which we have access during sleep. It strengthens our spiritual sensitivity while asleep, so that it can be more easily transferred into our waking consciousness.

TECHNIQUE SIX: DREAM CRYSTALS

The use of crystals, gems and stones has come into great prominence in the past few years. They are natural sources of a form of electrical energy, called piezoelectrical energy. "Piezo" comes from the Greek word "piezein" meaning to squeeze. Any stress upon the crystal releases its particular frequency of energy into our auric field.

It takes very little to release a crystal's energy. Even brain waves, generated by thought and focused in the direction of the crystal, will activate its release. Because of this, it is quite simple to program crystals and gems to work in a directed manner for us. Some crystals and stones work naturally with the process of dream alchemy. Others may need some programming for them to be effective.

When using crystals and stones for dream work, it is recommended that they be cleansed once per week. Setting the stone or crystal in sea salt, placing it in the earth, putting it in a running stream, or even running it through fire are effective means of clearing the crystals of negative energy and programming. The bibliography contains a number of sources on the effects of crystals, their uses and cleansing procedures.

You must also charge the crystals and stones you intend to use for dream work. This simply means that you want to bring their energy levels to the highest before you start to use them. In many ways they are like batteries. They become depleted with use, and they must be recharged. There are a number of effective ways of doing this. Placing the crystal or stone in sunlight and moonlight for 24 to 48 hours is one of the best. Place them outside during storms or changes of weather. Small stones can be charged by placing them in clusters of larger stones.

It is always good to have several that you use for dreams. While one is being cleansed, you still have others to assist you in your dream work processes. It is also better to have several crystals that you use solely for dream work. You may wish to use some of these as general boosters to your bedroom environment, while others you may wish to program for specific dream functions. These can all be part of the dream temple described in the next chapter.

The simplest manner of programming your dream crystals is to hold it in both hands while gazing into it. You may wish to put it on your lap and hold your hands over it. It is at this point that we employ the Universal Axiom of Energy: "All energy follows thought." Wherever we put our thoughts that is where energy will go. Thus at this point, clear your mind of everything other than what you wish to have programmed within your crystal. Concentrate on what you wish this crystal or stone to do for you in your dream work. See it, imagine it, feel it stimulating your dreams and your dream memory in dynamic ways. As you become filled with the visualization of it working for you exactly as you wish, project it out of your mind and into the crystal. See it in your mind's eye as if a beam of light is extending from your head and emptying into the crystal. Feel your hands pulsing out the energy, infusing the crystal with this thought.

Continue this process until you feel satisfied that the crystal is vibrating with this intention. Then repeat the process with your next dream crystal. This usually takes five minutes or so of uninterrupted focus and projection. This programming will stay with the crystal until you clean and clear it for some other use.

This method is especially effective in the upcoming mythic dream work process. You can infuse the crystal with the energy of a myth, legend or tale. You choose a myth according to your individual purpose, and you read the tale to the crystal, seeing its energies become a part of the energy pattern of the crystal itself. This infuses the crystal with the archetypal energy patterns of the myth, which in turn will stimulate dream correspondences.

Working with dream crystals requires some patience and practice. Just as with the herbs, fragrances, and flower essences, we are using a physical substance to assist us in shaping the more ethereal energies of the dream state.

In the beginning, double-terminated crystals (points at both ends) or herkimer diamonds are the most effective for acting as a bridge between the dream state and waking consciousness. Herkimer diamonds are stimulating to the astral body and serve to energize it. This gives the astral body greater mobility and consciousness while sleeping and dreaming. Double-terminated crystals are symbolic of linking one state of consciousness with the next.

Regardless of the crystal or stone you use, cleanse it first, program it and then only use it for one particular task. Give your crystal a singular purpose, and it will work more effectively. Don't use the same crystal for dreams that you are also using for healing and divination. You will confuse its programming and scatter its energies.

After programming the stone, place it under your pillow, on your headboard, or on a table next to your bed, close to the head. Before you turn off the lights to sleep, touch it, hold it and remember the programming you placed into it. Affirm that you will dream and remember the dream according to that program. Use your own affirmation or use one of the following which I was told a long time ago was translated from the Sanskrit:

> Lord, lift the veil that is between you and me this night and let me see reality. In my dreams this night may I be instructed in the goals of my life. May I meet in a dream tonight those experiences about to manifest, so that I might be prepared to handle those things in peace. May thy healing light shine through my being that those things not resolved be filled with light and healed.

When you are consistently remembering your dreams, try reprogramming your crystal to dream the same dream again to elicit greater information. With practice, you can program the crystal for a location in the dream state other than a physical one. This may be an ashram upon the etheric or astral plane, another planet, or another dimension entirely. The crystal can also be programmed to open doorways to the past and to the future. Here is a list of some stones and their properties.

Amethyst

This is an excellent stone for transmuting consciousness while in the dream state. It is good for bridging levels of consciousness. Its violet color is a combination of red and blue, symbolizing the dualities of physical and spiritual, waking and sleeping. It helps to balance and align our energies while asleep.

Chrysoprase

These stones are excellent for programming to clarify problems through dreams. They strengthen our inner vision, of which dreams are but one manifestation.

Clear Quartz

Any clear quartz crystal can be an effective dream crystal. They are easily programmable and size does not influence effectiveness. Small quartz points can be programmed and easily slipped into the pillow.

Double-terminated Quartz

As mentioned, this is an excellent stone for bridging waking and sleeping consciousness. It also facilitates memory of dreams.

Herkimer Diamonds

This is one of the best stones for mythic dream work. It stimulates great dream activity and if worked with consistently, it will lead to lucid dreaming. It can also be used to help develop conscious astral projection, of which the lucid dreaming is an excellent prelude. It energizes the etheric and astral energies, making dreams more vibrant and memorable.

Jade

Jade has a tradition of being associated with dreams and it is sometimes referred to as the dream stone. Red jade can stimulate connection with our master teachers in the dreams. Lavender jade stimulates a psychic understanding of our dreams. Jadeite is a stone which facilitates emotional release through dreams, and imperial jade stimulates prophetic dreams.

Onyx

Onyx is good general stone for increasing dream activity. If used properly, in a single night it will stimulate multiple dreams, often with the same theme.

Phantom Crystals

Phantom crystals are very powerful dream crystals. Their full power and significance is still somewhat veiled. They hint of realms and dimensions of true reality. Those which have earth elements within them forming the phantom are actually doorways to the world of dreams from the physical. These are powerful stones for mythic dream work. They open you to the archetypes of myths and tales which lie beyond our physical reality.

Quartz Clusters

I like to refer to these as dream clusters. They have a tremendous potential for stimulating multiple dream scenarios that are tied together. Many times the subconscious gives us many dreams at night, each different in the imagery and yet each the same in its theme. Clusters are excellent tools for relating the elements of a single dream or the elements of a variety of dreams. They assist in dream comprehension and interpretation.

Sapphire

Sapphire is a stone which can be used in dream work to lift the dream state from mundane reflections to higher spiritual imagery. It helps transform and lift the consciousness to higher realms through dream activity.

Tourmaline (black)

Black tourmaline is effective for sleep and all nightmare work. It is a powerfully protective stone which aids our inner search. It helps us in finding the light within the darkness, the significance within our dreams. It is an electrical transformer. While we are asleep, it can alter the energies of our dreams and our consciousness, enabling greater expression of light when awake.

CHAPTER FIVE

The Rite Of Dream Passage

The Rite of Dream Passage is a preparatory ritual to mythic dream work. It is a process that can powerfully dedicate a year of dream work initiation or a single night's efforts. It can be adjusted to your own dream purposes and goals. It is an excellent prelude to each night's retirement to the sleep and dream realms. It can also be renewed each month at the time of the full moon. (This will be elaborated upon in chapter twelve.)

This rite assists in stimulating dream activity. It helps to place your physical energies into synchronization with the more universal energies, which reveal themselves through our dreams. It is important to remember that it is a powerful knock on the doors of the subconscious mind.

Actions are empowered by the amount of significance we attach to them. With this exercise, we are infusing the entire dream work process with greater power, dedication and spiritual significance. We use this ritual to energize, bless and initiate our dream alchemy procedures. All rituals are only as powerful as the significance we imbue them with. Through them we learn to utilize and synthesize body, mind and spirit. They help us to imprint upon the deeper levels of our consciousness the command to integrate and activate energies according to the purpose of the ritual itself.

This ritual serves as an aid to crossing that threshold from the physical to the spiritual through our dreams. It inspires dynamic dream activity. A ritual is anything done with strong intention or emphasis. As it relates to our dream work, it takes on powerful dimensions. It utilizes an outer activity to enable us to experience inner realities. It opens the doors of passage to inner realms that operate beyond physical existence.

For any ritual to be effective, there are preliminary considerations. Know what your purpose is, and hold to it. Know why you want to be involved in it. Make sure that you know what you will need. Understand the significance of what you need and use. The more significance you can attribute to all aspects of the ritual, the more powerful the effect will be. Know when the best time for the ritual is. Gather together all that you will need before you start. Make sure it has a definite beginning and ending. You may wish to use a specific gesture or prayer for it. Approach it with great respect and reverence, for you are working with a method of invoking dynamic plays of energy into your life.

Preparation is the key to an effective ritual. This includes preparation of your self and your surroundings. Work out the specific details and significances prior to the actual working. This prevents energy being dissipated needlessly. Have any herbs, fragrances, crystals and stones that you intend to use present for this ritual. Prepare any sleep and dream sachets that you intend to use ahead of time. Also have your dream journal(s) available. You may also wish to have on hand any books on mythology that you may use in your future dream work activities.

Gather these items together, refreshing your memory on their significance. You may wish to perform this ritual for the first time on the night of the full moon. If you choose not to wait, that is fine as well. Regardless of when you choose to perform the ritual, make sure that you will not be disturbed once you start. Take the phone off of the hook, and inform others that there are to be no interruptions.

This ritual will take place within your bathroom. Run a bath of hot water in which you will be able to soak, meditate and bless the process you are about to initiate. As the bathtub fills, add any fragrance or herbs that you also used in making your sleep and dream sachets. As the fragrance fills the water and the room, know that it is going to permeate you as well. It will vibrate on both physical and spiritual levels, opening you to more memorable, powerful and beneficial dream activity.

Lay the tools for your dream work activity on a pillow beside the tub. In the corners of the bathtub, either resting on the tub or inside it, set your dream crystals and stones that you have programmed but not used yet. Light candles in the bathroom. Do everything by candle light—symbolic of the light of awareness that is reflected within your dreams. Step into the bath water, lowering yourself gently, as if easing yourself in full consciousness into the dream state. Imagine you are entering into the watery astral realm that exists between waking and sleeping.

This next step is optional, but it is very effective. There are many water soluble crayons on the market for children to use while bathing. Many are made of soap. You may wish to purchase a set of these for this part of the exercise. With a red crayon, draw a circle on the bathroom tiles in front of you and behind you. Make the circle about a foot to a foot and a half in diameter. Draw it so that it will be easily visible when you lie back within the water. In the center of the circle, draw the Sanskrit symbol of the Om, as discussed in chapter four.

Now we are ready to begin. Lie back in the water. Take a few moments and close your eyes. You may wish to perform some rhythmic breathing or a progressive relaxation. Inhale the fragrance of the bath and feel it permeating every cell and fiber of your being, opening you to greater awareness. If it helps you to relax, you may wish to have a piece of meditation music playing in the background.

As you begin to relax, visualize a ball of red light forming within your throat chakra, and in the center of it see the formation of the Sanskrit Om. When you feel this symbol alive in your throat center, open your eyes slowly and softly focus them upon the symbol on the wall in front of you. Imagine the wall as a mirror, reflecting this same symbol that is glowing within your throat center. And then allow your eyes to close again.

This is a good time to offer a prayer of thanks for the knowledge and awareness that is about to open to you every night hereafter. Give thanks for this in advance. Imagine it as if you have just placed an order from a catalogue and now will await its delivery every night.

Feel the dreamer in you come alive. We are all dreamers. When we were children, dream life was as important as waking. We want to reactivate that same kind of childlike wonder. Allow yourself a few moments to let your imagination run free, dreaming of things you still wish to do. Let these imaginings take whatever direction they wish.

After a few minutes of this, begin to direct your imaginings more specifically. Allow your mind to create images of dream revelations coming to you. See them healing, nurturing and teaching. See yourself easily remembering and understanding them. See yourself being able to control them. Imagine all that can open to you when you can control your dreams. Imagine all of the benefits that will come as a result. Visualize yourself growing stronger, more vibrant and more alive as you work with your dreams.

See other people acknowledging this new energy about you. Imagine yourself being able to control, handle and shape your physical life circumstances more fully. Imagine yourself becoming anything and everything that you desire. When you have worked these images up within your mind, allowing them to fill every pore and atom of your being, visualize it all being set in motion with this ritual.

See this energy filling and infusing your crystals, sachets, herbs and fragrances. See your dream journal becoming a manual of the alchemical arts. See yourself becoming a shapeshifter, able to mold your dream energies and images in any way you desire.

Imagine the symbol on the wall in front of you. If it helps, softly open your eyes briefly and gaze upon it. Visualize it beginning to grow larger, until it is life-size. Visualize it as being large enough to walk through. This symbol then becomes a threshold, separating waking and sleeping. Know that each night hereafter, all you will have to do is visualize this symbol within your throat and then reflect it outward, seeing it as a large passage into the dream state. Visualize yourself crossing over and into it, in complete control.

You have now created the doorway that leads to greater dream passage. With practice and persistence, this doorway will become more real and vibrant. When you are able to see this symbol as a doorway, give thanks for its manifestation and for all that you will experience because of it. Know that with its formation, everything associated with your dream work has become dedicated to greater self-awareness. Know that a new sense of self-empowerment is being stirred and awakened.

With a soft cloth, gently erase the symbol upon the wall. As you do that, visualize it as a closing of the door. Allow the symbol that you visualized within your throat center to gently dissipate, until called into activity again. Offer another prayer of thanks and extinguish the candles.

As you dry yourself, while the bath water empties from the tub, know that every part of your being is now more alive and sensitive. Know that you are about to start a new adventure, one that will return control of your life back to you.

Gather your crystals, pillows, sachets and other dream tools and place them in their designated spots within your bedroom. See your bedroom as becoming now a dream temple in which you will be able to meet the sacred in your sleep. Going directly from the bath to the bed and sleeping naked will bridge the ritual's energies more effectively the first time. As you turn your lights off to sleep, visualize the doorway to dream passage forming before you and inviting you through.

CREATING THE DREAM TEMPLE

Marking off sacred space, space in which spiritual activities can be blessed and augmented, has been a part of all ancient mystery teachings. In dream alchemy, we are consecrating our bedrooms to serve as this sacred space each night when we prepare to sleep. This is not to say that no other activities can go on in that space, but rather when we prepare to do a night of concentrated dream work, the room should be appropriately prepared.

For the best results, the room in which we sleep should be neat and clean. Clutter in the outer reflects clutter with the inner. As we bring order to the outer, we bring order to the inner.

There are many things that we can do to augment sleeping conditions and dream activity by working with the physical layout of the room. Have places near the bed where you can set your dream crystals. Clean sheets and bed clothing may seem like common sense, but it has a strong impact upon dream states. Prior to entering the room at night, have the appropriate incense or fragrance already filling the room, so that it can stimulate deeper levels of consciousness as you go to sleep.

You may wish to arrange the furniture in such a way that the bed is in the midst of a circle. The ancient shrines and temples were places that had specific geometric shapes so as to elicit specific responses in mind and body. Circular layouts generate negative ions which help relax the individual.

Science has shown that negative ions help induce altered states of consciousness, inducing alpha brain wave patterns. Circular shapes, waterfalls, candles and even rainfall and the rising moon produce negative ions in the atmosphere around us. They are calming to our system. Positive ions, on the other hand, wreak havoc upon the nervous system. Negative ion generators are now available. They can be run in the bedroom, creating a more peaceful and controlled sleep environment.

The room should be in such a state so that as we go to bed each night we know we will awaken rested. We should be in a state that re-enforces the thought that our dreams will be productive. Sleep then becomes part of our growth ritual, and the more preparations we make to remind us of this, the greater the effect.

In Part Four of this book we will discuss ways of creating sleep and dream mandalas which can be hung in the bedroom to empower you in your sleep and to protect you. We are learning through dream alchemy to empower an aspect of our life that we thought was beyond our control. We are learning to create a space in our home that is a temple doorway to wonders which lie beyond waking consciousness.

Using dream alchemy involves learning methods to consciously direct the creative imagination into dream awareness. Our dreams and their potential revelations are only limited by our conscious focus. This implies that we can dream about anything which we are in a position to do something about—if we can focus properly.

Before we can change the focus of our dreams and instigate the kind of changes we desire within our lives, we must employ some self-examination. How do we feel about our progress in life? How do we handle old weaknesses and problems when they resurface? Where do we need the most study and work to make our greatest progress? These and even more difficult questions may arise in the course of our dream work.

Our dreams are capable of providing extensive essays on aspects of our lives that we do not want to face. How can we tell that we may not want to face them? Our present dream activity is our clue. Our waking life is often paralleled in our dreams. How well do we recall our dreams? How well do we interpret our dreams? How we answer these can provide insight into whether we are truly facing certain aspects of our lives.

Our dreams are gifts to help us grow and change, to evolve to our highest potential. For this to occur, we may have to face aspects that may not be pleasant. To "know thyself" can be a painful process, but unless we locate and remove the thorns, they will fester and infect.

Our dreams force us to pay attention, to take greater responsibility. They force us to examine all aspects of ourselves. Only when we can see what must be faced can we create the new. As we clean out the debris, greater creativity emerges. Metamorphosis involves creation and change, and our dreams reflect that creative function and potential. It is part of our unconscious intuition.

PART TWO:

Mythic Dream Work

"Dreamtime is claimed to be a formative or creative period which existed at the beginning of things. Mythic beings shaped the land and brought forth the various species. The mythic beings no longer exist, but they did not die. They were transformed and became a part of ourselves."
— Stan Gooch, *Guardians of the Ancient Wisdom*

"Imagination has some way of lighting on Truth that the reason has not and that its commandments ... are the most binding we can ever know."
— William Butler Yeats

CHAPTER SIX

Dream Alchemy Through Creative Imagination

One of the best ways of furthering the educational process with dreams is through the study and use of myths, tales and legends. Like dreams, they manifest images and scenarios which show uncommon relationships. They reflect aspects of our lives—conscious and unconscious. They put us in touch with realities and dimensions of life that we do not consciously acknowledge.

Both myths and dreams touch the core of humanity. They touch those aspects of ourselves that are ultimate and universal. They are timeless, reflecting a flow of the past, present and future simultaneously. They are replete with symbolism linking universal archetypes to our everyday consciousness.

There are as many kinds of myths and tales as there are dreams and dreamers. Both can be used to build bridges between the physical and the more subtle planes of life. They both contain valuable sources of information. They both provide information about our attitudes regarding our relationships with other people and the world, our work and our spiritual growth.

Our inner self knows us and how we operate in all arenas of life, visible and invisible. It knows our strengths and weaknesses—past, present and future. These same teachings are expressed through many of our myths, just as they are through our dreams. Dreams and myths are able to reflect all things, in all lifetimes, for this lifetime.

This is not to say that the dream and mythic worlds have no limits. In dream and mythic realities, time shifts and alters according to the individual's sense of reality. In dreams and myths, probable events are quickly or instantly manifested. The events play themselves out in a combination of actual and symbolic forms. This is why dreams and myths must be considered from all aspects of our being—physical, emotional, mental, and spiritual. It is also why myths are such powerful tools for stimulating and shaping dream consciousness.

The fables, myths and tales of the past are replete with esoteric teachings. Many of the ancient masters used them to teach and open the minds of their students. In the Western world, this is most recognized in the parables of Jesus. The student has the responsibility of working with the tale, myth, or parable to find all of the hidden significance within it. Then they would be able to release the archetypal energies, operating through the story images, into their lives.

Work with tales and fables develops a form of thinking and relating that facilitates all dream work (as well as other forms of initiation) to bring us in contact with a higher consciousness. In ancient societies, fables and myths were often recited prior to major initiation rites, releasing even greater power into the ritual. In fact, in many of the ancient mystery traditions, students were not allowed to recite historical, religious or real events, except under strict conditions. This prevented the powers and energies connected with the events from being invoked unnecessarily.

The myths and tales were used to stimulate and enhance initiation rites and exercises of higher consciousness. The initiates would meditate upon the myths and use them in a very ritualistic, empowering manner. It was the students' responsibility to practice working with the symbolic material of the myths and tales. They had to learn to internalize them first and then translate them into specific actions. They learned in this process to use the mythic imagery to stimulate visions while awake and dreams while asleep.

It is for this reason that myths and tales are so effective in dream alchemy. They stir the creative imagination and stretch our image making ability. It is the image which then becomes a matrix for a dream scenario. One method of doing this ("mythic dream work") will be explored through most of the rest of this text. We will learn to combine the methods discussed in Part One of this book with techniques that use myths and tales to stimulate greater dream activity and higher dream consciousness. We will learn to shape the energies of the dreams to bring greater revelations and resolutions.

In mythic dream work, we learn to stimulate dream activity in a manner designed to elicit specific kinds of information. We manipulate the symbology and imagery of myths and tales to impact upon the subconscious mind, which in turn responds with a dream that is most appropriate for us in relation to the energies operating through the myth. In this manner, we can elaborate upon dream emotions, attitudes, and perspectives. We can clarify what we may not have understood. Remember that the symbols and images of *our dreams* are attempts by the subconscious to convey information and directions to the conscious mind. The symbols and images of *our myths* are a means by which the conscious mind can convey directions to the subconscious, so that it will respond according to those directions. Dream communication becomes two way.

We will learn to use myths and tales to stimulate dream activity that releases a specific kind of energy into our life. The symbols within myths and tales will be used in a ritual manner at night to trigger responses within the psyche. The ensuing dream response will reveal where those same mythic energies are currently playing important roles in our life circumstances. The myth and tale thus become the catalyst for greater dream realizations.

Learning to be the dream alchemist involves destruction and creation, two faculties of imagination. We cannot separate the two. We destroy one image so that another can be born. It reflects the process of birth and death. We die to one form to be born to another. This is reflected each night in our sleep. We die to physical consciousness as we are born into dream consciousness.

In the ancient myths and tales, there were primarily three ways to become a shapeshifter, or one who could metamorphose into another form or image. One way was to be trained as a magician or witch and learn to change at will. A second way was to become enchanted by a magic-maker, perhaps by eating something which caused one to change. A third way was to be born a natural shapeshifter, transforming by using the natural forces.

Through mythic dream work, we are taking steps to be all three. We are all born shapeshifters, adjusting our behaviors to our surroundings. Each night when we go to sleep, we are transformed into dream images and realities. We are also enchanted by the magic-makers of our environments, who so strongly influence us.

Other people and situations force us to change in order to live. And
we learned in Part One how to use herbs, fragrances, crystals and
flower essences to assist in our transformations. As we learn to
combine all of these and direct them, we are becoming the
magicians of our lives.

We are learning to transmute energies and forms so that we
shape the energies of dreams and realities in accordance with our
own desires, regardless of external influence. Developing shapeshifting ability through the use of dream alchemy involves
changing your life from the inside out. We change the inner activity,
and it will create repercussions in the outer world. That is the
significance of the scriptural phrase, "The kingdom of God is
within." The divine works through the inner first and then
manifests in an outer expression.

Everyday we change. When we work with mythic dream
work, we are acknowledging these changes and honoring them. We
are becoming an active participant in them. We are learning to
control and use symbols and images to access and invoke the
archetypal energies operating through them.

Joseph Campbell listed four primary functions of mythological
themes, all of which can be applied to dreams. The first is the
mystical or metaphysical, which involves the "reconciliation of
consciousness with the preconditions of its existence," redeeming
us from a sense of guilt in life. The second is the cosmological, which
involves the formulating of an image of the universe, one that helps
us to see that everything is part of a greater whole. The third was the
sociological, which helps us in understanding some social order and
our part in it, no matter how it was created. And the last was the
psychological theme which helps us to understand our individual
aims and ideals.

Most myths, tales and even dreams are problem-solving to
some degree. They are telling us it's time to carry out new
possibilities in our lives. They attempt to tell us to develop some
new quality. They show us ways to shake off the debris of our lives,
and they are definite calls to conscious decision and action.

Those who do very little work with their dreams will find that
most of the dreams they have will be this shaking off of the mental
and emotional debris of the day. Much of the dream activity will
center around the conscious worries. As they begin to work with the
alchemy process of dreams, those kind of dream scenarios will

diminish. The conscious worries will be reflected less within the dreams (although they will occasionally arise). Instead, the dreams will begin to reflect what they are consciously trying to unfold and develop in their lives.

Dream alchemy shows us that anyone can determine the significance of his or her dreams if there is a willingness to explore them. *Everyone who dreams is able to control, interpret, and learn from their dreams!* Using myths and tales is one of the simplest and most effective ways of doing so. Myths and tales are as multi-dimensional as our dreams, so it is easy to discover one or more to apply to your life circumstances or particular situations.

In Appendix B is an index to many myths and tales and some of the symbologies that have come to be associated with them. This index can be used with the mythic dream work techniques to stimulate dream activity which elaborates and clarifies those same energies that may be operating within your own life.

We are working toward a greater understanding of ourselves through dreams and myths. We are attempting to discover an explanation of something in our nature or to elaborate upon it for greater expression of it in our life. We are trying to uncover a narration of universal facts as they apply to and involve our mundane lives. As William Butler Yeats once said, "There is some myth for every man, which if we but knew it, would make us understand all he did and thought."

HOW MYTHIC DREAM WORK OPERATES

Symbols and images, like our dreams, are very chameleonlike. They assume forms according to the moods and attitudes of the individual. They shape themselves in scenarios that express and impress the individual. Our myths and tales are replete with a symbolism that we can use in a ritual/meditational manner to access deeper levels of mind and awaken an awareness of the universal energies that are translated through it in our dreams. We can employ altered states of consciousness to shape our dream energies.

Our dreams come to us through the subconscious mind. It is the bridge between the conscious mind and the archetypal energies playing within our life. The subconscious mind serves as a translator of those energies to conscious awareness through dreams. Through a directed form of meditation and guided imagery, we can consciously send messages to the subconscious, so that it will access, elaborate and clarify the archetypal energies in our life. Through mythic dream work we learn to work consciously in the subconscious.

SENDING MESSAGES THROUGH MYTHS

Archetypal Energies of the Universe

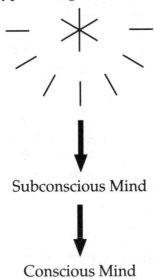

Subconscious Mind

Conscious Mind

We can use the mythic symbols and imagery to consciously send specific messages to the subconscious mind. The subconscious mind in turn accesses the appropriate archetypal force to which the image is connected, causing a greater release of its energies uniquely within our individual life circumstances. This energy release is translated by the subconscious into a meditation or dream scenario that the conscious mind can then more easily understand.

COMMUNICATING WITH UNIVERSAL MIND

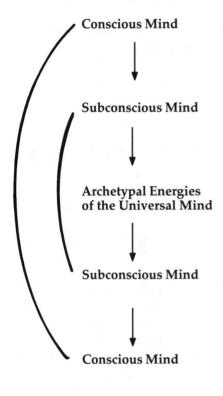

Conscious Mind (Communicates to the subconscious through symbols and images; ie. specific tales and myths.)

Subconscious Mind (Picks up these symbolic messages directed by the conscious mind and passes them on to the Universal Mind-Archetypal Energies.)

Archetypal Energies of the Universal Mind (The messages of the subconscious are picked up and responded to accordingly, releasing specific energies back to the subconscious.)

Subconscious Mind (Translates these new and expanded energies into images and dream scenarios that the conscious mind can relate to.)

Conscious Mind (Receives the new images and dreams, expanding the realization and play of universal energies within the normal, waking life.)

Now that you have learned how myths and dreams trigger appropriate information, and now that you know you can use that information to shapeshift, or change the form of your life, you are ready for the mythic dream work process.

STEP-BY-STEP: HOW TO DO MYTHIC DREAM WORK

1. Choose a myth or tale whose energies you wish to explore. This can be a specific archetypal energy that you have identified within your dream. If so, refer to the next chapter. It may be a myth or tale to help you understand the archetypal energies at play within your own life cycle. In cases such as this, refer to the guidelines in Part Three. You could choose to expand and elaborate upon a

particular symbology, emotion, or attitude. Choose a myth or tale that most corresponds to your purpose. The index in Appendix B will also assist you.

2. If you are using this process for a series of dreams, do not worry if the tale does not fit exactly or follow the content of an original dream explicitly. The primary symbolism will stimulate the mind to provide greater clarification through shaping dream scenarios that best apply to you.

3. Make preparations about an hour before you go to sleep. Once you become familiar with the process, it will not take as long to prepare. As a part of the preparation, you may wish to do any of the following, singularly or in combination:

- Prepare a ritual dream bath with appropriate fragrances.
- Program a crystal to assist you.
- Use an appropriate flower essence to amplify/assist the process.

4. Making sure you will not be disturbed, you begin the programming of the subconscious through meditation. Relax yourself, using guided visualization, progressive relaxation, etc. Alternately tensing and relaxing each muscle group is effective.

5. Close your eyes briefly, visualizing the symbol of the Om in the ball of red light within the throat center of your body. This is the same exercise you practiced in Part One. Visualize, imagine and feel the light emanating outward from this center to create a circular doorway through which you will visualize stepping through in a few moments. Do not step through yet.

6. Gently open your eyes, and softly read aloud to yourself the myth or tale you have selected.

7. Having read the story aloud, close your eyes and once more visualize this doorway. Make it more vibrant. (See the illustration in this chapter.)

8. As you create this mythic dream doorway, visualize, imagine and feel the leading character of your tale, standing within it. Have this character extend his or her hand, to lead you across the threshold. See yourself stepping through the doorway and into the scenery of the tale itself. As you do, allow the lead character (or the one to whom you most strongly relate) to melt into you. Visualize yourself now as this character, going through the activities and

events of the tale. Try and feel what the character felt. Experience it as strongly in your mind as you can.

9. As the tale comes to an end, imagine yourself back at the dream doorway. As you stand there, allow the character to separate from you. Offer your thanks, and step back through the doorway.

10. Allow the doorway to shrink back, fusing itself once more within the throat center. This serves two purposes. It develops the ability to mold and create energies on the more subtle levels, and it develops control of the will force.

11. You may wish to re-read the tale once more, aloud. Reading aloud grounds the mental energies into physical expression. It is a way of affirming that the archetypal energies behind the images and symbols will play themselves out within the physical more clearly. The messages you send and receive will be more clearly heard.

12. Now you have arrived at the end of the process. Just roll over and go to sleep, reminding yourself to remember your dreams. Do not be concerned if you fall asleep during the process. Having read the story and prepared the energy at the beginning will enable it to carry itself through even if not consciously finished.

13. When you are using this process for the first time, choose a story, myth, or tale that you have been drawn to since childhood. Usually there is a reason you are drawn to certain stories. The energies and emotions within them are very reflective of those within your own life. You will trigger dreams that will elaborate the energies of the myths as they are playing within your own life. You will still have to translate and interpret the dream scenario, but now you will have some guideposts. Different dream scenarios will ensue, but the basic archetypal energies will clarify themselves.

Repeat this process for three nights in a row, using the same myth or tale. Three is a creative number. When things are done in a rhythm of three, it activates our own creative energies more dynamically. In this case, we are releasing our creative energies to stimulate dreams along specific lines.

BENEFITS OF MYTHIC DREAM WORK

Using myths as catalysts for dream activities serves a variety of purposes, predominant among them is the elaboration of the content of previous dreams or even specific situations in life. I have

CREATING THE MYTHIC DREAM DOORWAY

As we go to sleep each night, we visualize our dream stimulation symbol within the throat chakra. We then visualize a doorway opening up for us in our dreams. It may be a regular door, a cave, or even a simple hole through which you can walk. On the door or over the opening, always visualize your dream symbol to link waking and sleeping.

often heard individuals say, "I wish I could go back into that dream and find out more about what it meant." Through mythic dream work, you can stimulate a dream or whole series of dreams that re-express the content of the original scenario, giving you more to work with and facilitating understanding.

You can use mythic dream work processes to stimulate revelations about specific aspects or qualities operating in your life. For example, using the mythic dream work technique outlined in the next chapter, you could use the tale of "King Midas and His Golden Touch" to elicit dreams that reveal where greed or carelessness might be operating in your life. It may even reveal around whom or what this greed is centered. The dream will not be a replication of the tale, but it will be translated into a scenario appropriate to you and your own individual life circumstances. This is part of the function of the index in Appendix B. In this way, each night can become an educational process of revelation and elaboration.

Dreams stimulated through mythic dream work can reveal opportunities to correct situations in your life or reveal where such opportunities exist. Choosing a myth that is tied to the symbologies and energies of new and unusual opportunities will trigger inspirational dreams around activities, people or events that are applicable to your life.

You can also use myths and tales to reveal where your energies are blocked. Choosing myths and tales that involve the symbols and images of overcoming restrictions and bonds will resonate with the subconscious. This will trigger dreams that reveal the restrictions in your own life that must be overcome or help clarify those restricting situations.

Mythic dream work awakens inspiration and creativity. Poets, writers, and artists from all times have told how inspiration was drawn from dreams. Coleridge, Goethe and Jung are but three. Mythic dream work stimulates the unconscious intuition so that inspiration can manifest through dream energies. It also awakens higher teachings through the dream imagery. Dream work can be a probationary path for the spiritual disciple, providing great symbolic instruction and eventual contact with masters.

Working with the mythic dream work process will increase dream activity in general. They will become more vivid and colorful, and it will lead to the development of lucid dreaming. This is the realization of being in a dream while you are dreaming. Remember that we are attempting to infuse conscious control over a state that we have allowed to occur unconsciously. Initially in dream scenarios the setting is involuntary, but in lucid dreaming, more and more volitional elements enter into it. As we become more aware of our role in the dream and the dream's purpose, we can change the outcome. We begin the ability to shape the course of the dream while in it. (Lucid dreaming is a dynamic prelude to consciously controlled out-of-body experiences.)

As we work with this, many opportunities for growth in our outer life will occur. This is part of what we are invoking through the dream alchemy process. Creativity will increase. Opportunities to face personality issues and fears will arise. There will be an increased awareness of karma and the path of correction. We will have greater opportunity to clear the subconscious of limitations and restriction, self-imposed or otherwise. We open ourselves to greater healing opportunities on all levels. We begin to harmonize the inner and outer worlds of our life. We also gain greater control, or opportunities for control, over our life circumstances.

MYTHIC DREAM WORK CASE HISTORIES

By looking at two case histories, we can see how individuals have benefited from using the mythic dream work process. These two case histories deal with people who were having problems with money or problems establishing the kind of relationships they wanted. Since these are common challenges faced by many of us, it is a good way to see how we can use the mythic dream work process to aid in our own metamorphosis.

Case History 1: Mythic Dream Work for Insight into Abundance
In this case, we have an individual who is in his late thirties. He has been trying to establish new areas of abundance and prosperity in his life. He would get so far and then the money flow would just stop. He was planning on initiating a new business, but was concerned about the best way to break down barriers that could prevent its success.

Myth Chosen for the Dream Work
Because he wanted to establish greater abundance, this man

used the "Tale of King Midas" to open insight as to the best things to avoid. He hoped it would clarify barriers that could be cleared.

Dreams Stimulated

(The first night of the mythic dream work stimulated a dream which he felt gave him his clearest insight into barriers in regards to the flow of money.) "I saw myself at a family gathering. It was like a reunion. I was one of the last to arrive. I was kind of happy about it because I wanted to make an entrance. As I entered the house, I saw it was the inside of a church. My father immediately jumped on me for being late. I told him I was not late that this is exactly the time I had said I would arrive. I even showed him my watch. He just turned his back, muttering that the rest of the family arrived early, why couldn't I.

"Then everyone started arguing and fighting. I don't remember all that was said, but several statements stayed strong. One was from my older brother who said: 'You've always thought you were better than the rest of us.' And another was 'You think you're going to out-do your old man, well you never will.' I remember grabbing my father, ready to hit him. I was crying. All I wanted to do was to be acknowledged for what I had accomplished. A pat on the back, a 'we're proud of you'—anything.

"I remember letting him go and turning my back on them. I stopped, faced them all and said, 'I don't need you. I can succeed without any of you. I've already got more than any of you.' I then proceeded to tell each of them why they would never succeed as much as I would. I said anything I could to make them hurt.

"I left, feeling angry and glad they were jealous of me. I also was very sad. The last thing I saw was the despair on their faces. I had crushed their only illusions. I woke up crying."

Insights and Impressions

This man remembered as he described his dream a time in childhood in which he had wanted to chip in to buy a Christmas present for his parents. Usually the brothers joined their money together, but this time the others in the family had decided to do their purchases separately, rather than as a group.

At the time, he was only about nine years old and had very little money of his own, not enough to buy any present by himself. He said he had felt so left out and so bad about not getting a present that it was one of the worst Christmases he had ever had. And no one had even noticed or seemed to care.

As he talked he began to clarify some old emotions and ideas about abundance. He saw a lot of his abundance tied up in relation to his family. He saw a conflict between having money and how it would appear to the others in his family.

He wanted to have more than anyone else in the family. He felt that being prosperous would make the others feel less successful. Part of him wanted that to happen, while another part didn't. There was that part of him that did not want to make the others feel poor because of how he remembered feeling when he had no money to buy a present as a child. Because he was pulled, he saw why his earlier business ventures would only succeed up to a point and then hit a limbo period.

There was also an issue in regards to spirituality and money. A part of him felt that he could not be spiritual and have money as well. This was reflected in the setting of the dream. He entered what he thought was his house, only to find himself in a church. His family had been very religious and with little money, other than for necessities.

As we talked we began to explore ways of resolving these conflicts. We began to explore ways of seeing wealth and family and prosperity and spirituality as not being mutually exclusive. He began to work on ways of avoiding pitfalls of emotions in regards to the family. We began to discuss ways of being and dealing with success without taking the responsibility for how others respond to it as well (particularly by not taking ownership of the guilt placed upon him for succeeding—whether placed upon him by himself or by others.)

Case History 2: Mythic Dream Work to Clarify Envy and Jealousy

In this individual's case, we have a mid-twenties female who was attracting a lot of negative jealousy and resentful responses from her coworkers. She was ambitious and motivated, and she felt like others resented her for it—even though she admittedly was accomplishing things in the work environment that she believed helped everyone. At the same time, she was confused that in spite of her work success, she still was having difficulty with establishing friends or finding someone for a deeper, more personal relationship.

Myth Chosen for the Dream Work

Because of the two predominant issues, (1) jealousy and envy and (2) the lack of personal, fulfilling relationships, the tale of "Snow White and the Seven Dwarves" was utilized with the mythic dream work process over a four day period.

Dreams Stimulated

Although she claimed that she rarely remembered her dreams, two small scenarios stayed with her during her mythic dream work.

Dream One: "I saw myself back home with my family. I was about twelve again. I was in the kitchen with my younger brother and sister. My brother is two years younger than I, and my sister is six years younger. I was packing them lunch for school. I remember rushing, as if we were late. I was worried that if we were late I would get in trouble.

"I was very upset, especially at my brother because he had not done the breakfast dishes right. I knew that if Mom came home from work and saw them in the state they were in, we'd all get in trouble, especially me. I was panicked, trying to redo the dishes and still take care of getting my brother and sister off to school. I didn't say anything to my brother, but I made noise with the dishes to let him know I was redoing what he had obviously not done right.

Dream Two: "The second dream I remembered took place at school. I remember being late for class and not even speaking to others as I ran into the school. I knew several were upset that I had not spoken in my hurry, but I remember thinking that I would straighten it out later.

"As I came to the hallway with my locker, I couldn't find it. I couldn't even remember the locker number. I was panicked. Finally I went to the area that I knew the locker was in and opened one— even though it didn't have my number on it. My books were inside, and as I pulled them out, I saw that my homework was only half done. I was scared to death. My work had never been late. How was I going to explain this. As I ran to my class, as the bell was ringing, I remember thinking that this was going to affect my overall grade. As I ran to the room, I woke up panicked."

Insights and Impressions

This individual was highly motivated and ambitious. She is also, admittedly, a bit of a perfectionist. She indicated that she remembered being put in charge of her younger brothers and sisters a lot in childhood because she was the oldest. She was the one in charge when her mother was not at home. This was even more dramatic for her as her mother and father divorced when she was ten. She was the one held responsible if things were out of line at home.

She felt that maybe she was not understanding how the others were responding to her own perfectionism. She realized they may be taking it as a reflection on themselves. Just as she banged the dishes, redoing the task of her brother, she felt she should see if maybe she was sending some of those same unspoken messages of disapproval to her coworkers.

With the second dream, she also saw how maybe her entire focus and manner at work—along with her absorption in it—may be putting the others off. She may be doing at work what she did in the dream. She was so focused on getting the job done and done well, that she forgot the common courtesies of the day—the greetings, etc. She felt she was probably being too stiff at work, and not taking enough time just to converse and share.

She assumed that the others understood, but apparently they didn't. Her failure to acknowledge the schoolmates in the dream caused her to reflect on her acknowledgment (or lack of) of her coworkers. She decided to pay more attention to them, and to begin working on eliminating the pattern of "If it's going to be done right, it will have to be done by me."

Within a month's time, there was a changing response in her coworkers to her, as she began to acknowledge them on levels other than just work. She began making suggestions for change for her coworkers to enforce, while refusing to take the responsibility of the changes upon herself. She is still working on this, but she is having more success.

Mythic dream work has been commonly practiced as long as humanity has existed. These case histories show us that by practicing it we learn to work with and manipulate mundane and spiritual energies through the language of symbology and the power of imagination.

Mythic dream work is an art form. It should be treated with reverence, for it reveals the nature of other worlds to us. The use of it is similar to times of prayer and spiritual upliftment, for it energizes the soul and aligns it with the physical. It is not a process of mindscapes or "let's pretend." It is a powerful process of transformation. It involves the alchemical process of molding old energies and the creating of new with greater, directed consciousness.

CHAPTER SEVEN

Archetypes and the Mythic Dream Work Process

In Part One we explored archetypal energies and how to identify them within our dreams. We examined how the role they play in our lives is reflected by the images and symbols in our dream scenarios. We will now learn how to use the mythic dream work process to stimulate dream scenarios that will elaborate upon those energies.

This process does not eliminate the need to interpret our dreams, but it will be easier to interpret them because the meditations and preparations will elicit dream responses along very discernible lines. The mythic dream work process enables us to expand dream activity to facilitate greater awareness. It also leads to the development of lucid dreaming, which can be then taken to the next step of out-of-body experiences. We use mythic dream work activities to further stimulate the subconscious mind along specific lines, so that the archetypal energies operating through them will be elaborated and expanded in our lives.

Dreams show us which areas of life we must face to develop certain strengths and qualities. The archetypal energies reflected in our dreams reveal the energies upon which we should focus. They may show where we have failed to develop certain qualities in the past. They may show us where we have failed to act successfully. They may reveal the attitudes that can prevent our strengths and abilities from manifesting in our outer lives.

The archetypes may not seem connected to our waking realities at all, but they may reflect symbolically that which is hindering fuller expression of our potentials. This is where the true importance of mythic dream work comes in. We may stimulate dreams through myths for greater revelations on achieving abundance in our lives. For example, as a result of our mythic dream work, we may dream of great anger. This anger, regardless of the scenario in which it is expressed during the dream, may then be the adversary that is preventing you from achieving the abundance you desire in your life.

With mythic dream work, there will always be a connection between your dream scenarios and your individual purpose for the dream shaping. The connection may not always be obvious or what we wish to know, but the dream scenario that results from this process will enable you to more fully examine and understand the way archetypal energies are manifesting within your own life circumstance. We can use myths and tales to elicit greater understanding of dreams that have already occurred and to stimulate and direct new dream activity along lines we choose to dream. In this chapter is a chart of basic tales and myths reflecting the seven archetypal energies previously discussed. These are general, of course, and any one myth or tale usually involves several archetypes.

In the rest of this chapter, we will explore how the mythic dream work process can be applied to specific archetypal energies. These can then be adapted for use with all of the other dream-shaping processes described throughout the rest of this book. The first technique involves using myths and tales to elaborate upon a previous dream, so that we can understand more fully the energies reflected in it. The mythic dream work process will *not* reactivate an identical dream scenario. It *will* stimulate dreams that reflect those same energies found in the original dream, only it will do so in different scenarios, so that we can explore them more fully.

The second mythic dream work technique employs myths and tales to stimulate new dream activity along particular archetypal lines. This enables us to awaken to a greater understanding and application of specific archetypal energies within our life. This is where the index of myths and tales in the appendix comes into play. While the second method may seem easier, the first actually is because with the first method we are simply exploring and elaborating upon what has already revealed itself to us.

The third technique is an even more specific example of using this process to stimulate revelations in accordance with specific archetypal energies. In this case, we will examine how to use it for an elaboration of the "Adversary Archetype," which will be especially useful when analyzing nightmares.

ARCHETYPE OF THE SELF	— French tale of "Master and the Pupil" — German tales of Tyll Ulenspiegel — Italian tale "Jump Into My Sack" — Egyptian tale "Promises of Three Sisters" — Story of Pinocchio — Irish tale "Man Who Had No Stories" — South African tale "Mbega Kgego"
ARCHETYPE OF THE FEMININE	— All tales of the goddesses — "Snow White and Rose Red" — American Indian tale "How Men and Women Got Together" — "Merlin and Nimue" — Grimm's "Old Woman in the Forest" — Egyptian tale "Promises of Three Sisters"
ARCHETYPE OF THE MASCULINE	— All tales of the gods — Tales of Odysseus — German tale "Master Thief" — "Merlin and Nimue" — American Indian tale "How Men and Women Got Together" — Labors of Hercules
ARCHETYPE OF THE HERO	— Tales of Odysseus — Greek tale of Atlanta and the Calydon Boar — "Rumpelstiltskin" — German tale of "Master Thief" — Grimm's tale of "Boy Who Went Forth to Find What Fear Was" — "Jason and the Argonauts"
ARCHETYPE OF THE ADVERSARY	— Refer to chapter one, "Nightmares" — Biblical tale of David and Goliath — Biblical tale of Jonah and the Whale — German tale "The Goose Girl" — "Cinderella" — "Snow White and the Seven Dwarves" — African tale "Old Crone and Iblees the Devil"
ARCHETYPE OF DEATH/REBIRTH	— "Rumpelstiltskin" — German Tale of "Goose Girl" — Dicken's *A Christmas Carol* — Crucifixion and resurrection of Jesus — "Sleeping Beauty" — "The Sword in the Stone" — African Bushman tale "Moon and the Hare"
ARCHETYPE OF THE JOURNEY	— Travels of Odysseus — Grimm's "Boy Who Went Forth to Find What Fear Was" — Biblical tale of Joseph and the Coat of Many Colors — *Alice in Wonderland* — *Through the Looking Glass*

TECHNIQUE ONE: ELABORATING UPON
THE ARCHETYPES OF OUR DREAMS

The first task in using this technique is to determine what major archetypal energies are reflected within the dream. In Part One we explored the seven major archetypal influences. Although there will be several, which seems to be the predominant archetype? Is this the one you wish to have elaborated? Is one of the minor archetypes reflected in your dreams what you wish to have elaborated through mythic dream work?

Remember that this elaboration process is just that. It is an opportunity to dream another dream related to the first one. It does not mean that the same dream will replay itself in an extended version. Instead a new dream scenario will be stimulated, involving greater reflections of that same archetypal influence. This will enable you to more fully articulate what its role is in your waking life circumstances. It will assist you in understanding the first dream more fully.

Induce a dream by repeating the mythic dream work process, as outlined in chapter six. When you record your dreams the next day, pay attention to the major figures in it. This often reveals where those archetypal energies are playing important roles in your life. Depending upon the scenario, it can reveal where and with whom those energies are most active. The events of the dream show us whether we may need to soften or strengthen that particular kind of energy.

This elaboration does not forgo the process of dream interpretation. It simply stimulates dream activity in relation to previous dreams, so that we have more to work with in the interpretive aspect. Something said in several different ways is more likely to be understood than that which is said in only one way.

The manner in which the archetypal energies reflect themselves in our dreams will vary. Opposite effects may occur. This is best understood by examining mythic figures which represent opposing archetypal energies. In greek mythology, Apollo is a male figure, a sun god. This is a *masculine* archetype. On the other hand, he is also the god of music, creativity and artistry which are *feminine* archetypal energies. Another example is Apollo's sister Artemis (*feminine*). She is skilled at the hunt which is *masculine*. We are all a combination of masculine and feminine energies in varying proportions at varying times. Do not rely on the obvious in your post-dream analysis.

The dreams stimulated by this technique will help you to discern the quality of a particular archetype. This is determined by the dream ego, along with the egos of the other dream characters. You may be playing all the parts in the dream.

The archetypal energies we invoke more dynamically through mythic dream work are neutral. However, they may reveal themselves in our lives in an unbalanced fashion. This enables us to correct our activities so that a more balanced and powerful expression of that energy unfolds.

Our personal roles in the dreams we stimulate through this technique determine the basic energies operating within your life. The actual dream activities provide clues as to where, how, when, why and with whom they most often manifest. They provide insight into our psychological behaviors in our waking life. They also provide a spiritual vision for calling up new strengths from the universal mind, to which we are all connected.

TECHNIQUE TWO: UNVEILING ALL
OF THE ARCHETYPES

In this second technique of working with and understanding the archetypes of our dreams, we will work with all seven archetypes more generally. This exercise is designed to reveal where the various archetypal forces are playing important roles in our lives. It is also designed to assist us in determining whether they are being experienced and expressed in a balanced manner. If we can reveal imbalance in an archetypal manifestation, we can set about correcting our course of action. We stimulate dream activity to provide insight into our daily life circumstances. We use this technique so that we will be able to enhance or to correct patterns that could otherwise disrupt or hinder.

Many myths and heroic tales start with a younger individual leaving home to seek a fortune (the *Self* in the form of the *Feminine* or *Masculine* upon the *Journey*). Esoteric lore and hero tales are actually giving us pictures of journeys we all must take in our lives, especially in the process of initiation into higher mysteries.

Along the way, the individual encounters obstacles to this journey (the *Adversary*), forcing a change in the individual (*Death/Rebirth*) so that the obstacle can be overcome and the rewards achieved (the *Heroic* archetype). Thus, most tales reflect the play of all seven major archetypal influences. To use an heroic tale in mythic dream work is a matter of deciding which myth or tale most reflects the circumstances of one's life. Although this quest will be explored more fully in Part Five ("Dream Time Initiation"), we can still use aspects of it in unveiling the general play of archetypal influence.

The call of the quest in most tales and legends is a call to adventure. It is the call to growth and maturity. In many heroic tales, the individual enters the service of a great king, symbolic of a greater force or the higher self. These tales often have older male/female characters who, when met, will offer advice. They are symbolic of elders working with the physical plane, available to us as we begin to expand our awareness. As we work with expanding our consciousness through dream work, the archetypal teachers and energies are more recognizable and accessible.

Whether a myth, legend, or a simple fairy tale, the stories are most often allegories for greater truth and awareness. They are ever-becoming and self-perpetuating. By aligning with a poignant myth, the psyche begins to expand. We see our lives in a grander perspective. We open to greater possibilities.

Finding our own mythic tale—the one which reflects our life most accurately—is difficult. We change, and as we change, the myths and tales to which we are drawn will change as well. The tales that appealed to us as children may not appeal to us as adults. So, begin with a mythic tale you have always felt drawn to, preferably one that involves an individual stepping out onto an adventure or journey. Listed below are a number of examples:

- "Jason and the Argonauts"
- Tales of Odysseus
- Tales of the Knights of the Round Table.
- *Alice's Adventures in Wonderland*
- Sumerian tale of Atalanta and the Calydon Boar
- Ishtar and the rescue of Tammuz
- African tale of Nana Miriam
- Biblical tale of Joseph and the Coat of Many Colors

The tales of the gods and goddesses are representative of archetypes. They strike the chords of our own inner music, and directly relate to our own images. In myths and tales, they were the models of behavior, and so our psyche will resonate with them in varying degrees.

It is beneficial to use the mythic dream work technique as a prelude to sleep for as many days as there are main characters within the tale. Remember that each character, and the events surrounding that character, reflect certain archetypes. You are trying to awaken as much revelation as you can about all of the seven major archetypes in your life. Thus, if a tale has seven major characters, perform the mythic dream work ritual for seven days.

Follow the usual procedure in setting up and performing the mythic dream work ritual. Each time that you step through the mythic dream doorway, you will assume the persona of a different character—even those who may not seem pleasant. Remember that you are trying to elicit as much information about as many archetypal energies within your life as you can. Assuming the persona of the major characters (including the adversary) stimulates dreams that reveal where those similar energies are active in your waking life. The dream scenario that ensues holds the key.

The post dream analysis is very important for this process, and it is important to do the analysis each day, after you have performed the exercise. Record your dreams as usual, listing the major events and images of your dreams. Align those major events with one of the seven archetypes. Begin a questioning process. Are there connections between the events in the dreams and the events of the tale you used? Do not worry if you are imagining or stretching the relationships. You would not be able to find them at all if they weren't operating on some level.

Which of the archetypes seem to be expressing themselves positively within your dream? Which are imbalanced? Who and what were these associated with? The answers to these questions provide clues to the manifestations of the archetypes in your waking life. It is important to apply them to your waking life. What emotions are strongest and who or what are they related to? Are you being told to change how you handle them or are you being shown that your efforts are ineffectual?

Are there archetypal energies that don't appear within the scenario? Is it then also missing within your life? If the dream scenario culminates positively, regardless of missing archetypal energies, then there is nothing to be overly concerned about. If the events are confused and unresolved, and if one or more of the archetypes are not found in the dream, then maybe we need to develop it more in our life.

We are still working with our dreams, but now we are learning to recognize the universal energies that touch us and affect us on very subtle and real levels. As we become more aware of them, we can then begin to manipulate them more fully. The alchemical process cannot take place if we are unaware of the elements involved. With the exercises in this chapter and those that follow through the rest of Part Two, we are stretching our subtle muscles of consciousness. We are learning to re-establish lines of communication so that we can begin to control and direct them more fully. We are acknowledging the archetypal influences in our lives.

Most dreams raise questions, not answers. However, you will find a number of correspondences between the tales and the contents of your dreams. You will also find increasing relationships between the dream content and your daily life situations. As we begin to recognize them and identify the various archetypal energies at play, the real adventure begins.

TECHNIQUE THREE: THE ADVERSARY
IN OUR NIGHTMARES

Some may think it strange to begin exploring the use myths and tales in dream work with nightmares. It is not so. Nightmares are strong messages to us. They demand attention. The methods we will explore are not designed to stimulate nightmares, but rather they are designed to stimulate dreams that help clarify what was so frightening.

Most people force themselves awake in nightmares. This is a form of avoidance. The individual runs from what they are being confronted with—usually the things most feared. We can use the myths and tales with the dream work techniques of re-immersion to arrive at a resolution of these energies. Using these techniques, you perform a meditation in which you attempt to re-enter the same nightmare scenario. In the meditation, you alter the scenario so that whatever you have been running from is confronted and overcome.

We have many fears to confront and overcome in life. In myths and tales they are symbolized by the monsters and demons that the hero must oppose. Most of these fears are excess baggage, so we can use tales and myths to heal ourselves of inner adversaries. We can exorcise ourselves in a conscious manner. The monsters of myths and legends assist us in meeting these inner demons. If we can confront them within our dreams, it will not only resolve the karma that has created them, but it will also manifest opportunities to remove their manifestation within our daily life situations. We can use myths and tales of monsters to show us where our own monsters are and how best to defeat them.

This kind of confrontation enacted within the physical life through the catalyst of mythic dream work does not occur in artificially contrived situations. It occurs in the normal course of our daily life. It may stir up old situations involving individuals who were the original source of our inner monsters and fears. It may also create new situations with new people that simply reflect those same old fears and monsters that we have not yet confronted. The old monsters simply arise under new conditions.

There is an old saying that dragons are not meant to be slain but controlled. Our fears, our old unresolved issues are monsters only as long as we allow them to be. Reading about the monsters in myths and tales helps us to uncover them within our own psyche. Dream work through myths stimulates the process of knowing ourselves. This includes shedding light upon those darker recesses of the mind. It involves allowing the light to shine on the old fears, issues, habits and behaviors that are not beneficial to us.

All mythologies contain monstrous beings, many of which are the most important aspect of the myths. They are symbols of the forces we must encounter in the natural world. We can use the mythic dream work process to stimulate dreams that reveal our own psychological monsters, along with the best means to overcome and control them. Monsters can only be fought in the mythical sense. In the human sense, they must be faced and transmuted.

In homeopathy, a rule of thumb is that "like cures like." We can use the ancient myths of monsters to bridge an awareness to our own "monstrous"aspects. We can use the myths where the hero overcomes the monster or demon to cure ourselves of our own nightmares. This usually occurs in one of three steps or a combination of these steps:

1. We awaken our awareness of our inner monsters and demons through the dream stimulation process. Sometimes this is all that is necessary to exorcise them.

2. We learn to correct and control the monsters and our responses to them by controlling all dream functions. If we develop lucid dreaming, we can change the elements of the dream while we are in the the dream itself. Thus, we are no longer at the mercy of that which is pursuing us.

3. The mythic dream stimulation will have repercussions in your physical life.The process serves as a ritual invocation, one that will create an opportunity to confront the real life counterpart in your waking life. It invokes the Hermetic Principle of Correspondence: "As above, so below; as below, so above."

Different monsters and demons represent different aspects. Knowing which aspects they represent helps us when working upon our own monsters and demons. We want to become the dream hero, overcoming all monsters, adversaries, and obstacles.

As always, certain preparations are necessary. Perform a meditation with the appropriate mythical monster first. Visualize yourself face to face with it, confronting it and overcoming it. As you prepare for bed, utilize any herbs or fragrances applicable. As you retire, create the dream doorway. Then cross through the doorway into the myth that contains the monster you wish to confront.

The dreams that follow can be very explicit or subtle but they will reveal the adversarial energy. You may see yourself in life situations that clearly reveal those monstrous qualities in you, or you may see someone else displaying them. You may see yourself running from a monster in a particular environment, reflecting where this inner monster most often will rear its head in your life. It will not be difficult to recognize this monster. It may be a predominant emotion, negativity, behavior or anything else that is unbalanced in your life.

You can also create your own tale involving the monster you need to control. If there is a quality you are desirous to change or confront, imagine it as a monster or as a being of some secretive aspect. Imagine a series of events in which you are brought face to face with it and must overcome it. Follow the pattern of the ancient myths. Imagine the joy, celebration and honor that comes as a result.

We do not have to always fight and kill our monsters. Sometimes our dreams may show us trying to do this in a very ineffectual manner. When this occurs, we should take the hint and find a different way of confronting and overcoming our fears and demons rather than through direct confrontation. The following list includes demons and monsters from various mythologies around the world, and descriptions of their basic energies and symbolic aspects.

Amazons

In Greek and Roman mythologies, these warrior women were powerful and knew how to deal with unwelcome advances. Their stories can serve to show you the best way to fend off outside intrusions and advances, as well as to help you see where they are occurring or are most likely to occur.

Animals

Animals have been symbols of many different qualities found in humanity, positive and negative. If we examine those qualities we fear most, we can usually liken them to certain animal characteristics. Using animals as symbols is an excellent way of creating your own dream myth to overcome adversaries, internal and external. Many of our fears, especially in childhood, appear as wild beasts of various sorts.

Boreas

In Greek mythology, Boreas is the North Wind. It can bring destruction and iciness to your life or represent those qualities. King Aeolus gave it to Odysseus to assist him in his journey. This is a good myth to overcome fears of stagnancy.

Charybdis

This is the daughter of Gaia and Poseidon in Greek legend. She was thrown into the sea by a thunderbolt from Zeus. She drinks in tremendous amounts of sea water and spits it out, creating giant whirlpools. In his travels, Odysseus had to face this danger. It is an excellent myth to use when we are feeling we have no control or are about to drown in our circumstances. It is also effective in working to escape the whirlpools of our past.

Calypso

Odysseus stayed with her for seven years. Although not a monster in and of herself, including her in a tale or reading tales associated with her assists in releasing energies to deal with fears of aging and the problems of youth. Its energy is effective in overcoming fears of overprotectiveness.

Echidne

In Greek mythology, she was killed by the many-eyed monster Argus. She gave birth to other terrifying monsters: Cerberus (the hound of Hades), the Chimaera, the Hydra, and the two-headed Orthrus. Working with her image is effective in dream work if we need to see if our actions and behaviors are giving birth to more trouble. It can also be used to reveal whether our present troubles are just the icing upon the cake.

Giant With No Head

In Chinese mythology there is a battle between this giant and the high god Tiandi. This tale assists in stimulating dreams for revealing and overcoming chaos and confusion.

Hercules

A hero of Greek mythology, his twelve labors involved overcoming monsters and beasts. His myth is an excellent tool for mythic dream work as applied to nightmares and fears.

Harpies

The Harpies were birdlike creatures who pecked and tore at Jason and the men of the Argonaut in Greek mythology. They are symbols of fierce winds, gossip and pettiness that can tear at us. They can represent an over-critical nature and feelings of guilt over the past which eats at us. Chasing them away is a means of eliminating those old feelings.

Fates

The three Fates of Greek mythology can assist us in our fears and problems involving time schedules—worry over time, our life span, etc. These three women spun the thread of life, measured it and cut it when they felt it necessary. Working with these images can ease stress over deadlines and aging which can easily manifest nightmares.

Hag of Ironwood

In Norse mythology, she was Loki's wife. She had the ability to alter reality to lead others astray. If our own life picture becomes distorted and confused, we can use her image to stimulate dreams that reveal where we are off track.

Maenads (Bacchae)

These were the madwomen of Greek mythology who allowed themselves to lose all rationality in their celebrations. Working with the myths and images of them assists us in seeing where we give into our emotions or where the emotions are unbalanced. The tale of Pentheus and Dionysus is particularly effective.

Marm

This is a witch in Australian folklore. The Marm would cast spells to drive others crazy, slowly. They caused others to hear voices and see shadowy menaces. She traded her eyes for her magical ability. This is an excellent image and tale to work with nightmares due to imbalanced psychism, paranoia, mistrust of friends and a lost sense of reality. Overcoming this image restores proper perspective.

Murga Muggui

Another monster from Australian lore, this is a giant spider who spins webs to entrap victims. The tale of Mullyan and Murgah is one of the best for this. If we feel we are being trapped into anything, claustrophobic, penned in, or threatened, this is the tale with which to work.

Sirens

In Greek mythology, the Sirens are sea nymphs who (through their hauntingly beautiful song) lure travelers to them and kill them. Odysseus encountered them in his journeys. This is a monster that can be used to represent any obsession. It can be used to reveal seduction and manipulation and ways to overcome them in our life.

These fifteen are by no means the only beasts and monsters appropriate to mythic dream work. Every society has its tales of monsters and beasts. From the Irish Banshee with its call to death (and thus its signal for transition) to the headless horseman in "The Legend of Sleepy Hollow"(again heralding death or transition) ghosts, demons, and beasts are a part of all traditions and all human psyches.

CHAPTER EIGHT

Four Exercises in Metamorphosis

The effect of mythic dream work is much deeper than you may initially realize. The energies of the myths will influence the dream state, but they also will bring a new kind of energy into your waking life as well. Through mythic dream work, you are learning to manipulate symbols and images to alter the energy circumstances of your waking life.

If you stimulate dreams through mythic dream work to provide information and opportunity to overcome anger, you may find that it affects your physical life. You may find yourself having to overcome anger in specific real life situations. It has been said that you should never pray for patience unless you wants to encounter situations that will try your patience. This can be a side benefit of mythic dream work. You may stimulate dreams for greater revelation of weaknesses to be overcome, but you may also release energies that manifest similar situations in real life, testing your ability to overcome them. When this does occur, you can use the dream scenario to help you know how to handle the situation.

The following exercises are preliminary stretching exercises for the psyche. They are meditations and they build a flexibility in your subtle energy fields. They stretch the creative imagination, develop concentration and visualization. They are effective for sending messages to the subconscious, messages that will become more active as you get deeper into the alchemical process.

These exercises are not just cute and fun. They each serve specific purposes and functions that assist in developing the ability to awaken full consciousness within the dream state. They strengthen the astral body so that it can become a dynamic vehicle for our consciousness while we are asleep. The more we infuse ourselves with thoughts of shapeshifting and alchemy, the greater the results. These exercises stimulate more creative versatility. These exercises help establish a mindset that enables us to discover new options within our life situations. We are working with basic universal principles. What we do on one level, carries over and affects us on all others.

Initially, perform these exercises on a regular basis. Doing them several times a week will quickly develop the ability to shift your attention and energy. Feel free to adapt them to your own needs. Some may say that they have no time to do all of these exercises and still handle the daily tasks. You do not have to perform all the meditations in a single day. They can be rotated, but performing these shapeshifting meditations strengthens our astral muscles, stimulating more vibrant dream activity. Also, as you become familiar with them, they will take little time to perform. As you develop your concentration, you can learn to shift consciousness and perform them in five to ten minutes.

Be aware that when we are working to control the subconscious mind, we will encounter resistance. For most people the subconscious mind is used to following whatever whim it encounters. When we use meditation, ritual and other methods of accessing and controlling it, it will resist. This resistance can take many forms to distract us from our purpose: an itch, a worry over a work or family matter, a thought that you don't have enough time to do it, etc. The mind may wander in fifty different directions.

When this occurs, do not get upset. Simply persist, and eventually the resistance will diminish. Resistance is actually a positive sign. We only encounter resistance when we have tapped into the subconscious. Recognize it as such, bring your attention back to the point of focus and continue with the exercise. You are training the subconscious to work along the lines you consciously decide— whether awake or asleep! For all three of these exercises in metamorphosis, take care to prepare:

1. Choose a time in which you can perform them un-interrupted.

2. You may wish to use soft, meditation music that is soothing to you. The more relaxed you are, the greater the benefits.

3. Perform slow rhythmic breathing or a progressive relaxation. Feel and imagine warm, relaxing energy melting over and through every part of your body—from your toes to your head. Take your time in doing this. With practice, you will find yourself shifting into a relaxed state the moment you start your rhythmic breathing.

There are many ways to work on developing a consciousness of shapeshifting and alchemy. Many myths and tales involve these transformative energies: The prince who turned into the frog, the story of Beauty and the Beast, etc. Remember that we are exercising our mental energies to create and expand consciousness while awake and asleep. Creativity works at all times; with these exercises we are accelerating its manifestation by working from the inner to the outer.

Most importantly, have fun with the exercises. They are infused with images and symbols to elicit dynamic effects, effects which prove themselves out in our physical life. Development and unfoldment do require energy and effort and a certain amount of time. There is no "fast-food" remedy. However, we can enjoy that effort. What is most essential and beneficial from these exercises is that they bring back to life the dreamer within us, the dreamer that lives while we are awake or asleep.

EXERCISE ONE: THE MAGICAL BUTTERFLY

The first exercise is one that is beneficial for children with nightmares. With practice, they can see themselves flying off to dreamland as a magical butterfly. If you work with a child on this exercise, you may wish to have the child act out the transformation that is described. For those who worry about neglecting their children by working on personal exercises, this provides an excellent opportunity to invite them into the activity. They thoroughly enjoy it.

As you begin to relax, allow your attention to be focused entirely upon yourself. You are alone and safe, warm and comfortable. Your eyes are closed and nothing can distract you or hurt you. The darkness that surrounds you is soothing.

You begin to notice that you are not in total darkness. It is more of a gray. You see within your mind's eye that you are sitting within a small spherical enclosure. It is formed of millions of thin threads, spiraling and winding around you, giving you just enough room to stretch if you need to. It appears as if these threads have frozen into a silvery form. What light there is shines through them and casts a grayish-silver shimmer within the dome.

This is your cocoon. It is a cocoon from which you emerge each night. It is the cocoon of your life. Its only colors are grays and silvers. It is comfortable, but it is also limiting.

The threads that form its sides are all the threads that you have sewn in life. The threads of your life have created a cocoon in which you can feel comfortable, safe, protected and closed off. And yet through some of the threads come slivers of light from another world, causing the silver threads to dance with new life. It makes you wonder what beauty this other world might hold.

You stand and move to a spot in the cocoon where a sliver of light from the outside sneaks through. You place your eye there, squinting through that tiny opening. For an instant, a rainbow of color flashes in your eye. It is almost blinding in its intensity. The brilliance of the color (greater than you have ever imagined) takes your breath away.

You step back, filled with awe. You must see this other world as it truly is. You know that only within its light will you be able to see who you really are.

You gently feel along the sides of the cocoon, searching for an opening. There are no doors and no windows. The sides do feel rubbery, and as you push and feel, they give with your touch. With your hands, you gently separate the threads slowly, like bands of elastic. You extend your hands and arms out through the walls. The outer light touches them, and you are filled with a sense of freedom and power. Moving your arms, you stretch the opening wider so that you can squeeze your head and shoulders out as well. The sight is breathtaking. You freeze, half in and half out.

Before you is every color upon the planet, and some you have never seen. There are shimmering emerald grasses, juxtaposed next to vibrant blue sky. The earth is speckled with flowers and plants of every variety. There is a soft sound as if the plants and the air are singing in harmony, greeting you.

Before you stretches an expanse of earth and sky so great that you wonder if you will ever be able to experience it all. You pull yourself through, and you lightly touch the earth. It sings as your feet brush the surface, and the sweet sound sends shivers of joy through your body. You inhale. The air is sweet with the smell of honey and new mown hay. You never felt so alive!

You spin quickly about, trying to take in all the sights simultaneously. The spinning motion lifts you off your feet. You feel light and free, unbound to the earth. It is then that you notice you have wings, wings of rainbow light. Emerging from the cocoon has given you the opportunity to fly!

The wings move with your thoughts, lifting you, lowering you. You begin to understand how magical the butterfly is. You float softly over the landscape, hovering over flowers and trees. Occasionally you light upon flowers and plants, so that your touch sends forth their songs into the air about you.

There is so much to see and learn. There is so much nectar to be savored, a nectar that has always been present but usually ignored. You are filled with a desire to share this nectar—this world—with others. Will they believe? Will others be able to see that there is a magical butterfly within each of us, waiting to emerge?

You know that you must take some of the nectar of light and creativity back with you. As your own life becomes filled with more color, others will notice and ask. Each must seek it out for themselves. To simply tell others will never do. It is only when they are able to see the effects in your life will their own desire to add color to their lives grow. Then it can be shared. When the desire is great enough, the butterfly will emerge from the cocoon.

You look about the field of flowers. You choose one in the center of the field. It is a flower with a special radiance for you at this time. Each flower is special. Each flower has its own unique energy and gift. You hover softly above it and then settle gently upon the outer edge of its petals. It sings to you at your touch. The sound carries through your ears and into every cell of your body, caressing them with joy.

In the heart of the flower is the sweet nectar. You cup your hands and sample its fragrant elixir. Your head spins with its dizzying effect. You are filled with joy. This flower has now become a part of you and you of it. You share its energy. It is a gift to take back with you. It may inspire creativity, insight, prosperity, or discernment. Each flower is different. Each is a gift and there are millions of flowers to sample.

You bow softly to the flower in gratitude. You rise up and float gently back to the cocoon. The sunlight shimmers a rainbow prism reflecting off of the surface of the cocoon. You spread the threads and enter, going back into the cocoon. You notice that it is a little brighter inside now. The light from the outside shines and penetrates a little more strongly now.

You know that as you allow the butterfly within you to emerge, the outer world and the inner world will blend more and more. With time, the rainbows of one realm will become the rainbows of the other. Every rainbow has two ends, bridging and linking the two worlds forever. You settle back into your chair in the center of the cocoon. The taste of the flower's nectar is still sweet in the mouth. You know that in the days ahead it will affect your life, sweetening it. You breathe deeply and allow your awareness of the room and your physical surroundings to return. You remember all that you have experienced.

An excellent way of grounding this energy more dynamically into physical life expression is by doing some research on the flower you touched. You may even wish to make a drawing of it. If it is a flower that you can identify, researching its magical, herbal and other aspects will provide insight as to how it will affect your life. It is a way of honoring the creative process that you have activated with the symbols and imagery of this exercise.

This exercise is good for stimulating the creative imagination. It is healing and nurturing. When used prior to sleep, it stimulates dreams that can show us where more creativity is needed, along with dreams that are freeing and healing. It is an exercise that is beneficial to developing an awareness of the out-of-body experiences that most of us do not remember each night.

EXERCISE TWO: THE PHOENIX RISING

For this exercise you may wish to sit so that a candle burns at eye level before you. This is often more effective if you are still having difficulty with visualization. It is extremely effective when performed in front of a fireplace.

This exercise is good for energizing the astral body so that it can be used as a separate vehicle of consciousness. It assists in developing lucid dreaming and an awareness of out-of-body experiences. When performed before sleep, it can stimulate dreams that show us where people and situations are tying us down and where transition is needed in order to free our more creative aspects.

Part of the purpose of all the exercises in dream alchemy involves learning to shift awareness more consciously from the waking to the sleeping, from the physical to the spiritual. For this to occur, we must develop the right muscles and energy states. This exercise works strongly on both aspects.

This exercise is beneficial for stimulating dreams that reveal past issues we have not fully dealt with and resolved. It can awaken dreams that you had in your youth and had forgotten. It stirs long forgotten memories so that we can see their effects upon who we are now. It can stimulate dreams that show old issues playing themselves out in our present life. This is going to be a time of examination, a time to discover how to resurrect yourself through shapeshifting your energies.

Again relax yourself. Allow yourself to focus upon the candle flame in front of you. See it dance and shimmer, creating form after form after form. Its light and energy is hypnotic and comforting in the darkness.

See before yourself a circle of fire. The flames dance and twist, each seeming to have a life and purpose of its own. You can feel the warmth it generates, and the flames create a myriad of shadows and shapes upon the walls surrounding you.

You watch the shadows. Memories are very much like shadows. You know they are there. They are a part of you and your surroundings, but they dance about you, haunting you at times.

You begin to reflect upon major incidents in your life. They begin to replay themselves within your mind. Some are the important incidents, and some you remember as trivial. Then you realize that because they are memories and have come to mind, they have also created change within your life.

You examine several of these. You think back to the time prior to the incidents. You remember how you were feeling, what you were doing and who was a part of your life then. You see these incidents occurring, interrupting those other energy patterns. As the flames dance, almost mocking you, you see and feel how you were never quite the same again. You understand that anything that created an emotional or mental response in you changed you by becoming a part of your very fabric.

As you review these incidents, the shadows upon the walls grow larger, as if taking on a life of their own. They are the ghosts of your past. They are the shadows of events that changed you in great and small ways. And they still haunt you.

You wonder how things would have—might have—turned out differently had you responded differently to those situations. If you had only had some guidance. If you had only done something different. If only ... You realize that you could "if only" yourself to death. It would not change a thing. You stare into the flames, and they continue their mocking dance.

Suddenly they calm. The flames are no longer dancing and mocking. They shift, pulling away from the center, creating a circle around a black hole. A single, yellow flame appears in the middle of the blackness. It shoots up a column of golden light that pushes back all shadows within the room. A sound builds with the light, until a roar fills the entire room and vibrates every cell of your being.

Then with a blinding flash, the column of light disappears. Where the column once stood there is now a beautiful golden Phoenix, the mythical being of light. Out of the ashes of the fire it rises up before you. The fires are gone and the room shines with crystalline light. You shrink back a little at its intensity. As if in response to you, the lights surrounding the Phoenix soften.

It fixes you with a stare and its voice fills your head in a manner that makes it impossible to determine if the sound is from without or from within. As the words echo within your mind, the plumage shimmers and changes colors, each more brilliant than the next.

"There are no 'if onlys.' We live our life and we grow from it. There are no right or wrong decisions or choices. Yes, some are easier than others, but all bring growth. All choices are gifts, gifts which create and shape you. You wish for guidance. What you wish for is someone or something to choose for you, to decide for you. Even no decision is a decision and even this will shift your life into certain patterns.

"The gift of experience is the gold of alchemy. It should be your guidance. It enables us to mold and shape and alter who we are and where we go. It alone provides true discernment.

"I am your mirror. You are seeing yourself in me. The Phoenix does not exist without you, for it lives within you. As you learn to see the Phoenix within you, as you learn to form the Phoenix about you, its energy will guard and guide you. You too will then rise from the ashes of your past to take flight within the heavens."

The Phoenix shifts and shimmers, and where it stood, there now stands a mirror. It reflects your image. As you gaze into the mirror, the outline of the golden Phoenix overlays your own image, and you feel old fires of inspiration coming to life within you.

"As you come to recognize me in all that you do and have done, you will see the gold by which you can shape the future and mold yourself anew." The image of the Phoenix disappears, followed by the mirror. In the circle of flame now lies a golden egg. You extend your hand through the flames, reaching for it. The flames are warm and give off light, but its fire does not burn. It is something you know you must meditate upon.

As you lift the egg, the circle of flames contracts and begins to dance and burn as it did initially. In the light of the fire you examine the gift. It really is a golden egg. In exquisite detail, it is engraved and set with jewels. It is an engraving of a Phoenix, rising forth out of the fires of life. It feels warm and smooth, and it causes a tingling to run up your arms and through your body. "Out of the egg comes new life. Out of experience comes anything you desire yourself to be, anytime you desire to be!"

As the words echo within your mind, the fire melts down. There is only the initial candle that you lit. You are left to your own inner fires and to the Phoenix that resides within the heart of you.

EXERCISE THREE: THE TALE OF
THE MASTER AND THE PUPIL

The tale which follows is an old tale, adapted from several sources. It is a tale of shapeshifting. More specifically, it is about a contest of shapeshifting. It has been told in many ways in most areas of the world. It has been called the "Wizard Battle" and "The Doctor and his Pupil." Although its origin is often given as France, versions of it appear everywhere. When it comes to folktales, it is often difficult to discern the origins.

This is an excellent exercise to do as part of the mythic dream work process, by creating the doorway and stepping through into this tale. It can also be used as a separate meditation, for a kind of waking dream. It is a means of activating the mythic energies through meditation, reflection, visualization and contemplation.

You use your creative imagination to empower altered states such as dream activity. It is comparable to the exercises used by Ignatius Loyola to bring a particular scene to life within the mind. It is comparable to what Carl Jung referred to as the active imagination, a "turning willfully to the unconscious while awake."

This is an excellent exercise with which to practice placing yourself in the different roles found in tales and myths, as described in the last chapter. Even though we may prefer to see ourselves as the hero or protagonist, we usually have qualities similar to the antagonist or other characters. This exercise can help you develop the power to visualize yourself as one of the characters.

This exercise has definite effects. It can be used prior to sleep to stimulate dreams for self-awareness, prophecy and initiation. It can also be used to create opportunities for their development in our life circumstances. It creates opportunities to develop versatility and flexibility of our creative energies. Here is the tale:

Once there was a poor boy who was looking for work. In his travels, he heard of a great wizard, a teacher who needed a servant. The boy sought out this man. He came to a large castle and banged loudly upon its door.

Before long, a man appeared at a window and called down to the boy, "What do you want?" he said. The boy replied "I am looking for work, kind sir, and I heard you were in need of a servant."

"Do you know how to read?"asked the wizard. The boy

hesitated. He was not sure how to answer, as the question sounded a bit like a test of a sort. "No," he lied, "But I am a quick learner if you are worried about being able to teach me." The wizard replied "I do not want anyone who can read, so I will hire you."

The boy entered the castle. The man greeted him at a tall stairwell and motioned for the boy to follow him up. They ascended the stairs in silence. At the top they entered a room which seemed a mix between a laboratory and a library. In the center of the room was a pedestal upon which sat a large book. "While I travel, I expect you to dust this room and to protect its belongings, particularly this one book," he said. The boy nodded, looking at the book with curiosity.

Before long the Master left on a long trip. He was no sooner out the door when the boy opened the large volume on the pedestal and began reading. It was a book of the magic and wonders of the universe. The boy studied voraciously and was always careful never to let the Master know what he was doing while he had been gone.

After three years, the boy had learned the entire book by heart. When the Master returned from his next trip, the boy said he must be on his way, and he left the castle. The boy returned home to his poor parents, anxious to try out his new knowledge.

On the eve of the village fair, the boy spoke to his father. "Tomorrow, you will find a magnificent steer in the stable. Take it to the fair and sell it, but make sure you return with its rope." The next day the father found this magnificent steer, took it to the fair and sold it for a good price. On his way home, he heard footsteps behind him. He turned and saw his son. The boy had turned himself into a steer and when he had been sold, at first opportunity he turned himself back.

Both he and his father were delighted with the deal they had made. Each time money ran low, the boy would transform himself into a steer or a horse or whatever could be sold. After the sale, at the first opportune time, he would transform himself back.

What the boy did not know was that to a Master of magic, any magic in the land would be recognized. It was only a matter of time before the Master for whom the boy worked would discern that something was amiss in the land. It did not take him long to find the boy. Then it was just a matter of waiting for the right opportunity.

The next time the father brought his transformed son into the village to sell, the Master recognized him and bought the horse from his father. He then took the father to a pub and made him drink so much that he forgot the rope by which he led the animal and which enabled the boy to return to his normal form.

While the father was passed out from too much drink, the Master took the horse to blacksmith. "Give my horse a good shoeing," he said, and then he left for a time. Before the blacksmith got a chance to do so, a young child came along and the horse spoke to her. "Untie me!" he ordered.

The child was so startled, that she did as told. No sooner was the horse untied, then he transformed himself into a rabbit and ran off. The Master saw this and transformed himself into a hunting dog, giving chase. The rabbit came to a river and turned into a fish. The Master bought the river and ordered that all the fish be cleaned. As the fish that was the boy was about to be cleaned, it turned into a lark and flew away. The Master then transformed himself into a hawk and gave chase.

Weary from flight, the lark dived down a chimney and turned itself into a gain of wheat which rolled under the table. The hawk followed, seeing the change. He immediately turned into a rooster, pecking at the loose grains upon the floor. The boy waited until just about to be eaten and then transformed himself once more. This time into a fox which ate the rooster.

And the boy lived out his days in wealth and prosperity in the castle of the old Master.

EXERCISE FOUR: MYTHIC TIME AND PLACE

Time travel takes great care, practice and effort. It is best to practice accessing other times and places, such as those described in myths and tales, through meditation first. When we can control them in meditation, it becomes easier to control time and locality in dreams.

We are learning through dream alchemy to work with the astral plane. This is a realm of great fluidity. Everything that has ever been felt or experienced has left its imprint upon this dimension, including mythical times and places. This is the realm of imagination, and we must not make the mistake of equating imagination with unreality. Images, and the energy behind them, are real and take form in other dimensions. It is only upon the physical that they are more ethereal and intangible. One of the reasons for dream work is to open this realm, to learn the laws within it and how it impacts upon the physical life.

There are many kinds of astral operations and processes that can connect us more fully with that dimension and its energies. Daydreaming, meditation and nocturnal dreaming are but a few. We are learning to connect with it in a directed manner. Meditation techniques and mythic dream work facilitate a more conscious awareness of its interaction with our life on a daily basis.

We are not our bodies. They are simply tools for the physical life, tools which we can set aside at night for more essential work. Part of this work involves learning how these subtle dimensions help shape the physical.

It can take time to control the time element and the locality of your dream experiences. To assist in this, you can use the symbology found within myths and tales. This next exercise is a meditation that can strengthen your energies to access ancient times and localities— real and mythical. As you learn to control them through meditation, you can learn to control the dream state. Persistence is the key.

As you learn to access other times, you may manifest dreams which reflect those energies as they are currently influencing you. Ultimately, you can develop the ability to access the past and correct the mistakes (and thus the karmic repercussions).

Initially, this exercise should not be performed too frequently. It is very powerful and may trigger a replay of situations from the past. This does not mean the same instances with the same parties will re-occur. More likely, similar kinds of situations will arise, infused with the same emotions and attitudes of the past, providing opportunity to handle them differently. In essence, you create an opportunity to tell the divine universe that you have learned that particular lesson. This eliminates the karma. Karma is a Sanskrit word which means "to do." Anything we do is a learning opportunity. If we do not learn the lesson the first time, it arises later to give us another opportunity. With this exercise and with application of it to mythic dream work, you are learning to manipulate symbols to accelerate your learning, while awake and asleep.

Uncontrolled fancy is a possible problem with this process. If our lives are not glamorous, we may create imaginings from the past to make us feel more important. Discrimination, discernment and common sense are critical to past exploration, particularly past life. If you find yourself rushing home from work to explore your past every night or find yourself becoming more dreamy and moody than usual, cease this activity. Physical plane life should *never* suffer because of exploration and work with subtler dimensions.

If performed properly, this exercise will open doors to the past. This kind of opening can release emotions and mental attitudes that you may have already come to terms with for the time being. This exercise will also stir up past life remembrances. These may reflect themselves in your dreams. Emotions and attitudes from these past lives may reveal themselves through your present dreams. Pay close attention to the predominant emotions you experience in your dreams for about a week following this exercise. They can indicate which energies you are carrying over from the past and are affecting you presently.

Also remember to apply common sense to what you receive in this exercise. Even if you get names, dates, places, it does not prove that you actually lived that life. That information may come from elsewhere. If it helps you to see your life from a new perspective or assist you in handling a situation in your life more productively, then it serves a purpose.

What is most important from this exercise is that we learn to infuse ourselves with the energies of different time periods. We are stretching those astral muscles even further. This exercise develops concentration and creative visualization. It utilizes the imagination in a manner that will teach us that we can traverse normal time parameters. We are learning to take quantum leaps to the past in order to correct, revise and shape the future. Here is the exercise:

As you breathe deeply, relax. Focus only upon yourself and how you are learning to shift your energy and awareness to suit your individual needs and desires. Imagine all that you will be able to accomplish by opening to an awareness of past times and places. Imagine how you will be able to review your past and rewrite it as it is affecting your present and your future.

Visualize yourself standing at the top of a tall stairway. The rail is ornate gold, and each stair is marbled. A soft mist hides the bottom from your sight, but you are not worried. In fact, you feel warm and safe and more than a little excited about the prospects that lie ahead. You begin to descend the stairs. You step down lightly, growing more relaxed as you do. With each step you grow lighter, until it feels as if you are floating upon puffs of billowy clouds. You relax deeper and deeper with each step. It feels so good to breathe. Every pore of your being is filled with warm relaxing feelings.

You are barely touching the stairs, you have grown so light and free. Each step down sheds the weight of the cares and tensions of the physical world. You feel free and relaxed and completely at peace. You glance down at the stairs themselves, and you see that you are no longer even touching them. You have grown so relaxed, so free and so light that you are now floating down.

You gently settle at the bottom of the stairs to find yourself in a large circular room. The floor is a soft violet and across from you is a large doorway. You step toward it and stand before it. The frame of the doorway is ornately carved. It is a relief carving of a vine that encircles the door. In the center of the wooden door is another carved symbol. It is the symbol of the Om within a circle. It has been stained scarlet, and the strong color seems to vibrate.

Above the door is a small plaque, upon which is an engraving of your name. As you look upon it and recognize it, the massive door begins to swing open. It spills out crystalline, golden light that surrounds you, pours through you and then emanates out from you. It is warm and nurturing. It is familiar in a very vague way.

You step through the doorway into the room beyond. The door closes softly behind you. Your eyes begin to adjust to the muted light of this room. You look about you and you see artifacts from every area of the world. Pictures, portraits, sculpture, clothing, and weaponry. Every time and locale seems to be represented here. Each has its own little cubicle. Some seem so familiar to you, while others are unrecognizable.

This is the Gallery of your Life. In it are the remnants from every lifetime and every memory that has gone into forming you. It includes the real and the mythical, the mundane and the fantastic—for all have helped to shape you. The cubicles closest to you are from special times and moments of your current life. Those that are farther away are from more distant times.

You step into a cubicle on your right. You remember these items. You pick up an article of clothing. You wore this as a child. And there is what was once your favorite toy. You remember how you first got it and how you felt. My, how things have changed since then! You remember the people who were closest to you at that time. You remember how you felt, what you did. It all comes flooding back.

On a shelf at the back of the cubicle is a book. You smile. Even though it may not be the exact same book, it is still the one story from childhood that you always enjoyed most. Fairy tale, myth, bedtime story, whatever—it was always your favorite. Because it was your favorite, it still affects you. It is a story you will use to heal and manifest greater power and joy in your life. You give yourself a mental note to find a new copy of that story for yourself.

Without thinking, you hold the book close to your chest and you make a wish. It is a wish about something that you may want to change, relive or feel again. The book begins to glow, and the title of the story stands out brightly upon the cover as if in response to that wish. Then it fades. You place the book back upon the shelf

You step out of the cubicle and look at the wide expanse of cubicles that form this Gallery. So much to explore. So much to relive. So much to remember.

It is then that the door through which you entered again opens. It is time to leave, but it is not forever. This is your Gallery. It is here for you to explore and open at any time. And each time hereafter, you know it will become easier and more fulfilling. You glance once more at the cubicle of your childhood, remembering the story, which reveals much about the magic of your current lifetime.

As you step out, the door closes behind you. You feel a little saddened. These are times past, but only past in the physical sense. They have left their imprints upon you and upon the ethers forever. It is comforting to know that you can relive them and maybe change events that saddened you to create a new future.

You reach out and gently touch the symbol of the Om upon the door and turn once more to the stairs. As you gently ascend, you bring back with you all of the memories that you have experienced from this.

As a way of grounding and activating the energy of this exercise more dynamically, try and find a copy of that story within the next two to three days and re-read it, only from an entirely new perspective: as a symbol of the magic of your life.

CHAPTER NINE

Awakening the Ancient
Dream Guardians

Many fear working with their dreams. They fear what may be uncovered, and thus the dream is not remembered. It is a way of not facing ourselves. Before we can truly meet the archetypes beyond the threshold, we must first meet the dwellers upon the threshold. These dwellers are the aspects of ourself we have refused to face, that we have painted over, glossed over and shoved to the back of our closets. They hinder and limit the free flow of our energies. Facing them is frightening at times, but our dreams assist us in facing them.

This meditation is filled with a symbology to awaken the self. It will reveal behaviors and situations that must be confronted once and for all. If we have a thorn in our foot and ignore it, it will fester and become infected. It may hurt to pull it out, but this is what will enable it to heal properly.

This meditation stimulates increased dream activity as well. It can awaken contact with spiritual teachers through the dream state. It can open you to new realms found in the dream state. It activates dreams that reveal new directions for your life.

Occasionally we hit limbo periods in our lives. Things become static and stale. This exercise will initiate new movement in your waking life. This exercise is especially effective when performed on the night of the full moon. In fact, it can be repeated every full moon to insure continual movement and growth. It is an exercise which proves that there are indeed meditations and exercises that affect dream states and which also ricochet into the waking life in order to create opportunities.

Make sure that you will be undisturbed when employing this

exercise. Take time to relax and prepare. Read through the meditation several times to familiarize yourself with it and its imagery. This will enable you to visualize it more fully later. If you think you will have difficulty remembering it, you may wish to read sections of it aloud, pausing to visualize yourself within the scene before moving to the next section.

At the end take a few moments to orient yourself. Reflect on how you would like this exercise to affect you. See yourself enjoying and experiencing its beneficial effects. See your dreams becoming more vivid as a result. See your dreams becoming more inspiring. See yourself beginning to encounter spiritual teachers through your dreams. See your subconscious becoming more active, strengthening your intuition and creativity. See yourself eliminating obstacles and hindrances to your movement while awake. See yourself becoming free to explore and seek out your greatest dreams.

Remember: "The world is a symbol of the permanence of God, life a symbol of the presence of God, and love a symbol of the understanding of God. To those who are able to sense the inner life of things and read into forms even a small part of that great agency which actually ensouls them, the all-sufficiency of Universal Good is all sufficing." *

As always, create a dream doorway by visualizing a ball of red light within the throat chakra. Within this ball of red light, visualize a scarlet Om or trident. When you fell this center come to life, visualize the red energy radiating out to form the dream doorway.

Imagine yourself stepping through this doorway into a bright meadow of summer flowers and green grasses. You are standing upon a path that leads down to a pool of clear water. At the far end of the pool, the path ends at a waterfall. Its spray is cool and misty, and as it touches the pool, it distorts whatever image is reflected. The sun is warm upon you as you stand next to the water.

You tilt your head slightly, listening to the environment. You are surprised. There is no other sound of life other than your own breathing and the soft splashing of the waterfall. The meadow looks pleasant enough, but where is all of the life? It is all form and no substance.

As you stand next to the waterfall, you notice a small cave

---

*Manly P. Hall, *Lectures on Ancient Philosophy* (Los Angeles: Philosophical Research Society, 1984), p. 359.

half-concealed behind it. You step carefully behind the waterfall and into the inner darkness of the mouth of the cave. What little light there is comes through the opening by the waterfall. It fills the cave with shadows.

The air inside the cave is cool and damp. The floor is moist from the mist of the waterfall. The only sound is that of the waterfall, until you step further into the cave. You begin to detect a soft sound, like the gentle splash of water against the shore.

You move deeper into the cave, leaving the light of the entrance behind you. You notice the ceiling sloping down, causing you to hunch. It is more difficult to see, and you move more by feel than by sight. The sound of the water becomes more distinct as the cave begins to enclose you. At the far end of the cave you discover a second opening. A pale diffused light emanates from the other side, illuminating this opening.

This opening has not been used in ages. It is thick with cobwebs, and you gingerly peel the silken threads back. You step through into an open area next to a large river. There is only one boat that you can see. The area is illuminated only by the light of the distant moon.

You step carefully down to the water. It is black and it stills itself as you approach. The moon reflects off of its surface, emphasizing the black depth, as if to tell you these are the waters from the womb of life.

You look out across the river. A vague outline of an island is barely visible through the soft fog that surrounds it. It is then that you notice the man. Tall and broad, he looks at you with piercing eyes. He motions to the boat, inviting silently. You hesitate, intimidated by this strange figure. He gestures a second time. Still you hesitate.

"We are never given a hope, wish or dream without also being given opportunities to make them a reality." His voice is soft, deep and gentle, belying his appearance. It touches a chord within you. You step forward and enter the boat. The trip is silent as he maneuvers you through the dark waters. Your only comfort is the soft reflection of the moon.

Soon you move into the fog. It blocks the view of the shore. You are cloaked in it. Not even the moonlight penetrates. It is so thick that you are not even sure you are moving. It is as if you are hanging in a cloud in limbo. You look toward your guide, but his face is stoic.

He merely goes about the business of working the oars as if you are not even there.

Then you feel a soft bump, and you know you have reached the island. The guide motions for you to stand. As you do, the fog and mist begins to thin. He steps forward and offers his assistance in stepping out upon the shore. It is then that you notice the medallion of wings that hangs around his neck. He nods in acknowledgment of your noticing and steps back.

Before you is a path leading up a slight incline out of the mist of the black river. As you move to the top, you find yourself at the entrance to an open air temple. It is lit by torches and the brilliance of the moon which is now directly overhead.

In the center of this temple area is an old stone altar. You move closer, and upon the altar you see a mirror, a small bowl of water and a medallion with wings, just as your guide had worn. Across the front of the altar, chiseled into the stone, are all the phases of the moon.

From behind the altar, as if appearing from the shadows, step three women: a young child, her mother and an old woman. All three wear robes of gray. The old woman has an insignia upon her robe of the dark of the moon. The mother has one of the full moon, and the child, the new. These are the creative forces of the earth and the moon. These are the feminine energies, the true Guardians of the Dreams. You are not sure how you know this, but you do. It is familiar, as if a replay from some distant dream of childhood.

The child steps forward, lifts the mirror from the altar and stands before you. She extends the mirror to you. "When we begin to open to new realms and new realizations, we are all like children. Those realizations need to be nurtured and coaxed. The mirror is a tool that you can use to see how all life reflects itself within your own life. It is a tool to help you see the night reflected within your days, and your days reflected within your nights." With these words, she steps forward and melts into you. It is a tie to the primordial energies of the universe that are coming to life as a child comes to life. You look within the mirror and you see the child outlined within your own reflection. She smiles at you.

The mother steps forward and raises the small bowl of water. "All cups, all bowls, all cauldrons contain the birth-giving energies. From out of the cup of life comes the new. Out of the depths of the waters comes birth. As you learn to touch the subtle areas of your consciousness, as you learn to stir the waters within, you too will not only see your energies reflected, but you shall be able to draw them forth into your life." She places the bowl within your hands and melts into you. You are reminded of the creative process that exists in all life. You look into the water within the bowl and you see your reflection overshadowed by hers.

As you look up from the bowl, the old woman stands before you. Aged and wrinkled though she may be, there is a vitality that is eternal. Her eyes pierce you, seeing all within you and yet loving you regardless of anything. She holds in her hands a necklace of leather, upon which is the medallion of silver wings. She holds it out to you, and as you lean forward, she places it around your neck. "There will come a time when these wings shall become wings of light. With them you shall be able to fly from one dimension to another, from night to day and back to night, all in the twinkling of an eye. These wings are the promise of the fulfillment of your dreams. It is the promise of love through the expression of light." In her face you see the young child. It shifts, becoming the mother and then once more back to the old wise woman. She smiles warmly and cups your face lovingly within her hands. Then she melts into you.

You raise your face to the night and to the moon above. You offer silent prayers of thanks for that which is about to open more fully within your life. As if in response, a beam of light issues forth from the moon above and forms a silver, sparkling path across the river. As you step upon the subtle light, you remember an old myth about walking upon the path of moonbeams, the path to your heart's desires.

The path ends at the mouth of the cave, just behind the waterfall. You step out from its opening and around the waterfall to the pool. The sunlight greets you warmly. You breathe deeply of the fresh sweet air. It is as if the cobwebs of your mind have been cleared, and you remember the cobwebs in the cave.

You pause, taking another deep breath, and then your breath catches. A flock of birds fly overhead. A fish jumps in the pool. You turn and look across the meadow. A deer walks serenely into the open. You smile. The meadow is alive! There is life and sounds of life all about you. Where there had been no life, now there is much life.

And it is this realization that is strongest as you follow the path back to your mythic dream doorway, stepping through. You close the doorway, drawing it back into the throat center. You allow yourself to return gently to your normal state of awareness, knowing that the bridge has once more been connected.

PART THREE:

Working With Dream Cycles

"Do we dream because we fear going to sleep and never waking up or do we dream to prove there is no death?"

— Anonymous

"To everything there is a season and a time for every purpose under heaven."

— Ecclesiastes 3:1

CHAPTER TEN

The Cycles of
Our Dreams

Every day is an adventure. Every night holds its own adventures as well. The more we immerse ourselves consciously in these adventures, the less we are at the mercy of our life circumstances. Learning to detect the subtle energies in our lives is the first step to controlling them. This is why dream work of any kind is so essential. It awakens us to that subtle play and shows us how to work within its rhythms.

Our entire incarnation is a quest for the unfoldment of our greatest potentials. Within the cycle of an incarnation, we will encounter major shifts in energy to prevent stagnancy. These shifts affect us on grand and small scales. Their affect on our lives is reflected in our dreams, providing clues for ways to work most effectively with these energy changes. When we can recognize universal rhythms at play and align ourselves with them, the veils between the physical and spiritual are laid aside.

In Part Three we will explore three cyclic shifts of energy: *the lifetime cycle*, which includes the seven crisis points often faced during an incarnation; *the year cycle*, which includes the influences of the solstices, equinoxes, and zodiac signs; and *the moon cycle*, which focuses on how the phases of the moon affect our energy levels. These cyclical shifts are reflected in corresponding dream changes. We can use mythic dream work techniques at the power points of these cycles to stimulate dreams that elaborate what new energy patterns we may be moving into.

THE QUEST OF A LIFETIME

Any particular incarnation can be seen as the great quest for fulfillment. Unfortunately, we can become so immersed in the daily trials and activities that we may lose sight of the big picture. We fail to realize that every person and situation is significant. We fail to recognize that nothing is inconsequential.

Our soul, with its grander wisdom, sets certain rhythmic changes to occur at specific times in our life. These changes keep us on track and assist the unfoldment of our potentials and lessons. These changes also occur with a determinable frequency. The specific times of these energy shifts can be pinpointed. Anyone working with dreams consistently will be aware of the corresponding changes within dream content, frequency, vibrancy and intensity at these special times.

These energy shifts are a part of everyone's experience. They are times which herald new growth and opportunity for growth in the physical and spiritual. Most people view such times as a nuisance, rather than as a call to new growth and maturity. They are times of choice and are often referred to as crises points.

At these crises points, a shift will occur in the universal energy acting in your life on physical and spiritual levels. There will be corresponding changes in chakra activity and overall sensitivity. A possible side-effect is the occurrence of some turmoil and an increase in opportunities to resolve conflicts. The daily situations will reveal definable patterns.

Although inner growth can create outer stress, it is in confronting such adversaries that the hero completes the journey with success. These crises points "evoke confidence when surmounted and produce greatly expanded vision. They foster compassion and understanding, for the pain and the inner conflict they have engendered is never forgotten, for they draw upon the resources of the heart. They release the light of wisdom within the field of knowledge and the world is thereby enriched."*

Crises points are times of specific adventures within the incarnation. They are periods that trigger specific patterns of learning circumstances. Each crises point has its own underlying

---

* Alice Bailey, *Discipleship in the New Age* (Albany: Lucis Trust, 1972.)

energy pattern that will play a unique part in the life of each individual. If we can identify our crises points, we can use myths and tales to stimulate dream activity and to clarify their energies. We can use mythic dream work to elaborate on an expression of those energies so that we can more easily discern them and understand how we may be affected by them during that period.

Most myths and tales don't show all of the circumstances of the hero's life. Most relate circumstances in which certain adversaries are met and overcome in order to achieve a reward. We only see a specific quest-adventure from a specific period within the protagonist's life. This is how we must look upon each crises point. Each is a period of specific adventures where certain activities and lessons are more likely to be encountered. Each crises point has its own adversary, an archetype which will play a predominant role in your life during that period. Being able to recognize the adversary in whatever guise it comes is the first step. Next comes the facing and overcoming of it. In both steps, mythic dream work assists us.

Throughout the rest of this chapter we will examine seven crises points within a single incarnation. There are others, of course, but these seven are the most recognizable and the most influential. Seven has a long history of mysticism associated with it. There are many associations with this number.

One theory for this mysticism is connected to the astrological influence of Saturn. Saturn is the teacher planet. Its influence is powerful. It makes a revolution around the sun approximately every 28 years. From an astrological point of view, this means that about every seven years it will aspect with our own astrological charts in a very noticeable way. A good astrologer can pinpoint these major shifts, as every seven years Saturn moves into a new part of the astrological chart, aspecting with different planets and creating new learning situations and opportunities.

Saturn is the teacher and the tester. It is through the lessons of Saturn that man is taught how to harmonize his imagination with the immediate circumstances of his life."* Thus by working with our dreams (the imagination), we can detect how teaching and testing will manifest in our lives during a particular cycle. This teaching and testing pattern changes every seven years when Saturn moves

---

*Alan Oken, *Alan Oken's Complete Astrology* (New York:Bantam Books,1980) p. 211.

into a new quadrant of the astrological chart.

The dates for these major crises points are approximate, but they are usually accurate within three years, either direction. The periods last approximately seven years. Our dreams will reflect the energies of these crisis points. This is not to say it is all we will dream of, but understanding these periods will provide insight into the energy changes and opportunities most likely to manifest. After we describe the seven crisis points, we will explore several techniques on attuning to them more fully through your dreams.

1. AGE 21

The first major crisis point is powerful. Many of our dreams will reflect the journey archetype, as well as how to come into one's self. At this age the individual begins to feel the touch of the soul upon the personality, and there occurs a drive toward expression of individuality and self worth. The personality begins to pick up the threads of past incarnations and integrate them into what has unfolded in this life.

For many, this is the age of stepping into the first true area of occupation. Many individuals have finished college, and there is a movement away from the friends and acquaintances of childhood and high school. There is a disassociation from peer pressure and a soul urging for individual expression.

Some myths and tales reflecting these energies are:
- West African tale of the fire children
- "The Tinder Box"
- *Romeo and Juliet*
- "The Labors of Hercules"
- Greek tale of the Zeus' overthrow by Kronos
- Tales of Chiron and the Centaurs (especially effective for those who are developing an interest in healing at this age)

2. AGE 28

Around the age of 28 another major shift of energy occurs. At this age there is a push for the soul to express its purpose. In the previous age the individuality was expressed by severing many connections with the past and by developing new friends and interests.

This period is a time in which the desire grows to express

oneself much more remarkably. For many, this may mean moving into a new profession. It is not that the old one did not serve its purpose, for it did demonstrate that you could survive as an individual. Now there is a growing desire to make a living at that which you would enjoy more fully.

For many, this period creates a desire and effort toward tasks that provide greater service. Many men and women begin to go back to school and explore aspects of healing service. There is a desire to be productive and creative at the same time. Some myths and tales can stimulate dreams to clarify our own unique issues in regards to this:

- Chinese tale of Tseng and the Holy Man
- English tale of "The Three Sillies"
- Italian tale "Jump Into My Sack"
- Adventures of Robin Hood
- Sumerian tale of Ishtar and Tammuz
- Icelandic tale of "The Father of 18 Elves"
- "The Shoemaker and the Elves"

3. AGE 35

This crises point stimulates a consolidation between the personality and the soul expression. At a point between age 25 and forty, usually around age 35, there occurs the crisis of opportunity. This involves determining choices that will lead to a distinctive nature of life service. It is not always reflected within the choice of living environment, kind of work, or kind of associates. It relates to life service and life commitment. There begins a clarification that your life is moving in a direction as yet indefinable, and yet it synthesizes many of your past experiences into new realizations.

The energy moving through your life during this point is beneficial to initiating original work and succeeding at it. This original work can be any avenue of work or life expression peculiar to you. Many people feel this drive for personal expression and develop an urge to move from the city, to get away from the hustle and bustle of extraneous rhythms to follow their own integral rhythms of individuality and creativity.

The field of endeavor is not as important as following your heart's desire. It is a time in which your creativity can most effectively be productive in the area which you desire. This is a good time to make changes in lifestyle.

This urge will be felt most strongly by those who have been living a lifestyle inappropriate to the soul's highest good. If the urges and energies of this cycle are fought against out of fear of change or other reasons, the crisis points following this one will be intensified.

These myths and tales can be used to stimulate dreams that can help clarify what kind of changes would be most beneficial at this crisis point:

- "Snow White and Rose Red"
- Greek tale of "Perseus and Andromeda"
- Greek tale of "Athena and the Aegis"
- Egyptian tale of "Promises of the Three Sisters"
- English tale of "Two Pickpockets"
- French Tale "The Master and the Pupil" (Refer to chapter eight)
- Greek tale of "Artemis and Endymion"

4. AGE 42

This is a very critical time. It is sometimes referred to as a death point. If the energies of the previous cycles have not been utilized properly, there will be a tremendous impulse toward radical change within one's life. While this period can be one of literal death, it is rare. For most, it involves a symbolic death of the personality in favor of the soul urges. That which is called the male mid-life crises occurs at this time, as do many of the first movements into menopause for women in this cycle.

For the men, there is an urge to chuck the old way of life and to start anew. Often this reflects itself through divorce and remarriage to someone new and often younger. This is a time in which the soul must express the innermost virtues to the highest degrees, for this is what is tested during this cycle.

For most, (men and women) it is a time of wrestling with the devil in whatever form it manifests. The individual must call upon the inner soul virtues of strength, self-sacrifice, serenity and balance—infusing them with prayer and faith. It institutes a time of tremendous testing in many areas. It is a time of self-assessment and evaluation. We are placed in a position of examining the people, situation and circumstances of our lives. We are faced with what has been lost, stolen or broken. It is an attic cleaning time, a time to sweep out that which is no longer beneficial so that it can be replaced by that which is.

This can be a time of great healing. It enables us to see the muck that may have settled within our life. It also presents opportunities to stir it up and clean it out. This may be reflected through physical cleansing or emotional/mental cleansing.

Here is a list of myths and tales can be used to stimulate dreams to clarify this energy:

- Crucifixion and resurrection of Jesus
- Biblical tale of Job
- Biblical tale of Jonah and the Whale
- Sumerian tale of Ishtar's descent to retrieve Tammuz
- Greek tale of Orpheus and Eurydice
- The Greek tale of "Pandora's Box"
- Egyptian tale of Isis and Osiris
- Charles Dicken's *A Christmas Carol*
- All myths where the hero descends into some world of darkness or death
- Tales of the quests for the Holy Grail in the Arthurian legends

5. AGE 49

This cycle is one in which the kind of energy playing an important role is that of usefulness. Opportunities occur for an increase in productivity and an increased outflow of usefulness in all areas of life. This period may provide the opportunities for productivity, but it is the task of the individual to seize the opportunity. Ideally, the soul and personality will be united, and together they can implement cooperative efforts, particularly if the tests and trials of the previous cycle were utilized properly.

During this cycle there is a drive toward the more spiritual and mystical aspects of life. There is an increased desire to do what is unique to oneself. If this is not pursued, a lifelong sense of failure may emerge.

This is an ideal time to expand, improve and extend yourself in any endeavor that brings joy into your life. This may mean moving into any area in which there has been a draw but has not been pursued until this time. This cycle also brings changes in lifestyle, leading to changes which are more relaxed and harmonious.

As with other crisis points, certain myths and tales are imbued with images and energies appropriate to this cycle:

- Hasidic tale of "Magic Mirror of Rabbi Adam"
- Tale of Joseph of Arimathea and the Holy Grail
- Tales of King Arthur and his knights (particularly in the period following the formation of the Round Table)
- The post-flood stories of Noah and the Ark
- Biblical tale of Moses and the forty years upon the desert
- Babylonian tales of Tiamut
- Sumerian tales of Ishtar and the rescue of Tammuz
- Greek tales of Apollo and the Delphic Oracles

6. AGE 56

This is a time of testing what to withdraw from and what to continue with in your life. It is a time of assessment. The energies moving through you at this time assist you in clarifying your purposes in life more distinctly. Part of this assessment involves ascertaining the need to remain within this incarnation.

For some, this may stimulate a period of rest and recreation, often reflected through early retirement. It may be a time to even more fully harmonize the personality and the soul. Preparations may be made to release the past. For some, preparations may be instituted on subconscious levels to begin loosing the energy ties to this incarnation.

Deep introspection often occurs as to one's self worth. This may be accompanied by decisions to take life much easier. Things can be generally more peaceful. The focus returns to yourself so that new decisions concerning the future can begin to be made.

Certain myths and tales can be used to assist you in the evaluation process:

- "Rip Van Winkle"
- The Irish tale "Half-a-Blanket"
- Hasidic tale "Magic Mirror of Rabbi Adam"
- Norwegian tale "Seventh Father of the House"
- German Tale of "The Boy Who Went Forth to Find What Fear Was"
- Greek tale of Demeter's search for Persephone
- Pueblo tale "The Spider Woman"

7. AGE 63

This is the crises point of true review. It is around this time that the energies of the soul are stimulated to view the personality and the unfoldment of the person's individuality. It is for many a time of nostalgia. The work accomplished and not accomplished is reviewed seriously by the individual. It can involve making decisions to withdraw from this incarnation or to initiate further useful expression of one's energies through new educational endeavors.

Illness and disease may manifest for those who are making decisions to leave the physical, to assist in loosening the ties to physical life. How long such a process lasts varies with the individual.

This phase can also institute radical changes in lifestyle. It is not uncommon for many of this age group (or older) to become involved in activities and endeavors that their children may not understand, creating family disruptions. For many, it can be a time of new birth with ensuing feelings that life is just beginning.

We can use myths and tales to stimulate dream scenarios that reveal the successes of our life and the options still available during this period:

- Turkish tale "Youth Without Age and Life Without Death"
- Crucifixion and resurrection of Jesus
- German tale of "The Old Man and the Grandson"
- Norwegian tale of "Snowdrop"
- Greek myth of Prometheus and the stealing of fire
- Greek myth of Orpheus and Eurydice
- Egyptian tale of "Promises of Three Sisters"
- "The Shoemaker and the Elves"

USING MYTHIC DREAM WORK WITH CRISIS POINTS

Examine your own age, and review the crisis point closest to it. If your present age falls between two crisis points, examine them both. You may wish to consult an astrologer to determine when Saturn moves into new quadrants of your chart to pinpoint the crisis period more specifically. Examining the events of your life in the previous two years will help you determine which point is affecting you the most at present.

Having determined your present crisis point, re-read the material pertinent to it. You may wish to keep a notebook handy. As you re-read the material, write down specific events that re-enforce it, life events that you recognize. Keep in mind that energy shifts affect everyone, but they will also adapt themselves to your own unique life circumstances.

Choose a myth from the crisis point that you are drawn to. You will work with this myth for seven days. We do this to activate the Hermetic Principle of Correspondence. The seven days are a microcosmic reflection of the seven year cycle we are exploring. The more significance we attach to every aspect of this process, the stronger we impress the subconscious mind with what we want it to do for us in our dreams.

Prior to going to sleep, perform a mythic dream work meditation. Make all the necessary preparations. Take a dream bath, choosing an appropriate fragrance. If you cannot decide which would be best, use one that is a general dream stimulant. You may wish to program a dream crystal cluster to use throughout the week. Prepare a dream sachet, along with any flower essences that may assist you. Remember: if the subconscious will becomes enamored of an idea it will respond accordingly. The more we do to prepare, the more intensely the subconscious is impressed with the idea!

As usual, create your mythic dream doorway. Step through the doorway into the tale's scenario. Each of the seven nights, you should visualize yourself as a different character. If there are not seven characters, simply rotate to a different one each night, even if it means repeating a character. In this manner, when the dreams unfold, you open yourself to greater revelations of where and how the crisis point energies are affecting your life.

When you complete the meditation, before stepping back out of the doorway, take a few moments and review the past year. Also, look ahead to the coming months. By adding this small aspect to the meditation, we are telling the subconscious mind to apply the myth symbols to events of your life associated with the recent past and the recent future.

Step out of the doorway, allowing it to shrink and draw back into your throat chakra. At this point it is good to go to sleep, reminding yourself to remember your dreams. At the end of the week, review the dreams, their archetypes, and the emotional content. Compare them to the energy patterns of the crisis points.

Do this review again one month after performing this week of dream rituals. It may take that long for all of the energies of this crisis point to reveal themselves to you through the dream state. Those basic energies will be the forces and energies most prominent in your life during this seven year period. You may wish to do this once per year. The birthday dream ritual, described in the next chapter, can be adapted to this process.

Anytime we work to understand what is going on in our lives on all levels, we are participating in the spiritual training and unfoldment process. In the ancient mystery traditions, the common precept was "KNOW THYSELF!" The purpose of mythic dream work in regard to the cyclic energies of our life is to learn about our own energy rhythms so we can direct them more consciously.

Knowing oneself is a purging process. It constitutes the first stage of training in awakening our divine potential. Desires and beliefs that we may not be willing to face must be approached impersonally. It is not always a pleasant task. It involves purging and stripping of pretense. It is a process that must often be repeated.

We can be our own worst enemy in this process. If we are unable to carry out the obligation of self-observation and judgment, then more preparation is necessary. We must develop a secure perception of our personal energies and those other energies playing upon us. This presupposes careful observation, discrimination and persistent effort.

Part of what unfoldment does is throw us back upon ourselves for our answers, for our miracles. It cannot be attained from books or teachers, although they can assist us. It must be drawn from the well of truth that resides within us. This is why dream work is essential. It helps us in understanding the universal rhythms and patterns of our individual lives.

CHAPTER ELEVEN

The Sun Quest of the Dream Walker

In the life quest of the true alchemist, there is an alignment with and an attunement to the energy rhythms of an incarnation, of a year, of a month and even a day. This enables the individual to use these rhythms to make each day one of growth and new adventure.

Part of the ancient mysteries involved teaching the sacredness of the seasons and the power available to us at those times. The seasonal changes are still powerful periods, times which initiate specific energy patterns that affect all of humanity in subtle ways. Each season marks a period when a particular manifestation of spiritual force becomes dominant upon the earth. These energy patterns can be attuned to and revealed through our dreams.

The three days before and the day of the equinox or solstice are holy intervals. It is a time when two seasonal forces intersect. They mark the beginning and ending of specific seasons. These are times when the veils between the physical and the spiritual are thinnest, and specific energies can be accessed at these times in ways that cannot be done at other times of the year.

There are many ways of looking at the year. Many look at the year as beginning January 1 and ending December 31. Others follow it according to the planting schedule. Many ancient societies looked upon the year from a different perspective. They viewed it in terms of what soul energies were predominant. Each year was considered a year of the soul, providing new growth for the soul—especially when the natural rhythms were utilized.

This year of the soul began with the autumn equinox and then followed the succession of the seasons, culminating with the summer. At each turning point in the year, the gates of the inner

133

spiritual temples open up to the earth and release a fresh outpouring of forces upon the planet.

Behind each physical phenomenon lies a specific spiritual archetype. For this reason, the physical sciences were sacred. Nature was the way God spoke to humanity. And Nature spoke through the ancient wisdoms of religion, science, art, and astronomy. The movement of the stars and the changes of the seasons all reflect specific interplays of energy between the divine world and the physical.

The atomic structure of all life is affected with each change of the season. With each seasonal change, conditions in each person's life are poised for opportunities for growth, expression and transition. Communication with other beings and dimensions occurs with greater ease. Each season is endowed with a new spiritual impulse which will affect us subtly and which will reveal itself to us through our dreams around the time of the holy interval.

The four seasons sound forth a call to come higher. They are times for giving birth to new expressions of our energy. They are times for increasing our psychic abilities. They are times for initiation.

AUTUMN EQUINOX

Autumn is the time when the energy is most appropriate for purification and the planting of new seeds. It is a time that is most beneficial for determining new values and for making new decisions. It is a harvesting time for what has passed previously and a time to set new goals for the coming year. It is an appropriate time for purifying the mind and transmuting emotions, attitudes and behaviors blocking our growth. The need for these kinds of changes is often apparent in our dream content around the time of the equinox.

Autumn manifests energies for transmuting the lower, for overcoming obstacles and for preparing the sacral center of the body, which is the center of our creative life force. It is a time for focusing upon regeneration. It is the time of harvest and recapitulation. It is the time for shedding of the old and preparing for the new. It offers opportunities for increased awareness of needed changes.

This can be reflected through our dreams. The emotional content of our dreams can show us what emotions most need to be worked upon during this season. The archetypes predominant in our dreams around the equinox help reveal what archetypal forces would be most beneficial for us to focus upon in the fall months.

Our dreams may show us how to take advantage of opportunities to balance our lives. We may find ourselves making decisions in our dreams, or we may find our judgment being tested. Past events and situations often resurface in dreams at this time of the year, providing clues for what we must still reap and sow.

How these autumn energies specifically affect your life will vary, but you can determine it to a great degree through mythic dream work. You can focus on those autumn energies by using your dream content to help you to determine what to extract from the past year's experiences. You can determine what still needs to be transmuted and cleansed. You can determine what new seeds still need to be sown. The dreams around this time of the year may reveal the kind of testing you may encounter throughout the season.

The following myths and tales can be used in meditation and mythic dream work to assist in revealing how the autumn season is most likely to affect you personally:

 - Tales of the Archangel Michael slaying the dragon
 - Tales of St. George and the dragon
 - Biblical tale of Joseph being sold into slavery
 - Greek tale of Ixion
 - New Testament tale of the gathering of the twelve apostles
 - Masonic legend of Hiram Abiff
 - Biblical book of Ruth
 - Greek tale of the return of Persephone
 - Egyptian tale of Horus
 - Tales of Parsifal and the Grail Knights
 - Milton's *Paradise Lost*

WINTER SOLSTICE

As the sun moves into the sign of Capricorn in the northern hemisphere, the winter season begins. This movement brings with it a corresponding change of energies that will affect us. The winter season is a time in which the etheric forces are aligned with the astral and both are pulled magnetically into alignment with the physical.

This is a time of year when love is pre-eminent, and many of the angelic hierarchies draw nearer to the earth. They are beheld and sensed by many—if only through the dream state. It is a time when our dreams reveal much about our abilities to give and receive love.

The energies of the winter solstice are connected to humanity's life of feeling and the heart chakra. It stimulates the feelings that come to us through our own astral energies, and it releases opportunities to bring peace to the soul. It plays strongly upon the hearts of all.

This is a time of the year in which the inner lights are kindled in spite of outer darkness. It is a time when it is beneficial to free ourselves from a sense of separateness. It is a time which stimulates the feminine energies in everyone. These energies stimulate introspection and inspire seriousness for greater depths of meditation. Anyone wishing to succeed in meditation and dream work could choose no better time to initiate new efforts along these lines.

This time of the year brings opportunities for healing and expansion of consciousness. Our dreams often reflect those areas of our life which most need healing and expanding. They open perceptions of that which we must still face in the growth process.

This is actually a beneficial time to withdraw from outer activities so that we can bring out our own personal, inner light. To bring new life from the darkness of the womb is the energy pattern of this season. It is a most appropriate time to learn how to balance our emotions through dream work.

The winter season is a time in which the universal energies facilitate illumination and the healing of petty resentments and great wrongs. Certain myths and tales can be utilized in meditation and mythic dream work to assist us in using these seasonal energies:

- Biblical tale of the birth of Jesus
- The Hebrew tale of Judah Maccabbee
- Biblical events in the life of Mary through the birth of Jesus
- The illumination of Rama of India
- The Roman tale of Cybele and Attis
- Egyptian tale of the birth of Horus to Isis
- Persian tale of the birth of Mithrus
- Greek tale of Kronos dethroning Uranus
- Tennyson's *Idylls of the King*

VERNAL EQUINOX

As the sun moves out of the sign of Pisces (water) and into the sign of Aries (fire), that which we were cleansing and conceiving through the winter can now be given greater expression. This shift of energy marks a time for greater activation of the masculine energies within all of our lives. It is a time that unveils how best to assert our creative aspects more productively.

During the spring season, the creative forces within us are stirred into expression. Aries is the sign of creative fire and new beginnings. Much esoteric significance has been attributed to this time of year through the literatures of the world—from the resurrection of Tammuz in Sumeria to the resurrection of Christ Jesus in the Christian tradition.

The keynote for this season is creation and expression of the new. It is an excellent time to initiate new endeavors and a new order in your life. It facilitates strengthening of the mental energy. There is an impulse to resurrect our lives—if only out of the doldrums of winter. The living waters of life (Pisces) are flooded with new radiance (Aries). If the cleansing and preparations have been accomplished through the winter, then this new radiance will effect changes in all avenues of life. It is a time that awakens the magic green fire of Gaelic legends: the alchemical force. Our dreams at this point often reflect how this transmutation is going to affect us personally. We can use legends, myths, and tales combined with meditation and mythic dream work to take advantage of this new pattern of universal energy:

- Biblical tale of God fashioning the world
- Crucifixion and resurrection of Jesus
- Egyptian tale of the resurrection of Isis
- Babylonian tale of the resurrection of Adonis
- Roman tale of the death and resurrection of Attis
- Sumerian tale of Ishtar and the resurrection of Tammuz
- Biblical tale of Israelites leaving the bondage of Egypt
- Masonic legend of the Son of the Forge
- Goethe's *Faust*
- Greek tale of "Jason and the Quest for the Golden Fleece"

Here is an example, a case history of how one individual used the mythic dream work process at the time of the vernal equinox. She was using the process to accomplish two purposes: (1) to clarify the death and rebirth process as it was operating in her life and (2) to show areas of beneficial focus for her throughout the spring season. This individual is one who was beginning to become very active in the metaphysical field.

Myth Chosen For The Dream Work

"Jason and the Quest for the Golden Fleece" was chosen as the myth. (This was chosen specifically to help the individual understand the new energies and opportunities most likely to have effects as the sun moved from the water sign of Pisces to the fire sign of Aries.)

Dreams Stimulated

Two dynamic dreams were experienced by the individual the first two nights of the spring season. The mythic dream work technique was applied three nights in a row. The first two nights elicited singular, dynamic dreams involving water, the third elicited a series of dreams involving animals.

Dream One: "I dreamt I was on a raft in a stream that flowed to a waterfall. The water was clear and clean. I did not intend to go over the waterfall, but as I did, I was filled with delight. It was a wonderful ride. Everyone was excited because the stream at the bottom of the waterfall carried me further than anyone else.

"As I climbed out of the water, an older man came over the waterfall, and he went even further downstream. I tried to dissuade the admirers of my trip and point out what this man had just accomplished. I was somewhat embarrassed by the attention I was receiving, especially after the other man's accomplishment. I told the crowd that this man had surpassed my ride, but they wouldn't hear me.

"The man smiled and shrugged. He wasn't concerned that he wasn't getting any attention or acknowledgment. There was no resentment on his part, and in fact, his attitude was more of encouragement for me to enjoy the attention I was receiving. I climbed back to the upper part of the stream and prepared to drop over the waterfall again."

Dream Two: "I was diving in the ocean with four or five others. As we came to the bottom of the ocean, we saw a giant whale-shark resting. It's eyes were closed and it seemed to be sleeping contentedly. The others were fearful of it, and I told them to relax, that there was nothing to be afraid of.

"We walked around the back of the whale-shark (no longer needing any breathing devices). On the other side were three steps leading to an open library. It was filled with many mystical books from every part of the world. There was a large number of them on the Qabala. I knew I wanted to check these out particularly.

"There was an overwhelming feeling of wanting to lose myself in the knowledge that was available here. There was also a feeling of being overwhelmed by the task of having so much to learn. I began leafing through the books, which was the last part of the dream I remembered upon awakening."

Dream Three: "On the third night I had a distinctive series of dreams involving animals. My sleep was extremely deep and the details of the dreams were fuzzy upon awakening and only the bare outlines of the three predominant images remained.

"In the first sequence, a large brown bear appears in the background. It is not always seen, but it is always felt, even when the other scenes come and go. There are faint memories of crocodiles, lining a muddy stream, but I was not afraid. In fact, I walked easily across their backs to the other side.

"On the other side the dream changed, and although I could see the bear, it always remained in the background. There was a small pond and pool of water surrounded by trees. There were a number of apes in the trees, and they came down and started playing in the mud. I thought this was really unusual to see them behave so playfully and comfortably in water and mud. It was almost as if I was to ape their actions."

Insights and Impressions

To this individual, these dreams were very meaningful and significant. The water has links to her own spiritual quest, reflecting new attention and notice for work accomplished. Although the individual expressed insecurity because of her youthfulness, the first dream seemed to indicate that that should not be a concern.

The second dream specifically has ties to the Qabala and to the level of Binah in the Tree of Life, particularly with its ocean and whale image. It also reflects an overcoming of fear in opening to the feminine energies, and as a result an awareness of new knowledge. Binah is the level of the Akashic records, reflected in the library images. The individual felt this was a signal to make sure that the studies continued in spite of more outward work. She has been working strongly with the Qabala and pathworking.

The animal images are significant as well. The bear is a totem of the feminine energies. The fact that it was awake and alert, reflected that this was not a time of hibernation. The crocodiles are fire totems, and the individual explained that there used to be many childhood nightmares involving crocodiles. The dream reflected the end of fears and the beginning of new play. Apes are playful, and the dreamer took them as a reminder to keep a playful spirit as she entered new waters that can sometimes get muddy.

Overall, the dreams reflected a shift resulting from the vernal equinox, a greater expression of abilities, and a greater recognition of these abilities. They provided much insight into the coming season of spring and the individual's own spiritual quest.

Our souls are always on a spiritual quest. When the year of the soul shifts from the new beginnings of the spring into the high energy time of summer, we call that the summer solstice. Of the four holy intervals occurring throughout the year of the soul, the summer solstice is the most powerful time for blending masculine and feminine energies.

SUMMER SOLSTICE

The summer solstice marks the high point of the year of the soul. For a brief time, all four planes of life and energy are aligned with the physical: etheric, astral, mental, and spiritual. Because of this, there is a more direct, dynamic flow of universal energies to us in our physical life.

The summer solstice and the ensuing season is a time when the forces of nature reach their peak in their annual cycle. The keynote is transformation toward spirituality. The energies affecting all of us at this time make it easier to commune with our angelic brethren. It is a time for opening to higher illumination.

This is the time of the year for the blending of the male and female within us. The glyph of the sign of Cancer provides much insight into this blending. The winter was a time when universal energies stimulated the feminine; the spring, the masculine. Summer is the time of bringing the two together to give birth to the Holy Child that resides within us. It is a time in which energies help reveal a new form of life expression in us.

The summer solstice is the time of the mystic marriage. This is the linking of the male and the female, the bridging of the pituitary and the pineal to open us to new realizations of our own intimate essence.

Many will find they dream of childhood events at this time of the year, reminding them of what may have been lost. It may stimulate dreams showing issues that need to be left behind so that the new child within can be born. It stimulates dreams that brings contact with higher guidance (i.e. spiritual teachers). It is a time when dreams often reveal what must be harvested and enjoyed in the months ahead, what qualities are still beneficial to you and how to bring a new sense of balance and fruition to all aspects of your life.

Certain myths, tales and legends can assist us in our meditations and mythic dream work to awaken us to the light and beauty of the child that still lives within us and in our life circumstances:

- Greek tale of Ceres, Persephone, and Dionysus
- Shakespeare's *Midsummer Night's Dream*
- Greek tale of Theseus and Hippolyta
- Biblical tale of the ascension of Jesus
- Biblical tale of Marriage Feast at Cana
- Biblical tale of the Sermon on the Mount
- Chinese tale of the ascension of Kwan Yin.

Meditation and mythic dream work at each change of the season will help you to recognize how the universal energies of that season will affect your individual life circumstances. Begin this process three days before the actual change of the season and complete it on the actual day of the equinox or solstice. (If you feel the need, you may extend it for three days following the equinox or solstice. This makes a seven day ritual, and the significance of the number seven has already been discussed.)

Each night of the holy interval, immerse yourself in one of the myths or tales appropriate to the season. This does not have to be done just prior to sleep, although that does make it more powerful. If you do not perform the mythic dream work ritual before retiring, at least take time to re-read the tale before turning out the lights for the night. It is also beneficial to read all of the tales and myths associated with the season at some time during the holy interval. This empowers the individual mythic dream work ritual.

Pay close attention to the dreams, moods and events of your life for the next several weeks. Pay particularly close attention to the events of your day-to-day life the week prior to and for several weeks after the equinox/solstice. These events often reflect the major issues, emotions and energies that are best to deal with during this season. Remember that part of bringing ourselves into the rhythms of the universe requires that we recognize that nothing is insignificant.

DREAMS OF THE STARS

As we meditate upon and apply myths to dream work activities, we attune ourselves to the more subtle rhythms of universal energies occurring in our lives. Just as there are energy shifts within the seasonal cycles, so there are also subtle shifts each solar month as well. Every month the sun moves into a new sign of the zodiac. As the sun moves into each sign, unique patterns of astrological influences are set into motion, in accordance with the seasonal variations in energies.

We can categorize specific tales and myths according to astrological aspects. Each month has an astrological energy which helps attune us to the archetypal energies influencing the entire earth, as well as our individual lives.

We may use the same myths (reflecting certain archetypal forces) but they will interact and express themselves in a manner unique to each of us. The myths and tales of the astrological signs can be used to trigger awareness of those energies within our own life. Simply reading the tales during the month begins the process of attuning to their energies and influence. If we dynamize them through meditation and mythic dream work, the realizations are enhanced. In this way, each month becomes an adventure, revealing energies we may never have noticed or acknowledged.

ARIES

Using the following myths and tales in meditation and dream work will assist in revealing information about your personal process of SEEKING SELF. They will show you where there is initiative, courage and movement out of the dark. Or, they may show you where those qualities are needed in your life. They may reveal foolhardiness and lack of forethought in regards to people and situations.

- Story of the birth of Moses and the exodus from Egypt
- Greek tale of "Jason and the Golden Fleece"
- Crucifixion and resurrection of Jesus
- Babylonian tale of the resurrection of Tammuz
- Egyptian tale of the resurrection of Osiris
- Roman tale of Attis
- Chinese tale of "One Honest Man"
- Grimm's tale "Boy Who Went Forth to Find What fear Was"
- "Sleeping Beauty"/"Briar Rose"
- African tale of "Child in the Reeds"

TAURUS

Using the following tales for meditation and dream work while the sun enters and is in the sign of Taurus can reveal awareness of our individual process of HAVING AND POSSESSING. These reveal areas and lessons of loyalty, practicality, and fertility. They help reveal where there is stubbornness, sensuality, and materiality within your life. They can reveal where those qualities are lacking or where they are imbalanced.

- Egyptian stories of the god Osiris
- Greek tale of King Minos
- Greek tale of Hercules and the Cretan Bull
- Greek tale of Europa
- Grimm's tales of "Water of Life" and "The Three Languages."

GEMINI

Using the following tales in meditation and dream work while the sun is in this sign will stimulate revelations about our THINKING processes. Our dreams often reveal our degree of versatility, precision and sensitivity. They also reveal areas around which there is nervousness and an inability to discriminate, especially in relationship to others.

These tales can assist us in seeing where work is needed in communication, as well as where it is already productive:

- All tales of the pairs of gods and goddesses
- Assyrian tale of Nebo and Tasmit
- Roman tale of Romulus and Remus
- Greek tale of Castor and Pollux
- Folktale of "Beauty and the Beast"
- Twain's *Prince and the Pauper*
- Grimm's tale "Old Woman in the Forest"

CANCER

When the sun moves into the sign of cancer, meditation and dream work associated with the following tales will elicit information concerning our individual processes of FEELING. They can reveal areas of sensitivity and understanding in our life. They can reveal areas of great emotion and even selfishness. They also reveal much about our ability to be nurtured and nurturing, our mother aspects:

- Greek tale of Hercules and the Hydra of Lernea
- Babylonian tales of the Tortoise
- "The Shoemaker and the Elves"
- Grimm's tale "The Seven Ravens"
- Grimm's tale of "Fisherman and His Wife"
- Tale of St. George and the dragon
- Biblical tale of Moses and the parting of the Red Sea

LEO

When the sun moves into the sign of Leo, it is a good time to meditate and use dream work with the following tales and myths. They can help reveal how the archetypes will be affecting your individual process of CREATING. They can reveal areas and degrees of self-assurance, protectiveness and inspiration, along with new avenues of personal expression. They may also reveal areas and degrees of vanity and dictatorship, along with hindrances to new avenues of personal expression.

- Tale of the Buddhic Lion
- Greek tale of Hercules and the Nemean Lion
- Biblical tale of Daniel in the Lion's Den
- Greek tale of Theseus and the Minotaur
- Folktale of "Beauty and the Beast"
- English tales of Richard the Lion-hearted

VIRGO

When the sun moves into and through the sign of Virgo, we can use myths and tales in meditation and dream work to reveal our individual LEARNING process. They can reveal areas and degrees of helpfulness, dependability, meticulousness and self-reliance. They can teach us how to utilize these qualities more effectively with particular people and situations that we are likely to encounter during the month. They may also reveal areas and degrees of manipulation, secretiveness, fault-finding and old lessons not yet learned.

- All legends and tales of virgins
- Egyptian tales of Isis and the Sphinx
- Greek story of Astraea
- Greek tale of Ceres and Demeter
- Tale of the night journey of Muhammed
- Greek tale of Demeter, Persephone and the eating of six seeds
- Biblical tale of Mary, the mother of Jesus
- Biblical tale of Ruth

LIBRA

When the sun moves into this sign, we can meditate and use dream work to reveal its affect on the life process of UNITING. This is the area of balancing and expressing in balance. The tales reveal areas and degrees of impartiality, sociability, and inspiration in your life. They may also reveal areas and degrees of indecision, manipulation, and self-centeredness. They can be used to reveal how to unite all of your abilities for your greatest benefits:

- Egyptian tale of the Goddess Maat
- Greek tales of Pluto and Hades
- Arabian tale of "Ali Baba and the Forty Thieves"
- Biblical tale of Elijah and the Prophets of Baal
- Grimm's tale of "Briar Rose"
- Greek tale of the judgment of Themis

SCORPIO

With the sun in this sign, we can use certain tales in meditation and dream work to help us understand our life processes of DESIRING. They help us to understand the archetypes that assist us with areas and degrees of creativity, rebuilding, inner strengths, and wishes. The tales also help reveal areas where transformation of destructive and seductive elements is necessary for our greatest creativity to manifest:

- All tales of serpents (i.e. Adam and Eve, etc.)
- Greek tale of Apollo and Phaethon
- Greek tale of Orion
- Dickens' *A Christmas Carol*
- Sumerian tale of Gilgamesh
- Teutonic tale of "Death of Siegfried"
- Eastern tale of Upnapishtam and the Flood.

SAGITTARIUS

When the sun is in this sign, we can use tales and myths to reveal insight into our individual process of BEING. Meditation and dream work will reveal areas and degrees of inspiration and higher mind explorations, as well as areas of exaggerations and dissatisfaction. We will be able to see areas and people that distract from the higher purposes in our life:

- Biblical tale of Joseph (Old Testament)
- Greek tales of Chiron and the Centaurs
- English tales of Robin Hood
- Folktales of William Tell
- Chinese tale of Tseng and the Holy Man
- Biblical tale of David and Goliath
- Grimm's tale of Rapunzel
- Andersen's tale "The Little Mermaid"

CAPRICORN

During this month, we can open to revelations about how we process energy for USING in all areas of our life. The meditations and dream work will reveal areas and degrees of self-sacrifice, spiritual understanding and industriousness. They will also reveal tendencies and areas for miserliness, dictatorial aspects and opportunistic endeavors. It can reveal where we are being used or are using others.

- Greek tale of Pan, the war of the gods of Olympus and the Fall of the Titans
- Greek tales of Vesta or Hestia
- Hindu tale of "Krishna and the Serpent"
- Biblical tale of Adam and Eve
- Greek tale of Amalthea and Zeus
- Zoroastrian tale of Ahura Mazda and Ahriman
- Arabian tale of "Alladin and His Lamp"

AQUARIUS

The myths and tales associated with this sign can help us find insight to how these energies will affect us in areas of our HUMANITY. They can reveal areas and degrees of our sociability, loyalty, and intuitive understanding of others—or our lack of any or all of these qualities. They can also reveal flightiness, coldness, aloofness and any tendency toward being a zealot, whether it's with ourselves or others in our life.

- Biblical story of Noah
- Greek tale of Deucalion, son of Prometheus, and the deluge
- Biblical tales of John the Baptist
- Greek tale of Zeus and Ganymede
- "The Elves and the Shoemaker"
- American folktale "Rip Van Winkle"

PISCES

When the sun moves into the sign of Pisces, myths and tales can be used in meditation and dream work to stimulate information centered around our individual process of SEEKING OR NOT SEEKING.

These may reveal varying degrees and areas of unselfishness, imagination and universality of efforts, as well as areas in which we or others may be attempting to control through giving and sensuality. They can help reveal any locked in potential, along with the area of life it is found most strongly in.

- Biblical tale of Jonah and the Whale
- Biblical tales of John the Baptist
- Greek tales of Eros and Psyche (i.e. the rescue of Aphrodite and Eros from Typhon, etc.)
- Shakespeare's *Romeo and Juliet*
- Navajo tale of "Coyote the Trickster"
- All tales of mermaids
- Teutonic "Tale of Tontlawald"

Begin paying close attention to your dreams two to three nights before the sun moves into the new astrological sign. These new energies and changes will be felt most strongly at this time. It is easier to see how they will play within your own life circumstances in the coming month. Use the same techniques as we described for the life cycles of energy and the seasonal. Create your mythic doorway and enter into the tale, immersing yourself as fully as you can. An effective variation is to place a necklace about yourself once you step through the doorway. Upon the necklace should be an insignia for the astrological sign. This activates its archetypal energies even more dynamically.

BIRTHDAY DREAM RITUAL

One of the most effective means of obtaining insight into these astrological energies is to use the mythic dream work process during the week of your birthday. This ritual is designed especially for understanding the energies of your own astrological sign. Birthdays are power points within the year of any individual. It is a point of the solar return. It is an excellent time to access and reveal energies that will play important roles in your life during the coming year.

Seven days before your birthday, begin your preparations. Review the crises point you are presently within, along with the seasonal energies. Read through as many of the myths and tales associated with your month and your seasonal cycle as you can. Most libraries have books containing the majority of them.

Choose one tale to which you feel most drawn to or enjoy the most, from those associated with your month. For seven days, you will immerse yourself in that tale, using the mythic dream work technique. Create your doorway, using the appropriate symbol and allow yourself to step through into the myth or tale you have chosen. Each night, immerse yourself as a different character within the tale. Make sure you are the protagonist on the first night, as well as on the last.

On the last night before your birthday, perform the mythic dream meditation while taking a ritual bath. Immerse yourself within the tale, while immersed within the water of the bath. This should be done the last thing prior to going to sleep. Think of it as a special time in preparation for your birthday celebration.

Record all dreams through this whole process. Pay attention to the predominant emotions and the archetypes within the dream scenarios. These will reflect what issues most affecting you and predominant in your life in the year to come.

This is a powerful time to access the energies of your present cycle. Birthdays are points in which the veil between the physical and the spiritual thins and the archetypal forces within your life reveal themselves more clearly. Birthdays are not just times to bake a cake. They are times for enlightenment and revelation of the year to come.

CHAPTER TWELVE

Dreams Within the
Tides of the Moon

The third major cycle of energy in our life is associated with the moon. The moon governs the tides, the tides of water and the tides of change. Each phase has its own magic. Each phase corresponds to changes within the tides of our own feminine energies.

The moon reflects the sun. It reflects the more grandiose energies of solar and life cycles in a more finite and tangible manner. While the sun is often a symbol for our spirit, the moon is a symbol for our soul. The soul is what bridges the physical with the spiritual, and thus it has many similarities to dreams and the bridging of the conscious and unconscious mind.

The moon is referred to as the giver of form. As it passes through its stages (its various forms) so will our individual energies. I often recommend that individuals take time at each phase of the moon to assess their energy. At the new moon, what are you feeling physically, emotionally, mentally, and spiritually? At the quarter phase following? At the full moon? At the quarter phase following it? Performing this easy assessment for several months will enable you to detect patterns of high and low points. This will enable you to adjust your activities accordingly. Watching the patterns of your dreams at these phases will also help you to determine your emotional rhythms within each month.

By harmonizing your own rhythms to those of the moon, the moon becomes what it was often worshipped as—a giver of gifts. These gifts may be dreams, feelings, intuition, psychism, inspiration, revelation, and even lessons in birth and death.

The moon has a light and dark aspect—the inner and the outer, the physical and the spiritual. It is the feminine side of us that is

151

active at night. It is the symbol for our intuitive side that influences our dreams, so that greater light can be shed into our waking life. In mythic dream work we are learning to draw down the moon into our waking life.*

There have always been certain myths, images and forces associated with the various phases of the moon. Some of these were briefly touched upon in chapter nine. We can use these and others to bring our feminine energies to life more dynamically at night. There are always those who scoff, believing that the moon is nothing more than an orb in the sky. They believe it has no more of an effect upon us than a tree upon the earth. It doesn't matter whether you accept or believe in the power of the moon to affect you. By consciously performing certain exercises, you re-program the subconscious to affect the dream state. If it makes you feel better to simply look upon the dream work done at the phases of the moon as a re-programming rather than as a ritual invocation of power, that is fine. Either way the results will be the same. The image-forming power of the mind will be consciously used to activate and shape dream activity. The more we consciously make these activities significant, the stronger they affect the subconscious.

Moon goddess images powerfully affect the subconscious, and moon goddesses have been associated with most societies. Traditionally, they inspire wisdom and are often referred to as the keepers of dreams. They have the ability to weave spells and reveal that which is hidden. In short, they operate in much the same manner as our dreams. These goddesses often teach mortals to walk the silvery threads of the moon to all the lands of time. The moon goddesses awaken second sight and etheric vision. The tales of the moon goddesses are as varied as the societies that held them in high esteem, and in spite of differing personalities, they held the same basic powers and gifts.

Most mother myths are tied to the moon in some form, from Kwan Yin in Chinese lore to the Christian Mary with the moon at her feet. In Egypt, Isis was the queen of moon magic, but in most societies the moon goddesses were not confined to a single individual. There was often more than one moon goddess, often in

---

* This ritual of drawing down the moon is performed around the time of the full moon. It involves using a mirror to reflect the moonlight into a chalice or cauldron or upon a talisman to energize it with the moon's energies.

association with the various moon phases.

The three aspects of feminine energy have their correspond-ence to the phases of the moon. These three aspects have a uni-versality in mythology: virgin, mother, and wise woman/crone. They symbolize the creative forces of the moon.

The virgin is associated with the new or waxing moon. The virgin child is a symbol to remind us that we are like children whose realizations must be nurtured and coaxed into expression. The symbol of the young maiden or child is appropriate to use in mythic dream work and meditation at this time of the month. It will reveal scenarios that are healing and that show us how to unfold and develop ourselves. It is an excellent time to stimulate insight about new endeavors and how to meet their challenges. Using these images helps us see new obstacles in our lives and what we can expect in the coming days regarding new situations and people. These images also help to re-awaken the child within us.

Around the time of the full moon, the mother images are appropriate to use in meditation and mythic dream work. This is a time to open to insight on how to give new birth and new expression to various areas of our life. The images are tied to archetypes that show us where our inner adversaries may be and how best to confront them. (Remember that the moon shines brightest when it is full.) Mythic dream work in relation to understanding nightmares is effective at this time of the month.

The full moon is a time to open our consciousness to communication with higher energies and for bringing them to light in our life. We can use this time of the month to stimulate revelations of how best to bring forth our creative energies. The full moon can bring forth revelations concerning family matters, the unfoldment of psychic and healing energies, and enlightenment concerning what our emotions are giving birth to in our lives.

The old wise woman is an image associated with the waning and dark phase of the moon. The wise woman, often depicted as a crone or hag, is a symbol of a time in which the psychic forces within us are powerful and when ancient knowledge can be revealed through dream work and meditation. This image brings insight, truth, and knowledge into our dreams and meditations. These qualities must be brought out into our lives. The crone reveals what we may not wish to see but which must be confronted if we are to grow.

The crone has the look of eternal life, and as intimidating as she can be, she is the true teacher of how to walk the silvery threads of time. She brings the promise of the fulfillment of our dreams—of childhood or adulthood. She can open knowledge of the past, reveal hidden truths, help us to recognize and resolve childhood issues, and provide insight into discord.

THE MOON GODDESSES IN MYTHIC
DREAM WORK AND MEDITATION

You do not have to confine yourself to the use of the three guardians—the virgin, mother and old wise woman. You can also use images of the other moon goddesses to stimulate awareness in meditation and dream work. The ancient goddesses reflect specific archetypal energies to which we have access through those images. We can choose a goddess to be our guide. Many of them align very well with dream work of any kind.

ARTEMIS (Greek): New Moon
Mistress of magic and hunting, she corresponds to the Roman Diana. This goddess is tied to the archetypal energies of strength and independence. She provides strong energies against psychic attack. She is a protector of children. Her image can be used with children to ease and overcome nightmares. Her images and tales stimulate dreams that show us the secret places and people in our lives where we can rest and gather strength for our daily trials. Using her myths and imagery for mythic dream work is most effective in revealing our animal totems in our dreams.

BOMU RAMBI (West African): All Phases of the Moon
This is a goddess of the moon associated with the Zimbabwe peoples. She is the giver of wisdom and comfort. Her energies are calming to emotional stress, and with her as a guide in meditation and mythic dream work, we can release stress and gain comfort. She can be used as a guide and guardian for any phase of lunar dream work, although her followers were noted for wearing necklaces with a crescent shaped moon upon it.

CERRIDWEN (Celtic): Full Moon and All Phases

One of the mother goddesses, Cerridwen is noted for her abilities in magic, enchantment, and divination. She stimulates wisdom and prophetic foresight. She is also a master shapeshifter. For this latter reason alone, she is a wonderful image to use in mythic dream work. The cauldron, a symbol of the container for the divine essence of life, is her primary symbol. She oversees all initiation rites, and thus her image in meditation and dream work can help reveal upcoming initiations of our own.

CHANGING WOMAN (Navajo): Full Moon

This mythic character is excellent for all facets of dream work and shapeshifting. Changing Woman is the Mother of All in this American Indian tradition. She is the one who brings brilliance and joy into life. She can stimulate dreams to teach us about the flow or stagnancy of our lives. She brings dreams and insight concerning the wisdom. A bed of flowers and rainbows are often associated with her. She is always involved in the blessing-way of new birth.

CIRCE (Greek): Dark of the Moon

Often associated with the magic of the moon, Circe can stimulate dreams of premonition. Her dreams are not always seen as beneficial, as they can often stir our deepest and greatest demons. For anyone wishing to stir the depths of his or her psyche to reveal itself through dreams and meditations, her image should be used. Her face is often seen veiled and cloaked in darkness.

FATES (Greek): All Phases of the Moon

The Fates are ladies, not truly goddesses, but their imagery is most appropriate for dream work with moon cycles. They spin the thread of destiny by the light of the moon itself. The spinning loom and threads are some of their strongest symbols. These three ladies are often depicted spinning, measuring, and cutting the threads of life. Their imagery can stimulate dreams and meditations that reveal the time element in regard to various goals and efforts in our day to day life. Their imagery stimulates a strong sense of destiny.

FRIGGA (Scandinavian): Full Moon

This mother goddess of Teutonic lore is often depicted with the Brisingamen necklace. She holds in her hands the threads of fate.

Her imagery and myths can stimulate vision that helps us to see the patterns of our life and to weave them into a new design. Meditation and dream work with her image helps us perceive our own life patterns—past, present, and future.

HATHOR (Egyptian): The Full Moon

Egypt has many images associated with the moon energies. Hathor is often symbolized by the sacred cow which contains the milk of life. Her image can be used in meditation and dream work to help us understand abundance or lack of it in our life. She opens us to insight about the lack and reveals areas and people that can stimulate more abundance. The milk of life flows in rhythms and with joy, and she can reveal to us how to suckle upon that flow of abundance.

HECATE (Greek): Dark of the Moon

Hecate is the goddess of witches and magic. She stimulates the magickal power of the word, which resides behind all life. Her image and energy is strongest at the dark of the moon, at which time meditation and dream work can reveal how to renew the cycle of our life. She brings insight into our personal process of birth, death, and rebirth as it is reflected in our own life circumstances. She opens us to hidden knowledge in order to add enchantment to our lives. She stirs our circumstances in her cauldron of knowledge to reveal the new.

HESTIA (Greek): New and Waxing Moon

Hestia is the goddess of home and hearth. She can be used in mythic dream work and meditation to stimulate awareness about that which is closest to us, i.e. home and family. Hers is the energy of the home fires and how they affect other areas of our lives. A virgin goddess, it is easiest to activate the archetypal forces behind her image at the time of the new moon. The hearth fire is a symbol for her, as is a flaming circle. She can stimulate dreams that reveal to us how and where to be a better servant to others.

HUITACA (Columbian): All Phases of the Moon

This moon goddess can stimulate revelation about stress and how to relieve it in our life. It is said that she spins and weaves our dreams for us. These dreams can be designed to sober us or to lighten us. She is active in dream-making in all phases of the moon.

IDUNA (Scandinavian): New and Full Moon

This goddess of the Land of the Giants is the bearer of the golden apple which gave eternal youth. She is pre-eminent in celebrations of spring time and in childbirth. She can be used in meditation and mythic dream work to open the vision of newborns, especially during the time of pregnancy. This is especially effective the month before and the month following birth. Hers is an excellent image to reveal areas of our lives in which we are becoming too serious.

ISHTAR (Sumerian): Full Moon

This powerful mother goddess has been associated with almost every archetypal energy in the universe. She is the producer of life, the guardian of the laws, the protector, the warrior, and the teacher. She descended into the underworld to retrieve her lover Tammuz. Her image can be used in meditation and mythic dream work to reveal how to recover the eternal loves of your life, or to find out if they can be recovered. She brings dreams that open access to the deepest reaches of your essence. Her image helps reveal aspects of your life that hinder your progress and wisdom on how to overcome them. Her symbols are the double-serpent scepter, the breast that produces milk, and the lion.

ISIS (Egyptian): All Phases of the Moon

The greatest of the Egyptian goddesses, Isis is the patroness of magic and healing. She protects women in childbirth, restores sight (physical and spiritual) and stimulates great healing through meditation and dreams. Her image can be used to reveal areas of our lives that need compassion and maternal love. Her images open awareness to making the impossible possible. The throne is one of her symbols. Visualize her on the other side of the mythic dream doorway, sitting upon her throne, waiting to part the veils between the worlds.

IX CHEL (Mayan): Full Moon

This Mayan goddess of the moon is a powerful one to invoke in meditation and dream work concerning pregnancy. She eases childbirth. For those who are pregnant, her image awakens knowledge about the child they carry. She holds great knowledge of the healing arts and can reveal areas in our lives that need healing. Her image eases menstrual imbalances while sleeping. She is known as the eagle woman and can be visualized that way.

JEZANNA (West African): Full Moon

This is the goddess of the golden moon. She was prominent to the people of Zimbabwe, and great reverence and wisdom are associated with her. She awakens psychic and spiritual vision through meditation and mythic dream work. Her image stimulates understanding and comfort regarding the great sacrifices of life. The image of the moon aglow with golden fire helps to awaken the archetypal force behind her.

KALI (East Indian): Dark of the Moon

Kali is known as the dark goddess. She is associated with time and its influence in our lives. The yoni or womb are her symbols, for they give form and shape to time. Her image in meditation and mythic dream work awakens intuition and insight into the darkness of our lives and our dreams. Although often seen as fierce, hers is the energy of primal feminine force. She nurtures and sustains, and reveals to us where these qualities are lacking and how to attain them. She rules the dark and our dreams. She is the blackness of the womb and the night in which our dreams are born.

KWAN YIN (Chinese): Full Moon and All Phases

Kwan Yin is the great spiritual teacher. As much reverence is given to her in the East as is given to Mary in the Judeo-Christian tradition. One legend tells how she achieved enlightenment and choose to stay close to the earth to assist humanity. She is known as the merciful mother, with purity so strong that she can walk through legions of demons and never flinch or be affected. She is often depicted upon a throne with lotus flowers and children about her. Sometimes she is depicted sitting upon the lotus herself. Her image is powerful to use in meditation and dream work to ease nightmares, especially those of children. She reveals areas where greater purification is needed, and she provides insight into what still must be done for us to achieve enlightenment.

MUSES (Greek): All Phases of the Moon

The Muses were supernatural beings. Nine was usually their number, although some sources quote three, seven, and even eight. Each had her own unique ability and energy, overseeing a specific area of human activity. They were often associated with the sun god Apollo. The tablet and stylus are symbols associated with them, as they bring learning to us in all forms through our dreams and meditations. Each reveals insight and knowledge into a particular area of our life. Each Muse has its own individual symbol, which can be used in meditation and dream work to open us to insight into that corresponding area: trumpet (history), flute (music), comic mask (comedy of our life), club of Hercules (the tragedy of our life), cithara (poetry and music), meditative pose (heroic hymns and art), globe (astronomy and astrology), and the tablet and stylus (poetry and eloquence of speech). They can be used to reveal our artistic energies, abilities, and potential endeavors.

MAWA (West African): All Phases of the Moon

This goddess is considered the omnipotent creator of all life. Her powers are almost unlimited, and her magic always significant. Her image in meditation and dream work helps stimulate renewed awe and reverence for life. It opens us to revelations of the mysteries of life and death—especially how and where these forces are playing within our own unique circumstances. Her image awakens memories of dreams. Her image assists us in being mindful of the divine influence in all areas of our lives, no matter how they are initially perceived.

She can be visualized as breathing forth new life into our world. In mythic dream work, she can be visualized on the other side of the doorway. As you stand opposite, you feel her breath, sweet and cool, instilling new life into you as you step through the doorway itself. Her image is powerful all month, for the cycle of birth and death is continual.

MORGAN LE FAY (Celtic): All Phases of the Moon

This powerful goddess of magic was the queen of Avalon. Merlin taught her all of his magical knowledge. She is strongly connected to the fairy kingdom, and many legends tell how she is of fairy blood herself. She could separate the veils between the kingdoms of the world and her powers are great. She is an enchantress, and some stories speak of her as the Lady of the Lake who gave King Arthur the sword Excalibur. Whether as goddess or fairy queen, her image in meditation and dream work is powerful. She is associated with the waters of dreams. Her image can be used to reveal what circumstances of your life are off course and how to get them back on course. She can be visualized in the mythic dream doorway standing upon the Isle of Avalon. She holds the keys to shapeshifting our lives.

NEPTHYS (Egyptian): Waning and Dark of the Moon

Nepthys is the great revealer, the giver of dreams. She seduced Osiris in order to have his son Anubis, who is the jackal guardian of all inner realms. Nepthys is also a guardian, but of things hidden, things that are revealed to us through our dreams. She is a goddess of obscurity and invisibility, and she is powerful in meditation and mythic dream work in clarifying the meaning and significance of our dream contents. Through her image and her son's we are able to chart our way through the uncharted realms of our sleep. She guides us through the dark worlds. Her symbols are the cup and lotus, and she is often depicted with a basket upon her head. She can reveal to us how best to walk the circumstances of our life when the way is not clear.

INVOKING THE GODDESSES IN OUR
LUNAR DREAMS & MEDITATIONS

1. Determine which phase of the moon you are presently in. An ephemeris or moon calendar will assist you. Make sure that the phase of the moon is appropriate to your own dream/meditation purpose.

2. Next determine what it is you wish to know about yourself through your meditation and/or dreams. Is there some aspect of your life you wish to develop? Is there some aspect you wish to overcome? Do you wish to see how best to heal yourself? Do you wish to see what area(s) of your life most needs healing?

3. Read through the list of goddesses or explore others whose archetypal energies can most easily create the effect you desire. Read through several myths about the goddess to familiarize yourself more with her energies.

4. Make preparations for a pre-sleep meditation.

5. Create your mythic dream doorway. On the other side of the doorway, visualize the moon goddess you are working with. Allow her to guide you through the myth itself, helping you to immerse yourself in it.

6. At the end, sit before the goddess, and allow her to reveal how these same energies are playing in your life. Imagine it as a conversation. Imagine her presenting you with a symbol or even a gift. Then have her assist you to your feet and as she stares into your eyes, allow her image to melt into you, symbolic of her energies coming to life within you.

7. Step back through the doorway, aware of the goddess' presence within you.

8. Before going to sleep, again create the doorway. Lie upon your right side, so as to further activate the feminine energies. Feel the goddess alive within you. Know that as you go to sleep, she will stimulate dreams that will help you know what you wish to know, in a scenario that you can relate to.

9. Repeat this for three nights in a row, planning it so that the middle night occurs at or around the strongest point of the lunar phase. For dream work appropriate to the new moon and the full moon, the strongest points occur the day before, the day itself and the day following the new moon or the full moon. These are the most effective times. For dream work associated with the dark of the moon, the days just prior to the new moon are most effective.

10. Other variations can be used as well. Use your own creativity. Learn to work with these images and the archetypal forces behind them on a level that you find most beneficial and effective.

PART FOUR:

Dream Totems and Mandalas

"But ask now the beasts and they shall teach thee; and the fowls of the air, and they shall teach thee; or speak to the earth, and it shall teach thee."
—Book of Job, 12:7-8

"Once every people in the world believed that trees were divine and could take a human or grotesque shape and dance among the shadows; and that deer and ravens and foxes and wolves and bears and clouds and pools, almost all things under sun and moon, were not less divine and changeable."
—Stephen Larsen, *The Shaman's Doorway*

CHAPTER THIRTEEN

Dream Totems

Two things which all shamans hold in common are an awareness of the power of myth and strong work in dream interpretation. They recognize that there is a power behind the images of their tales. They know myths can be used as a bridge between the realm of sleep and the world of the awake.

In more ancient societies, the shamans were the keepers of the sacred knowledge. They were held in high esteem and recognized as the true shapeshifters and dreamwalkers. They were able to use their dream time as effectively as they used the time they were awake. They were tied to the rhythms and forces of nature.

Shamanism is an experiential growth process. It involves becoming the master of your own initiation. In shamanism, the individual ultimately answers to no human or totem and is alone with the supernatural. Yet, he or she maintains a true sense of belonging and connectedness to all life. This individual is able to visit the heavens and the underworld. This individual is able to learn from all life forms. They learn to control the mind stuff, what in traditional yoga is called the "citta." By stilling the mind, they become aware of the inner realms and develop conscious interaction with them.

A person becomes a shaman by one of three methods: (1) by inheriting the profession, (2) by a special calling, or (3) by a personal quest. The process of following that personal quest and unfolding the innate powers begins with two steps. The first is the overcoming of preconceived notions and limitations. It is comparable to what Edgar Cayce taught: "There is as much to unlearn as there is to learn."

The most difficult part of this step is seeing through the maya, the illusions of our lives. Becoming the shamanic shapeshifter develops a strong sense of not truly belonging to reality. We are often taught that we should belong to something. Many people spend their whole lives attempting to belong. Most of the time it leads to disappointment.The shapeshifter and dream alchemist must develop a sense of individuality that is strong. You must be able to be alone without being lonely. This involves mastering the paradox of opposites:

- Keeping silent and talking.
- Receptivity and resistance to influence.
- Obeying and ruling.
- Humility and self-confidence.
- Lightning-like speed and circumspection.
- To accept all and yet retain the ability to discriminate/ differentiate.
- Ability to fight and the ability to establish peace.
- Caution and courage.
- To possess nothing and to command everything.
- To have no ties and to be loyal.
- No fear of death and high regard for life.
- Indifference and love.

The second step in the shamanic quest is building a bridge between our waking life and the more subtle realms beyond it. This involves unfolding our intuition, creativity, and creative imagination. This bridging process is described through myth in a variety of ways. The individual learns to visit the heavens and the underworld by means of an axis. This axis can be the image of climbing a rope, climbing a tree, being carried or led by an animal, by becoming a bird or an animal, following a cave through a labyrinth, etc. Ancient societies employed mythic imagination to facilitate this step.

The resurgence of the shamanic tradition is breathing new life into the modern mythic imagination. It is awakening that part of our mind which can still feel the archetypal forces behind the mythic imagery. Working with the mythic imagination exercises our more subtle and undeveloped levels of consciousness.

We must move beyond the orthodox treatment of mythic imagery as found in modern religions. These images and their associations to outer reality are held to a fixed, unchangeable dogma. They have grown stale. They have lost their ability to touch each of us uniquely. We must restore the experiential aspect to the mythic images of our life. Only then can we imbue the imagination with the energies of transformation and renewal.

ARCHETYPAL ENERGIES OF ANIMALS

Part of the shamanic tradition is connecting to the energies of the earth and all life upon it. To assist with this, animal imagery is strongly utilized. In the East, it is often said that the way to heaven is through the feet. By connecting with the energies and rhythms of the earth we give greater impulse to our life.

Animals fascinate people because they are a tie to the earth. They are a symbol of greater power and energy. There is an unconscious recognition that they reflect archetypal forces within the world, reminding us of the primal sources from which we came. We can use animal imagery to learn about ourselves and to actualize archetypal energies.

Animals hold a great purpose in the development of the true shapeshifter and dream alchemist. In many myths and tales, animals speak, deliver messages, and call the hero to awareness. They lead individuals into and out of the wildernesses of life. They are a manifest part of the initiation process. Animal totems and guides can assist us in breaking down barriers and in opening up to the new. Carl Jung tells us that animals are representatives of the unconscious, and all animals belong to Mother Earth. We also belong to Mother Earth, and part of the shamanic tradition in dream work is to re-establish the ties to the Great Mother which had become temporarily lost.

In some societies, the power of an animal (its "medicine") is obtained by killing it. When we use animal imagery in dream work, we are participating in a symbolic and yet ritual killing. We are killing our orthodox and stagnant view of life and power for one that is primal and alive. We learn to merge with the archetypal energy of the animal. Thus, it is no longer the same and neither are we.

It is not enough to keep our images autistic and undeveloped. We must breathe new life into them. Begin by recognizing that all forms and images—including animals—reflect archetypal energies.

We do not have to believe that these animals are beings of great intelligence, but there is an archetypal force behind them, one that oversees them. These archetypes have their own qualities and expressions of energies and these are evident through the behaviors and activities of specific life forms.

When we honor an animal, we are honoring the creative essence behind it. When we open and attune to that essence, we begin to manifest it. The animal then becomes our totem, our power or medicine. It is a symbol of a specific kind of energy we are inviting and manifesting.

Humanity has lost that instinctive tie to the rhythms and patterns of nature. However, we can develop an intuitive tie to enhance our lives. Each animal reflects specific energy patterns. By aligning yourself with the animal, you align yourself with the energy pattern that works through it. When we use the mythic imagery of animals in meditation or dream work we are asking to be drawn into harmony with the essence behind it.

Our myths and tales are filled with animal-people who teach, guide and protect. From Aesop's fables to Navajo tales of Coyote the Trickster, animals and creatures perform in the same way humans do. Although allegory on one level, they also stimulate the realization that dynamic forces operate through other kingdoms of life. It is this realization which helped some societies develop an animal mythology that explains everything from creation to how and why dreams operate.

One of the most striking examples is found in African Bushmen tales of the Mantis. The stories of the praying mantis deal with the time when animals and birds were supernatural beings that later became what they are today. The praying mantis is conceived of as a kind of dreaming bushman. He was endowed with supernatural powers, along with human qualities. He taught the bushmen that big things come from the small, and thus they paid great attention to everything in their dreams.

The Mantis worked his magic through other person-animals. When disaster was impending, the Mantis would always have a dream that revealed what to do, and the disaster would be averted. Since the Mantis had the ability to bring the dead back to life, there was a strong belief that their dreams could restore their lives as well. If danger threatened the Mantis, it would form wings and fly to water. Water is a symbol of life to the Bushmen, but it is also an archetypal symbol for the astral plane and the dream state.

Animals in myths and in dream work serve as symbols of that which we have not expressed or even acknowledged. If we can discover our dream animals, they can serve to lead us into dream time, using the mythic dream work techniques already explored.

That faculty in us which responds to and generates images is a dynamic creative faculty. We can choose to develop it and apply it constructively, or we can ignore it, allowing it to manifest as a device for uncontrolled fantasy and daydreams.

Images lead us to meanings that are valid in our life. Discovering those meanings is sometimes difficult, which is why dream work and animal imagery are so compatible. Dream imagery is natural to everyone, and animal imagery triggers our own primordial faculty of imagination. Together they liberate the mind. We then become aware of what Jean Houston refers to as the lure of becoming. The dreams begin to change the dreamer.

There was a time when humanity saw itself as part of nature and nature as part of it. Dreaming and waking were inseparable, the natural and the supernatural merged and blended. Shamans used the symbols of nature to express this unity and to instill that transpersonal kind of experience. These totems help individuals to see themselves as part of the universe.

A totem is any natural object, being, or animal with which we feel closely associated and whose phenomena and energy seem related to us in some way. Some totems reflect energies operative for only a short time in our lives, and some remain with us from birth, through death, and beyond. They are symbols for integration, expression, and transformation.

Animals in particular play a strong role in symbology. They reflect the emotional life of humanity, often representing qualities of our own nature that must be overcome, controlled, and re-expressed as a tool of power. They are symbols of the archetypal power that we can learn to draw upon when pure reason no longer serves.

Adopting the guise of animals and wearing their skins or masks, symbolized the endowing of ourselves with that primordial wisdom and instinct. Terrestrial animals are often symbols of fertility and creativity that must be re-manifested in our evolvement process. Thus, each species has its own characteristics and powers to remind us of the archetypal power we must learn to manifest more consciously. They help us to build bridges between the natural and the supernatural. They awaken us to the realities of both.

Birds in myths and tales are often symbols of the soul. Their ability to fly reflects our ability to rise to new awareness. It reflects the ability to link the physical realms with those of the sky (heavens). Birds reflect the linking of the waking with the dreaming, and thus are powerful totems for all dream work. We are all given to flights of fancy, a phrase often used to describe our dreaming. As totems, each bird has its own peculiar characteristic, but they all can be used in meditation and dream work for inspiration, hope, and new ideas.

Aquatic life also serves a role as a powerful totem. It can also be very effective in dream work. Water is the symbol of the astral plane experience, much of which reflects itself in our dreams. Water totems return us to our origins. There are many myths of life springing from primordial waters. Water is the creative element, reflecting the feminine archetype of the Mother.

It is the feminine, the intuitive, and the creative that is brought to life each night when we dream. The moon, a symbol of the feminine, controls the tides of water upon the earth. The quality of water in our dreams often reflects the character of our present life events. Journeys in or upon water reflects the journey archetype, the seeking for transformation.

Various fish and other forms of aquatic life make dynamic totems for meditation and dream work. In myths, they often symbolize guidance from our intuitive aspects. One of the most dynamic totems is the shell, reflecting the powers of water and the feminine force. It is often a symbol of the journey across the sea to new life and the sounding forth of that new life, like the trumpeting upon a conch shell.

Insects are also a part of nature, and they can make powerful totems. Michael Harner, an anthropologist who teaches shamanism, warns against their use, but they have ancient mythological histories. From the bee of fertility in Egyptian tales to the Mantis of the African Bushmen to the many tales of the Spider Woman who created the universe, they are as much a part of the mythic power of life as any animal form.

Most people look upon insects as pests, but they serve a powerful purpose in the chain of life. They each have unique qualities, reflecting archetypal influences with which we can align.

One of the most common tales is that of the "Ant and the Grasshopper." The ant is industrious and works to survive the upcoming winter, while the grasshopper relaxes and enjoys the summer.

Shamanism teaches us that *all* forms of life can teach us. By studying and reading about animals, birds, fish, and insects, we can learn much about the qualities they can reflect in our lives. This is especially essential when you discover your dream totem. The more we learn of our totems, the more we honor the archetypal energies that affect us through them. Remember that each species has its own unique qualities. An ant may not seem as glamourous as a bear, but an ant is industrious and has a strength that far exceeds its size.

Part of working with nature and our dreams is to break down the outworn preconceptions. Our individual totems in meditation and dream work assist us in this.

> If you talk to the animals,
> they will talk with you
> and you will know each other.
> If you do not talk to them,
> you will not know them.
> And what you do not know,
> you will fear.
> What one fears,
> one destroys.
> —Chief Dan George

DISCOVERING DREAM TOTEMS

In this meditation exercise, you can begin to discover your animal totems. It is a beneficial exercise for healing and meditation groups seeking to discover spirit and totem guides. As in all meditations, music and fragrances can enhance the effects. If there is someone who drums or uses rattles, they can be effective for calling forth the energies of nature.

The drum and the rattle are instruments connected to the heartbeat of the earth, and they are commonplace tools in shamanic journeys. "In aboriginal drumming, it is the echo of the drumbeat that is important, for they say that the sound circulates around the mountaintops where the reverberation bumps the spirits surviving on cosmic planes, circles around the mountains back to the human world. And of course it helps the shaman to enter the expanded state of consciousness. Thus the drum is a tool for journeying in the dream time in order to perform certain kinds of work . . ."*

The drumbeat should be slow and steady, and the participants should allow the drumbeat to lead them. "Riding the drumbeat" to the dream time worlds is part of all shamanic experiences. With practice, it is easy to allow the drumbeat to escort you to the inner realms. You may even wish to use an audio tape of a drumbeat at night to assist you in your mythic dream work.

With the following kinds of exercises, individuals sometimes wonder if they are experiencing a true shamanic journey. The difference between a meditation and a true journey is the depth of experience. In the journey you are actually in it, feeling it and experiencing it first hand. It also will not always follow a predescribed pattern. On the other hand, in meditation exercises, you often observe yourself experiencing the situation or imagining how it should be experienced. Imaging practices and meditation exercises leads to an ability to immerse yourself fully in the midst of the experience itself. You become the part, rather than just playing the part. The meditation aspects lead us to the control and experience of the true shamanic journey.

This difference is reflected in the contrast between mediumistic trance experiences and shamanic trance experiences. In the former, the individual leaves the body and allows another entity or being to work through the physical vehicle. It involves achieving a passive and receptive condition. In shamanic trance, the individual leaves the physical body (leaving it protected), goes out upon the inner planes, experiences them firsthand and brings back the knowledge for themselves. It is an active form of trance.

EXCERCISE: DISCOVERING YOUR TOTEM

As you relax, pull your energies and attention into yourself. You are going to go deep within yourself to discover the totem that lives there. Imagine yourself standing in a wide field. The air is still, and there is a calmness around you. The sun is still visible, although it is setting. The moon has already risen.

---

* Dr. Nandisvara Nayake Thero, "The Dreamtime Mysticism and Liberation: Shamanism in Australia," in *Shamanism*. Shirley Nicholson, ed., (Wheaton: Theosophical Publishing House, 1987) p. 227.

It is dusk, that powerful time between day and night. It is the time in which the sun and the moon share the sky. It is where day and night mingle. It is the intersection of light and dark, waking and sleeping.

Before you stands a tall oak tree. Its bark is gnarled and twisted. Its roots extend far into the heart of the earth itself. Its branches block your view of the sky as you stand beneath it. You are unable to see its uppermost branches.

There is a small opening at its base, just large enough to squeeze through if you bend over. With one last look toward the setting sun, you step carefully into the inner darkness of the tree. There is the smell of moss and moist wood. As you squeeze through the narrow opening, you find that it widens as you move further within. Soon you are able to stand erect, and you breathe a little easier. You pause, catching your breath and summoning your courage to inch further inside. It is then that you hear the sound.

At first it is faint, hardly discernible. You hold perfectly still to insure that the sound is not your own movement. It is soft, but as you move forward, feeling your way in the darkness, the sound grows louder. It is the sound of a distant drum. In the darkness of the inner tree, its sound is hollow and primal. For a moment you imagine it as the heartbeat of the tree itself.

The beat is slow and regular, and yet its hollow tone touches the core of you. It coaxes you through the dark, deeper into the tree itself. It is hypnotic, and you know that it is sounding forth that which you have awaited a long time. You are not sure what it will be. You have never been sure, but you know you will recognize the reality of it when confronted with it.

You continue forward, knowing it is better to go forward than to return. You are beginning to feel as if you are in a dream which has its own reality. As you move further in, you notice it grows lighter. At first you are not sure whether it is due to your eyes adjusting to the dark or whether something new is being introduced into this walking dream.

Ahead of you there is a torch burning, illuminating the path you are upon. Now you can see that the path is narrow. The sides of the tree are steep and ridged with its inner veins and arteries. You touch your hand to the sides, and surprisingly it feels warm. You understand. Blood runs warmly through all living things. It is comforting.

As you approach the torch, you find it is at the top of a steep, descending path. It is illuminated by sporadic torches, leading down into that which can only be experienced. You place your feet carefully, as the path is covered in spots with a slick moss. Fortunately, the illumination grows brighter with each step.

The path spirals down, leading you deep into the inner heart of the planet. You feel as if you are following one of the roots of the tree to the very core of the earth, to the center of life. You know you are being led to a primal point of life and energy within yourself. You are reconnecting with your own roots.

The drum beat has grown to a steady volume. It has become a part of your own rhythm—or you have become a part of its rhythm. You are not sure which is true. As you move down, another sound begins to reach you, enticing you even more deeply into the heart of life itself. It is the sound of running water. A stream maybe, or a waterfall. It is not quite discernible.

It is then that you see the end of the tunnel. Ahead of you is a cave-like opening. You step out through the opening. The sunshine is bright and warm. It is as if you have stepped out of the womb into new life. You are surrounded with bright sunlight and the soft greens of nature. In the distance is a river of crystalline waters, running through what appears to be the heart of the meadow. Wildflowers of every color and fragrance fill your senses with their beauty. The greens of the grasses are emerald, and at the edge of the meadow is a forest of rich dark greens, the color of primeval life at its purest.

You move into the meadow, allowing the sun to fill your body with a fire that warms and soothes, chasing away all fears. You fill your lungs with air that is sweet and fresh. You had almost forgotten how wonderful breathing could be.

You move to the edge of the river, and you watch hypnotically as it flows over rocks, creating eddies and spirals of myriad shapes. The sun glints off the waters in rainbow hues. You look down the river, and you see it widen and spill out into the deep blues of an ocean. All waters are here. You bend down and gently cup your hand into the river, bringing its cool elixir to your mouth. It quenches your thirst and refreshes your body.

Next to the river is a stone, shaped a little like a chair. You settle upon it, feeling how the sun has warmed it. From here you can take in the entire meadow scene. You are filled with a sense of peace.

Surely there could be no better place to get in touch with yourself. This is a place where dreams meet reality. Here you can connect with your core. Here you can discover the power that is yours to claim in life.

Your eyes slowly look over the area: the river, the distant ocean, the meadow, the forest. And your breath catches. As if in response to your thoughts, there is a movement. It may come from the waters. It may come winging across the skies. It may step out from the woods. You sit still watching as an animal appears in your vision. Its eyes seek you out and hold your gaze.

Never have you seen anything so wonderful, so unique. Such animals have always seemed wild and out of touch. There is no fear. There is only recognition and wonder. Surely this must be a dream! Again as if in response to your thought, it makes a sound, a movement, a gesture—indicating its own unique power and strength. And then it disappears!

You stand, looking about you. Had you been dreaming? Was it all in your imagination? You scan the skies; your eyes search the edges of the forest, trying to penetrate. You look to the waters. Nothing.

Have you done or thought something to offend it? You stand confused, unsure. It was so beautiful, so noble, such a unique expression of life. It deserved to be honored and respected—not just by you, but by all of humanity.

Your thoughts are shattered by a trumpeting that echoes through the meadow. You turn towards the mouth of the cave that emptied you into the meadow. There in the darkness of the opening was the outline of your animal. Its image freezes briefly, its eyes holding yours once more. Then it fades from view. You laugh, running toward the opening. You understand. As you give it honor and respect, its energies come alive for you, to guide you between the worlds. Its energies are yours to claim, but they can only be claimed through honor, love, and respect.

As you reach the opening, there upon the ground lies a large conch shell. A part of you knows that this is the symbol of the calling forth of new energy. The trumpeting upon the conch shell is a reminder that new life can be called forth to enable us to walk the dream time. You pick up the conch shell, your gift, and with a silent prayer of gratitude, you step back into the cave. It is now well lit, and its path is wide and clear. In the distance, you see the outline of your new-found friend, leading the way. Soon you see the light that leads you from the tree itself.

As you step from the tree, you see that the sun is coming up. It is dawn, and the moon is still visible. You look back into the opening, and your guide retreats into its depth. You understand that as you claim your own power, as you connect with your true self, your path becomes clearer and more easily managed. You cradle the conch shell within your arms, a reminder of all you have learned.

Once we discover our totem(s), it is easy to apply them to the mythic dream work process. When you create your dream doorway and are about to immerse yourself in a particular myth, visualize your totem on the other side of your door. Allow the guide to accompany you throughout the mythical imagining.

As you work with your dream totems, you will find they come to you in your dreams more often, along with other guides who are important to you. It is always a wonderful confirmation, and it helps you to remember your dreams better.

CASE HISTORY: USING DREAM TOTEMS

The following account is an example of how one woman effectively used the mythic dream work process to uncover her dream totems, using the method just described in the "Discovering Your Totem" exercise. It helped the individual discover several significant spirit totems.

Dreams Stimulated

The dream-totem meditation, in conjunction with the mythic dream work process, stimulated two significant dream scenarios. In both dreams, the common thread of bird totems appeared, reflecting much about air, new knowledge, and mental changes that were occurring and about to occur in her life.

Dream One: "The whole dream had a feel for new things coming my way and a need to honor them. I had just returned home from shopping and I got out of the car. I immediately saw a large white feather from a snowy owl, along side another twelve-inch tail feather of rich browns. The second [feather] I knew had to be either a hawk or an eagle feather.

"In my front yard was an open circular area with a tree in the center. Although there was no such area in my yard, I wasn't surprised by it. Inside the edge of the perimeter was a small cluster of hawk feathers. As I picked it up, I noticed it was clustered around a bird's foot, and I knew this was a true fetish.

"The foot was smoldering. In the dream I seemed to know that the children in the neighborhood had burnt it for fun. I tapped it against a rock to knock off the charred pieces and the cluster and foot all fell apart. I was disappointed, but I knew it had been dishonored. Several small feathers still remained, but I gave them up, figuring that it was best to give it all back to the earth. As I turned from the circle, I knew that I still had my two larger feathers."

Dream Two: "I was walking along the street, and I encountered a dead crow. I knew I had to stop and honor it by taking some feathers and by burying it. There was initially a full wingspread, but as I began to gather it up, there were only three feathers.

"The top feather was not entirely a rich black, but it was large and in good condition. The second feather was also large but it was a very deep, rich black. I knew it would have to be cleaned of blood though—especially at the stem. Underneath it was a large feather of bright red. It was a red crow feather—even though I knew that that did not make sense. When I picked it up, there was no doubt about it being a crow feather. I knew that even more would fly my way."

Insights and Impressions

The most obvious insight is the revealing of specific bird totems. This includes the snowy owl, the crow, the hawk, and the eagle. She began to examine these birds more closely, to discover what they could teach her.

She was opening to new knowledge and was at a point in her life when she was afraid of not being able to experience the spiritual realm. She was having difficulty integrating various metaphysical lessons with her traditional religious background.

She was at a point where she needed something much more universal, something that didn't deny her traditional beliefs but simply added to them. This is somewhat reflected in the balance of the bird feathers she first found. The owl is the symbol of the moon and the night; the eagle and hawk are symbols of the sun and day. She was beginning to come into balance. She was also beginning to truly express her creativity and artistic energies. She was overcoming her fears and insecurities.

There were also several sexuality issues she was dealing with which were reflected in her dreams. The crows reflected the cleansing of old sexual issues, a new honoring of her own femininity, and a reclaiming of her own power.

HONORING THE DREAM TOTEMS

The use of animal imagery in meditation and dream work assists us in transcending physical consciousness. It draws our attention toward those energies influencing physical life. The biggest difficulty is interpreting those images. Since these images are received in altered states, we must employ the conscious mind to determine their significance. Reading, studying, and learning about these images helps us to relate them to ourselves.

We must also combine this thinking aspect with our feelings. Amber Wolfe, author of *In the Shadow of the Shaman*, defines this process as a focusing of our awareness (thinking), going within to our own inner sources to verify (intuitive), checking our own heartfelt connections or disconnections to these images and totems (feeling), and finally learning to sense and activate that image (sensational).

This kind of meditation can stimulate encounters with mythical animals and creatures. Mythical creatures can be powerful totems, especially in the mythic dream work process. They assist us in transcending from normal dreams to those which can be more easily directed. We create the mythical dream doorway, and then we ride the mythical creature to the dream state or into a specific myth or tale.

Mythical creatures do have powerful thoughtforms and energies associated with them, so a little caution may be necessary. It is good to learn as much about them and the mythology surrounding them as you can. We do not have to accept the images and totems without question. We can demand that the energies be expressed to us in images we can relate to. If we are uncomfortable with an animal totem and have already put it through a verification process, we should just send it on its way. At the same time, the animal images and totems that we receive should not be haphazard-

MYTHICAL CREATURES BRING DREAMS

Mythical creatures can be powerful dream totems, as they are often a combination of the real and the fantastic. Their images serve to shelp us transform normal dreams into those which are more easily controlled and directed for our benefit. From Pegasus, to the unicorn, to Chiron, to dragons, they can be discovered just as our animal totems can. They are very effective with all mythic dream work.

ly discarded simply because they are not as glamorous or as powerful as what the ego wanted. The image or totem may be quite appropriate, but only study and exploration of that animal will reveal its significance to you. Discovering that significance is a means of honoring that totem.

Don't jump to conclusions. The totem may be much more than what you imagined. An eagle is a totem that many perceive as powerful, and it is often desired. Its image speaks louder than a simple wren. Totems naturally seek us out and reveal themselves to us. They will also change as we change, although some stay with us through life. Be careful about trying to predetermine your totems. You can open yourself to delusion, and when this occurs it reflects more interest in filling a need of the ego rather than that of growth. Take heed from the old tale of "The Eagle and the Wren":

The eagle was known as the strongest of the birds. No other could fly as high into the heavens. No other had even come close—not the hawk, the crane, the goose, the robin or any of the bird kingdom. One day Wren overheard Eagle bragging how it could fly higher and see more than any one else. Softly, Wren interrupted Eagle's speech. "I have heard of one who flies higher."

All the birds stopped their chatter. Eagle looked at Wren and stretched its powerful wings out. "There is no one powerful enough to fly as high. No one!"

Wren watched Eagle flex his massive wings. "You may be right Eagle," said Wren. "But to be sure I would have to see exactly how high you can fly."

"That is no problem," answered Eagle. "You are a tiny thing; climb onto my back, and I will fly you to the heights so you can see for yourself."

This Wren did, and Eagle immediately took to the air. He flew upwards, climbing higher and higher, working his wings to limits as he had never done before. He forced himself ever higher. When his powerful wings had reached the limits of their endurance, he turned his head and mocked Wren.

"I am the strongest and most powerful, no bird will ever be able to reach these heights much less go beyond." Wren smiled. "You are wrong, Eagle, for I can fly higher by far." Then Wren, who was not tired and who had allowed Eagle to carry him to the heavens, flapped his own wings and lifted off of the back of Eagle. He flew even higher into the heavens. With a laugh, he disappeared beyond the clouds, leaving Eagle far below.

All totems—animals, birds, fish, mythical creatures—must be honored. The more significance and honor that you attribute to them, the more effective their images become. Here are some ways to honor your totem:

1. Learn as much about your totem as possible. Read about it, learn its qualities and behaviors. Research myths and tales associated with it. All of these activitites will help you to understand those same energies within you.

2. Find a picture of your totem(s). Make a collage, in which your totems are encircling a picture of yourself. Draw and sketch pictures of it. Artistic endeavors access the right hemisphere of the brain, re-enforcing our connection to the image and the archetypal energies that operate through it.

3. Buy figurines for yourself. You may also wish to purchase small tokens and images of your totem and present them as gifts to friends. As you give the gift, you are honoring the universality of the totem's energies and its ability to help everyone. You do not have to tell everyone why you are doing this, nor the esoteric significance of it. Most will not understand. Let them enjoy the gift on their own level.

4. Give an anonymous donation to a wildlife fund or a specific organization associated with your totem. As you promote the life of your totem, you promote all life. The anonymity insures that the honoring is for the sake of honoring rather than for the recognition.

5. Be creative in the ways you show respect and honor for your totem. Acknowledge it, giving thanks to divine sources for bringing this totem to you.

Once we discover our totems, a unique process is set in motion. You will start encountering your totem(s). You will find pictures, postcards, curios in which they are depicted. You will discover television programs exploring their habitats and behaviors with greater frequency. Books, myths and other depictions of them will cross your path. You do not have to indulge them all, but by noticing them and taking advantage of these instances, you show honor and respect. Initially, it is important to do so to more fully ground the energy into your physical life.

Do not brag or reveal to others what your totem does for you. Disbelief on their parts, expressed or not, can hinder your connection to the archetypal force behind the totem. An old axiom teaches "there is strength in silence." Speaking of your relationship with the totem, and how much it does for you, can dissipate its energy before it has an opportunity to work its real magic for you.

There is nothing wrong with letting others know that you like certain animals or that you are fascinated with such animals. A totem, however, is personal. Yes, other individuals may have the same "generic" kind of animal, but the manner in which it works for you will be unique. It is neither better nor worse—just different.

CHAPTER FOURTEEN

Making and Using Dream Talismans and Mandalas

A totem is a natural object or animal, and you may feel naturally attracted to its energy, or feel somehow associated with it. A talisman, according to the Golden Dawn, is a "magical figure charged with the force which it is intended to represent." It is a sacred object whose energies serve as symbols and means for integrating and transforming our own energies in a unique manner.

Talismans and amulets are often used synonymously, but the amulet is thought of more as a form of protection. The talisman, however, is a symbol of specific energies you wish to attract. Talismans have been used in many forms. The St. Christopher medal and the rosary are but two. One who wears a cross about the neck is using a talismanic image. This image is a physical reminder and a profession of one's beliefs and faith. Talismans serve as reminders and stimulators of the creative forces associated with them.

Many of the oldest charms are derived from nature: stones, feathers, and herbs are common natural amulets. Each takes on its own unique significance to the individual. That which helps us to develop a strong connection to a force inside or outside of us can be considered a talismanic tool.

Talismanic images, especially mythic ones, serve several purposes. They awaken a sense of our relationships to the mysterious dimensions of the universe. They help us to recognize that we are related to and can connect with all things within it. They are a great resource and can provide bridges to archetypal forces. They open astral doorways and help orient us to the spiritual train of thought. They help us link the past to the present, so as to build

183

new energies and perceptions for the future. They link the physical world to the spiritual dimensions which influence us.

The most effective talismans are those personally made. The process is neither esoteric nor complicated. It is important, however, to know why you are making them. The more significance you associate with the images and symbols, the more they will be able to work for you. You must know what everything on the talisman represents. You must know what energies will be stimulated when you align with them.

Most esoteric systems teach access to magical states of consciousness through basic meditation and visualization. These same processes can be applied to talismans to affect the dream consciousness. Such a talisman can be just a general dream stimulant, or it may be designed to stimulate dreams to reveal transformational processes.

All images, all symbols, all geometric shapes alter the electromagnetic field in which they exist to varying degrees. They interact with our own personal electromagnetic fields. For example, a pyramid shape amplifies electromagnetic fields around it. This is why the pyramid is stimulating to the physical and spiritual energies of an individual. Talismans made in this shape accentuate and amplify the specific electromagnetic energy patterns represented by the talisman.

To work with the dream consciousness, we will construct talismans of circular shapes. The circle alters the electromagnetic field of an individual to facilitate integration of the conscious mind with the subconscious (the outer circle with the inner). Basic physics does play a part in this process, especially in understanding the interaction of various energy fields. We are working with the biochemical, electromagnetic properties of the mind and body. We are also working with thought, will and feeling.

These dream talismans can be worn, carried or placed under the pillow. It is recommended that they be used only when sleeping. This exclusive use keeps them special. During the waking hours, place them in a small box, wrap them in silk or place them inside your pillow.

Talismans can be made of various materials: parchment, wood, paper, cloth. Dream talismans are effective when made from clean cotton material. When worn about the neck at night, they are relatively unnoticed during sleep. Although silver is the metal associated with the moon and its influence, it is also rather expensive and requires skill and training to craft it properly. Cotton cloth works effectively and it can be fashioned into an effective pendant.

Astrologically, the moon influences dream states. Choose the color of the material according to how the moon is associated with your dream purpose. If the mythic dream work is to be performed at the dark of the moon, you may wish to use black material. If you are wanting to stimulate the psychic energies that are powerful at this time of the month, choose symbols that apply to those goddesses associated with psychic energies, such as Hecate or Circe.

Be as creative as possible. Make the talisman fit your individual needs. Choose your symbols carefully and accordingly. This includes the color. Seven colors in particular are effective for the foundation colors of dream talismans: blue-greens, indigo, silver-grays, black, sea greens, aqua, white. All of these colors are associated with aspects of the moon and our own subconscious energy. A little study of color will provide great insight into the mixing and matching of these for your own specific purposes.

It is also good to personalize one side of your talisman. This means have your name on it or a symbol for your name. We will learn how to create a name sigil based upon magical squares. This, in conjunction with three aspects of your astrological chart, will personalize the talisman very well. The three aspects to use are your sun sign, your moon sign and your rising sign.

On the opposite side of the talisman, you should inscribe symbols and images associated with dreaming. These can be arranged in any manner you desire. They can be sewn in different colored threads, or they may be drawn with permanent markers. The making of your dream talisman is an individual creative process. There are no limits other than your own creativity. Here are some helpful steps to help you create your own talismans:

CREATING THE DREAM TALISMAN

1. Decide what kind of dream stimulation you desire. Choose symbols to align with your purpose. Use the "Dictionary of Dream Symbols for Talismans" found in this chapter to help you.

2. Choose the color of the material that is most appropriate for your purpose. If unsure, simply go with white.

3. On the cloth, draw a double circle, approximately two inches in diameter, connected by a half-inch square section. Refer to the example found in the diagram "Creating the Dream Talisman."

4. Convert your name to a sigil, as described in the next section of this chapter.

5. On one of the two circles, write or sew your name sigil and other personally identifying symbols, such as the astrological symbols just discussed. If you wish, you may use the "Dictionary of Talisman and symbols to add to this.

6. On the other circle, inscribe any particular dream symbols and images appropriate to your dream purpose.

7. Cut the talisman out of the cloth. Do not cut the circles out separately. Leave them connected by the half-inch square section of cloth. Fold the talisman at the half-inch square section and align the two circles.

8. Before sewing, you may wish to place a dream crystal inside or some specific dream herbs to further activate and charge the talisman toward your purpose.

9. Sew around the edges of the circle, binding the front and the back together. The half-inch square now forms a loop through which you can slip a necklace of some sort so that the talisman can be worn about the neck.

10. The more exact in your choice of symbols, the better. It is beneficial to construct this when you will not be disturbed. Visualize the symbols as you work on each step, and see each symbol assisting you with your dream work. At its completion, perform a small blessing and meditation ritual with it. Smudging it or running it through incense is appropriate. Visualize everything it will do for you. Dedicate it with thought and prayer for your growth and enlightenment.

THE USE OF MAGICAL SQUARES

The use of magical squares in talisman making comes to us through various sources. The most prominent is *The Sacred Power of*

CREATING THE DREAM TALISMAN

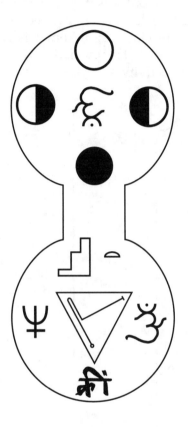

One one side of the material will be symbols and designs to stimulate whatever dream activity you are desiring.

On the other side of the talisman will be the personalized symbols and sigils: your name sigils and any other dream symbols you wish to employ.

The talisman is cut and folded over, to be sewn along the edges of the circle. You may wish to place a dream crystal between the two sides prior to sewing. You now have a talisman to wear at night.

Abramelin the Mage by S.L. MacGregor Mathers. Magical squares are based upon numerological correspondences drawn from the Hebrew Qabala. This ancient form of mysticism breaks the universe down into ten levels of consciousness, tied together in a diagram known as the Tree of Life. Each level has its own energies associated with it. The ninth level of consciousness is known is Yesod, and it is that level of our consciousness that is associated with the influences of the moon and all dream activity.

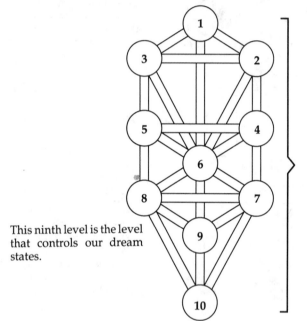

This ninth level is the level that controls our dream states.

The levels of consciousness, as depicted within the Tree of Life. Each can be viewed as a different level of subconscious activity.

The magical squares consist of numbers that are arranged so that no matter which direction they are added—horizontally, vertically, or diagonally—the total will always be the same. Each of the seven major planets has its own magical square. By aligning our name to that square, and marking it off according to the numbers, we create a name sigil that symbolically aligns us with the planetary energy. The sigil is our personal connection to the energy. It becomes a bridge to the archetypal forces represented by that planet.

MAKING YOUR OWN MAGICAL DREAM SQUARES

Here are the steps to make your own magical squares for use on your dream talismans:

1. There are several ways that we can convert our name to numbers. One way involves traditional numerology, in which the letters of the alphabet are assigned to one of the nine basic digits:

1	2	3	4	5	6	7	8	9
a	b	c	d	e	f	g	h	i
j	k	l	m	n	o	p	q	r
s	t	u	v	w	x	y	z	

In this method, take your first name, write out the letters and find the corresponding number.

EXAMPLE: J   O   H   N
           1   6   8   5

You can also use your last name. This will give you a second sigil, but it is the first name that is your predominant energy signature. Your first name is what most uniquely reflects you.

Since the magical square for the moon has 81 numbers, there are enough individual numbers to cover the entire alphabet. We can thus use a second method of converting the name to numbers:

A	B	C	D	E	F	G	H	I	J	K	L	M
1	2	3	4	5	6	7	8	9	10	11	12	13
N	O	P	Q	R	S	T	U	V	W	X	Y	Z
14	15	16	17	18	19	20	21	22	23	24	25	26

EXAMPLE: J   O   H   N
           10   15   8   14

One way is no better nor worse than the other. They are simply different ways of converting your name to numbers so that he talisman can be personalized. What is important is the significance you attribute to it.

2. Having converted your name to numbers, locate them upon the magical square. Refer to the example given in the diagram entitled "Magical Square for the Moon." Find the square that has the number for the first letter of your name. Draw a small circle in it to indicate the beginning of your name. Next locate the squares that hold the number for the other letters in your name—in the order they fall within the name. Draw a continuous line from the small circle to each numerical square for the letters in your name.

3. For names with double letters in them, such as BILLY, make a loop in the square for the double letter and move on to the next.

```
B   I   L   L   Y
2   9   3   3   7
```

4. In the box for the last letter in your name, draw a small perpendicular line, to indicate the end of the name.

5. You can also take the names of various goddesses associated with dreams (as described in chapter twelve) and convert them into a sigil as well. Placing that sigil beside your own is powerfully effective in aligning your own energies with the archetypal force behind the mythical goddesses.

MAGICAL SQUARE FOR THE MOON

37	78	29	70	21	62	13	54	5
6	38	79	30	71	22	63	14	46
47	7	39	80	31	72	23	55	15
16	48	8	40	81	32	64	24	56
57	17	49	9	41	73	33	65	25
26	58	18	50	1	42	74	34	66
67	27	59	10	51	2	43	75	35
36	68	19	60	11	52	3	44	76
77	28	69	20	61	12	53	4	45

SIGIL FOR "JOHN"
The name John converts to four numbers (1, 6, 8, 5) Starting with number 1, lines are drawn connecting each number in sequence. At the beginning number, draw a circle. At the ending number, draw a line.

The sigil for John is now drawn upon the talisman, along with any other symbols appropriate to it.

Once you have converted your name to numbers, draw it on the magic square to elicit the sigil or symbol for your name. A smaller duplication of it is then drawn upon your dream talisman, along with any other personal symbols (such as astrological correspondence)—as depicted above.

DICTIONARY OF DREAM SYMBOLS FOR TALISMANS

 The Sanskrit symbol of the Om. A powerful dream stimulant, used in forms of dream tantra and in creative dream activity. The Om is the sound from which all sounds came.

 The trident is a symbol for Neptune in astrology, the unconscious mind. In dream tantra, it was worn, painted and visualized in the throat area to stimulate this psychic center to create greater dream activity.

 The four phases of the moon, representing the monthly cycle of our psychic and feminine energy which controls our dreams. From top to bottom: new moon, waxing moon, the full moon and the waning moon. Each phase of the moon influences our dream activities differently. The phase known as the "dark of the moon" occurs just before the new moon.

 The equal-armed cross is an ancient symbol of the intersection of two planes and the balancing of the four elements in dream work, it symbolizes the intersection of waking and sleeping, which is dream time.

 The circle is the meeting point of the inner and the outer. It ties all consciousness, symbolizing that all is connected. In dream work, it is the circle of sleeping and waking united.

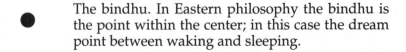 The bindhu. In Eastern philosophy the bindhu is the point within the center; in this case the dream point between waking and sleeping.

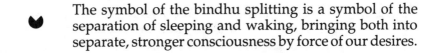

The symbol of the bindhu splitting is a symbol of the separation of sleeping and waking, bringing both into separate, stronger consciousness by force of our desires.

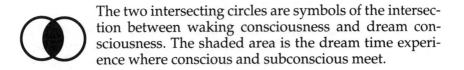

The point within the circle is ourselves within the inner workings of our dream consciousness. It is the symbol of that point in our dream where we become conscious of the dream's inner workings and thus can begin to control them.

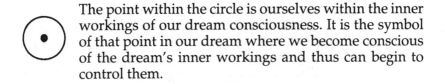

The two intersecting circles are symbols of the intersection between waking consciousness and dream consciousness. The shaded area is the dream time experience where conscious and subconscious meet.

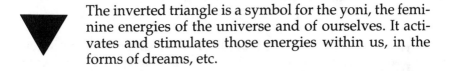

The spiral is an ancient symbol of creation and creativity. The spiral of life (reflected in the spiraling helix of the DNA molecule) is a symbol for spiraling into new consciousness, new dimensions and new perceptions.

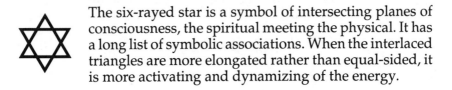

The inverted triangle is a symbol for the yoni, the feminine energies of the universe and of ourselves. It activates and stimulates those energies within us, in the forms of dreams, etc.

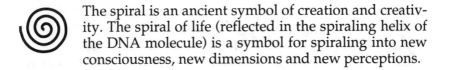

The six-rayed star is a symbol of intersecting planes of consciousness, the spiritual meeting the physical. It has a long list of symbolic associations. When the interlaced triangles are more elongated rather than equal-sided, it is more activating and dynamizing of the energy.

The square is the foundation of creation. When we begin dreamwork, we are building a new foundation of the inner and the outer. All enclosed shapes are a merging of inner and outer forces and energies.

 An Eastern symbol for Nada Yoga, the yoga of sound. It is a symbol associated with and stimulating to the creative will force of the throat chakra, which we try and bring to greater manifestations through mythic dream work.

 The diamond shape is the activating of the creative Foundation of the square. It is activating and stimulating to new dream foundations that are being established.

 The triangle within the triangle within the triangle is the symbol for the interaction between the male and female energies within us in order to access deeper levels of consciousness. It is a symbol for asserting the will to manifest the creative feminine.

 The Krim. This is a Sanskrit symbol for the feminine energies of the goddess Kali. Kali holds the power of creation and dissolution—awake and asleep. A dynamic symbol for awakening the creative feminine in the dream state.

RUNE SYMBOLS FOR DREAM TALISMANS

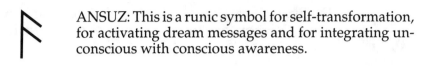

ANSUZ: This is a runic symbol for self-transformation, for activating dream messages and for integrating unconscious with conscious awareness.

PERTH: This symbol has an energy comparable to that of the Phoenix. It aids in releasing something which is hidden within. It can stimulate dreams of initiation and is used for releasing our deepest blocks.

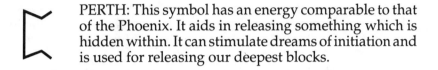

INGUZ: The runic symbol for new beginnings and for stimulating dreams which can reveal new beginnings and/or preparations necessary for new beginnings.

LAGUZ: The runic symbol for water (dream element). It awakens the unseen powers of our nature and stimulates dreams that are cleansing.

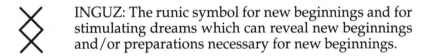

RAIDO: The runic symbol for the journey. In talismanic dream stimulation, it stimulates general dream activity and communicates to us through dreams how best to begin new journeys.

THURISAZ: This is the symbol for the place of non-action. In dream talismans it stimulates dreams that can reveal what is hidden and what needs to be experienced by the individual to grow.

SOWELU: The rune for wholeness and self-realization. It is a powerful symbol for making the forces of dreams more available to you.

All of the runic symbols should be inscribed on the talisman in an upright manner. When worn they should appear upright!

EGYPTIAN SYMBOLS FOR DREAM TALISMANS

The Eye of Horus is a powerful symbol for protection against nightmares and for seeing into the significances of our dreams.

The Egyptian hieroglyph for Isis, the goddess of magical arts, inner vision and guardian of the veils between the physical and spiritual. This symbol is beneficial for children as it protects against nightmares.

The Egyptian hieroglyph of the chalice is a symbol for Nepthys, the psychic bringer of dreams. It is protective and brings revelations. It is often a symbol for that part of us which is active at night. It is the symbol of the revealer.

The Egyptian symbol of the jackel is a symbol for the god Anubis. It is the shadow. Anubis helps one to navigate the dream state safely. It is a symbol that opens the inner paths of dreams and all journeys of life.

The crook and flail is an excellent symbol for those who are bothered by continuing nightmares. It helps when confronting something frightening in your dreams.

The Egyptian hieroglyph of the obelisk and the star is a symbol for the star Sirius. It is a symbol of universal awareness, the opening of the unconscious. It is excellent for understanding the archetypes that are playing within dreams.

These three symbols (hieroglyphs) symbolize life, health, and prosperity, respectively. They bring peaceful sleep and nurturing dreams.

DREAM MANDALAS

A mandala is a visual doorway between two worlds. It is a tool for focusing and concentrating the mind in order to pass through the usual blocks and fetters. In Eastern philosophy, they are known as yantras. In the Native American tradition, they are known as medicine shields. They can be a mixture of associated symbolic pictures, or they can be a series of geometric patterns designed to elicit a specific effect.

A mandala holds the essence of a specific thought or concept, and it is designed to draw our consciousness more fully into that concept. It is a vehicle for bringing us to the center of our universe or to the center of some aspect in it. A mandala stimulates the inner creative forces in a manner peculiar to its design. It can be constructed to arouse any inner force we desire. A mandala is a symbol for integration and transformation, a form of action and interaction with ourselves.

Carl Jung said that symbols are not manufactured, but are discovered through primal inner sources. Mandalas serve to stimulate those primal inner sources imprinted upon the deeper levels of our consciousness. They are psychic transformers, helping us to connect with our own missing parts. They are a way of miniaturizing the archetypal energies. They help us to withdraw from the outer to the inner realities. Through a visual process we are put in touch with those realities. We trigger an inner visual experience.

Dream mandalas are designed to stimulate specific dream activities. When placed within the dream temple of your bedroom and focused upon prior to sleep, they influence the consciousness in a manner appropriate to the mandala's design.

MAKING A MANDALA

The construction process is simple. All you need is a small variety of drawing utensils (colored pencils, markers, etc.) and poster board. You use the same images that you would in making a dream talisman. The first step is to decide which images and symbols you wish to employ.

In the middle of the poster board, draw a large circle, keeping in mind its symbolic significance. All of your other dream symbology and imagery will be placed inside this circle. (We are

A DREAM MANDALA

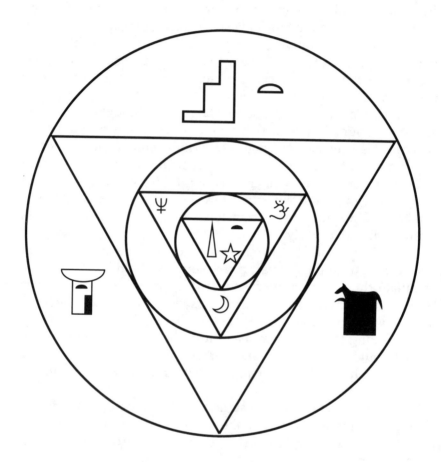

Dream mandalas do not have to be complicated. The one above is very effective for stimulating dreams that show us where there has or has not been growth since the past. In this one, Egyptian symbols have been predominantly used. It is perfectly all right to mix and match, as long as you are aware of what energy will be invoked by what symbols. Hanging them so that they are seen as you go to sleep is very effective. They can be drawn on simple poster board, parchment or even painted on wood or canvas.

using symbols and images in order to go into our own consciousness.) Concentrate as you construct it. Make sure you are undisturbed while working upon it. Take as many precautions as necessary to be uninterrupted.

Arranging the symbols in the mandala is a creative process. Draw and sketch them in the manner best for you. Make sure that you know what the purpose is for each aspect. Use colors for different sections of it, colors you feel are appropriate. The more significance you attribute to every aspect of the drawing, the more it will work for you. You are activating the right brain, programming it to respond to the mandala and its symbolic energies. The creation of the mandala is a form of creative meditation.

Avoid critical judgment. You are not trying to demonstrate artistic expertise. You are working to tap hidden levels of consciousness and manifest them more dynamically. The early shamans could not be called technical artists with the figures and images they drew, but they did imbue their images with energy and significance that was tremendously primal. As you create your mandala and imbue all aspects of it with significance, it will be both beautiful and powerful.

Feel free to add to your mandala from time to time. Create new ones as well, designing them for a specific kind of dream stimulation. If you reach a point in your mandala construction where you do not know what to add next, just stop. You have probably created one that is appropriate for you at the moment, but one that will also evolve and change as you evolve and change.

When it is finished, set it across the floor from you and just sit and look at it for ten to fifteen minutes. Feel its energies. Review its significances. Visualize what it will do for you.

It is important to consecrate mandalas and talismans. This is not a complicated process. Burning incense associated with sleep and dream work helps. Simply smudge the mandala and talisman, visualizing them coming to life, charged full of energy. You can also take crystals you have dedicated to your dream work and attach them to the mandala within the circle. Meditate upon its image, and give thanks for its effectiveness in advance.

Once completed and consecrated, hang it in your bedroom across the room from you. You should be able to lie in your bed and view it. You may want to attach small lights to illuminate it in the dark.

The dream mandala is a doorway to the dream state consciousness. As you go to sleep, that doorway opens and the energies impact you throughout the sleeping hours. This charges your dreams with new life, imparting new energy and a new sense of reality to them. You are affecting the entire electromagnetic pattern of the bedroom. You imbue your room with a power field that creates a sacred space where dream time can come to life.

PART FIVE:

Dream Time Initiation

"A hero ventures forth from the world of common day into a region of supernatural wonder: fabulous forces are there encountered and a decisive victory is won. The hero comes back from this mysterious adventure with the power to bestow boons on his fellow man."

—Joseph Campbell,
The Hero with a Thousand Faces

CHAPTER FIFTEEN

Becoming the Dream Hero

The cycle of life is at the heart of all worship and unfoldment. Birth, death and rebirth are repeated, literally, symbolically and ritually in all life patterns. These mysteries and their cycles hold the keys to higher forms of consciousness and existence. In consciously directed dream work, we are deliberately invoking these cyclic energies to play more important, vibrant roles in our lives.

New life and transformations have to be earned. This is the law of sacrifice operating in death and rebirth. We lay down the old for the new. In more ancient times, the individual offered to the deity what he or she most treasured. Today, if we wish to intensify and transform the life experience, we must face the inner self with a greater understanding of the richness that exists within.

Mythic dream work and meditation assist us in understanding sacrifice, death, and rebirth as they operate in our own lives. Each night we sacrifice our waking self. The conscious mind dies so that the subconscious can be reborn. Ideally, we will manifest those innate energies in our waking world.

To become a dream walker, we must develop access to all levels of our consciousness at all times. That part of us which does not seem alive when we are awake and going about our daily business must be kept vibrant. That part of us which does not seem alive while we are asleep must be coaxed into activity. The human vehicle is the place where the spiritual meets the physical. It is within the mind that we meet all our demons and our gods. We are our greatest adventures.

With dream alchemy, we use the mythic imagination to

expand awareness. We are taking on a lifelong process of initiation. Initiation has been given many meanings. Simply put, it is a beginning, a beginning of new perceptions. It leads to the awakening of deeper levels of consciousness.

Any initiation, whether in the form of a new job or in a new study, reflects the cycle of sacrifice, death, and rebirth. The new light is preceded by veils of darkness and often bewilderment. The darkness is a time of conquest of the self, so that the new can be liberated. We must confront our inner demons to awaken the divine. We must search for the hidden divinity that lives in humanity, in the planet earth, and in the universe. As we do this, we come to understand the hidden significance of our lives.

The student of life participates at all levels, awake and asleep. The student works to break down the walls of separateness to see that both dimensions are connected. The student works to see the significance of everything and everyone at all times. As we involve ourselves in the process of daily dream alchemy, we begin to see that which has been hidden from us. Those hidden mysteries are often reflected in the circumstances of our waking life and our dream consciousness.

Traditionally, these mysteries are divided into three categories—Lesser, Greater and Supreme. The adventures in our dreams reveal the effect of these mysteries on our individual life circumstances. If we come to recognize them in the dream state, we can facilitate a new birth in our waking life.

The Lesser Mysteries in our dream scenarios are those dealing with the development of the personality. We are presented with situations that test and reveal our character and moral fiber. They are those scenarios that reveal imbalances in our personality. The Lesser Mysteries always involve other people and our relationships to them because our greatest learning comes through them. These dream scenarios reveal the characteristics still needing to be developed and those needing to be corrected. The dreams provide teachings to assist us in maintaining sound body and mind, along with control of instincts and passions.

Our dream scenarios also reveal aspects of the Greater Mysteries operating in our lives. The Greater Mysteries involve teachings about the development of our individuality and our own unique expression of creativity. These are the energies and abilities we strengthen and add on to each incarnation. Dreams reflecting these mysteries involve lessons of faith and facing our fears.

Many nightmares are reflections of the Greater Mysteries revealing themselves to you through the dream scenario. It shows us what we must face before new birth can occur. We must sacrifice our fear. The Greater Mysteries, when reflected in dreams, involve scenarios in which inner principals are tested, along with dedication to various goals in your life. The scenarios help teach the need to fulfill obligations and to act upon our own resources.

The Supreme Mysteries of life also reveal themselves in our dreams. These mysteries, when active in our lives, stimulate dream scenarios that help us to understand the relationships between our spiritual essence and our physical life. The dreams inspire us to set new activities in motion for the good of all, rather than for some immediate goal. We begin to see hidden aspects of our lives and we are able to put events into a bigger picture.

At any one point, at least one or more of the three mysteries will be active in your life. A dream scenario can reveal that all three are active. The people, the environment, and the situation of the dream scenario helps us pinpoint what we are being taught. If we have a nightmare, we know that the Greater Mysteries are active. The other people and the locale of the dream scenario can help us pinpoint where in our waking life we most need to face the inner fear to have new birth occur.

We can use the mythic dream work techniques and meditations to elaborate upon these mysteries. Certain myths and tales reflect many of the same aspects traditionally associated with each of the three mysteries. The following tales and myths can be used to stimulate revelations about the activity of the Lesser Mysteries within our life and in the development of the personality:

- Norse tales of Loki
- Greek tales of Pan and his conflicts with gods/goddesses
- "Beauty and the Beast"
- "The Pied Piper"
- The tales of King Arthur (prior to the Round Table)
- African tale of "Departure of the Giants"
- Irish tale of "Bridget and Lurikeen"
- English tale "Old Woman Who Lived in a Vinegar Bottle"
- Spanish tale of "The Serpent Woman"
- Grimm's tale of "Hansel and Gretel"

The following tales can be used in meditation and dream work to reveal the activity of the Greater Mysteries in our life circumstances, regarding the development of our individuality:

- Greek tales of Apollo and his music
- Hindu Tale of "Dance of Shiva."
- Sumerian tale of "Ishtar and the Rescue of Tammuz."
- Tale of "Jack The Giant-Killer."
- Greek Tale of Orpheus and Eurydice
- Celtic tale of "Cerridwen and Gwion."
- Celtic tales of Morgan Le Fay and Merlin.
- Irish tale of "The Lawyer and the Devil."
- Anderson's tale "The Little Mermaid"
- Babylonian tales of the Goddess Tiamat.

The Supreme Mysteries actually involve aspects of the other two, but myths and tales associated with sacrifice, death, and rebirth specifically will stimulate revelations of their affect on our own life circumstances:

- Babylonian tale of the death of Tiamat
- Sumerian tale of Ishtar and the rescue of Tammuz
- Greek tale of Demeter and Persephone
- Greek tale of Zeus and Kronos
- Biblical tale of the death and resurrection of Jesus
- African tales "Why There is Death in the World" and "Tortoise and Dog Messengers of God"
- African Bushmen tale "Moon and the Hare"
- American Indian tale of "Woman Who Chose Death"
- American Indian tale of "The End of the World"
- German tale "Godfather Death"
- Hindu tales of Kali
- Chinese tale of "Gum Lin and Loy Yi Lung"

BECOMING THE DREAM HERO

Part of initiation and the art of dream alchemy is solving our problems, confronting aspects of ourselves and others, and opening to new realms. This is why myths and tales are so beneficial. They teach us how to become the heroes of our lives regardless of the circumstances. We can choose any quality we would like to unfold or eliminate from our lives, and there is a myth or tale associated with it. Those myths and tales can be used to stimulate dream scenarios that reveal more clearly where these qualities are operating in our lives.

If you can see where these qualities are manifesting in your daily life through dreams, you can initiate a process of conscious change. For example, you may use the mythic immersion meditation in the tale of King Midas to show where greed exists in your life. As a result, you may stimulate dream scenarios that reveal you vying for attention in the family situation. The myth helped stimulate a revelation as to where greed is manifesting most strongly. In this case, it was in the family and in the desire for attention.

In most mythic quests, the hero encounters an older person who gives advice and counsel. How the hero acts upon that advice determines how easily and successfully the quest is achieved. With mythic dream work and meditation, the dreams become our counsel. How we act in response to them determines how successfully we meet our individual adversaries and achieve our own goals.

There are many myths of initiation and heroic tales of destiny in which we can immerse ourselves. These can be anything from "Ali Baba and the Forty Thieves" to adventures of Robin Hood to the folktale of John Henry. We must begin to recognize that our myths and tales have much greater import in our lives than mere entertainment. Archibald MacLeish in the *Hypocrite Auteur* stated that "a world ends when its metaphor has died. It perishes when those images, though seen, no longer mean."

There have been many heroic epics written in the past that you can use in meditation and dream work to understand your individual quest in life. Archetypal energies work through epic tales and heroic myths. They not only affect you through meditation but through your dreams as well. Using the mythic immersion technique, if you confront something in a dream or meditation, it is a safe bet that you will be brought into confrontation with similar energies somewhere in your outer life. We are learning that the worlds really are not separate. We are learning to shift our awareness of one realm to give ourselves greater impact in the other. We are learning to walk within our dreams to transform our lives.

Initially, choose a tale or mythic hero that you feel personally drawn to. What hero or heroine have you always related to most strongly? You may also choose a heroic myth to assist you in those personal issues that are strongly affecting you now. It is good to become familiar with a number of the heroic tales and epics. As we change, the energies of our individual quests will also change. Because of this, certain epics and tales may resonate more strongly than others. Different tales and myths will correspond to different times and places in our lives.

It is a good practice to periodically review some of the great tales and quests, determining which most reflects your life circumstances at that time. Some of the most effective heroic tales and epics for mythic dream work and meditation are:

- German tale of Siegfried
- Sumerian epic of Ishtar and the rescue of Tammuz
- Celtic tales of King Arthur and the quests for the Holy Grail
- Celtic tales of Cerridwen and Gwion
- Celtic tale of Morgan Le Fay and the death of Merlin
- Egyptian tale of Hassan the Brave
- Nigerian epic of Nana Miriam
- West African tale "The Great Mwindo Epic"
- Greek tale of the labors of Hercules
- Greek tales of the travels of Odysseus
- Greek tale of Jason and the quest for the Golden Fleece
- Greek tale of Demeter and Persephone
- Greek tale of Perseus and the rescue of Andromeda
- Greek Tale of Theseus and the Minotaur
- Arabian tales of the "Voyages of Sinbad"
- Apache myth of "Wild Pony."
- American Indian tale of "Spider Grandmother"
- American Indian Tale of "Changing Woman"
- Scandinavian tale of "Necklace of Brisingamen"
- Teutonic "Tale of Tontlawald"
- Teutonic tale of "Beowulf"
- Grimm's tale of "Snowdrop"
- Chinese myth of "Gum Lin and Loy Yi Lung"
- East Indian tale of "Devi and the Buffalo Demon"
- Babylonian epic of Tiamat

- Biblical tale of Jacob
- Biblical tale of Job
- Biblical tale of Joseph and the Coat of Many Colors
- Biblical tale of death and resurrection of Jesus
- All descent and death myths

In using myths and tales of initiation for meditation and dream work, choose the mythic hero according to your temperament at the time. Choose the myth that most closely symbolizes your present conflicts and your goals. Don't be afraid to alter it to fit your own unique situation. When you immerse yourself in the mythic content, you do not have to hold to the literalness of the tale. You may even wish to place individuals of your present life into the various roles of the myth to give it stronger correspondence.

Always resolve the mythic situation in your pre-sleep meditations and preparations. Have yourself discover the resolution to your problems. If you leave them hanging in the meditation, your dreams may not provide the resolution. Remember we are sending a message to the subconscious about what you would like it to communicate to you. This includes a resolution, even if it is not the one you create yourself.

Through the mythic meditations, you are incubating dreams. This is especially true when the tale or myth involves the initiation archetypes. You are strongly stimulating the subconscious mind. The more you visualize, the greater the effects.

This kind of dynamic stimulation of the subconscious may elicit certain effects, for which it is best to be prepared. You may experience strong unsettled feelings. This is because you are stirring up debris within the subconscious so that you can clear it out, providing a freer flow of creative energies and perceptions. You could temporarily have more of a tendency to be over-critical and fault-finding. Remember your dreams may reveal things in an amplified manner to make sure you get the message. It does not mean that you have that quality or characteristic to that intensity, nor that you will encounter identical situations with that intensity.

It is important to process those feelings. Begin first with acknowledging them. Then recognize that the human part of us will make mistakes as we grow and learn. We must forgive and love ourselves in spite of mistakes, realizing that our intentions do carry weight.

Using artwork (in the form of mandalas or dream symbols) can also help you to synthesize the meditation and dream experiences. Try to convey the feelings and energy of the dreams into some art form. By doing so, you force the subconscious to elicit greater insight into those feelings and their energies. If you do not feel you can convey it properly with art, write out the feelings that are stimulated and how those feelings will help you in the future.

As you work with meditations and mythic dream work, you will find that lucid dreaming experiences will occur and be strengthened. All of the techniques in this book are designed to lead to this process. If we can work out issues and conflicts within the inner life, we will be less likely to encounter them in our outer lives.

CREATING YOUR OWN DREAM MYTH

When we follow a mythic path, we follow the destiny of another. No two destinies are ever truly alike, because no two people are ever exactly alike. Our own path may be similar to another's, but there will be differences as well.

There comes a time when the need for greater responsibility manifests. At this point it doesn't matter what we decide or choose, but rather that we *do* decide and choose. Either way, circumstances will unfold to help us learn and grow. We must become active in our lives, rather than passively allowing life to play upon us. We must be mature enough to say, "This is what I choose. If it works out, wonderful! If it doesn't, then I am willing to suffer the consequences because even then I will learn."

Dream alchemy will reveal much of our life path to us if we allow it. The imprint of our life and its impact upon others is recorded within the ethers. We can learn to walk the way of the shaman through our dreams to read these recordings. We can create our own myths to assist us in this process.

It has been said that there are two orders of mythology, that of the Village and that of the Forest of Adventure. When we create our own mythical story, it is best to choose one of these settings. The Village setting has to do with the mythology of day to day life, understanding its circumstances and its ability to shape and mold who we are. The Forest of Adventure can be used to discern the grander picture of our life and our destiny. One is no more important than the other, and both often rely on each other for existence. We are all involved in both at various points in our lives.

Components Of Your Personal Myth:
1. Hero or Heroine (this is you).
This is the archetype of the self, reflected through your image of you.

2. Setting
The Village setting is not necessarily a village. It can be a castle, a home of many and varied rooms, or anything in a relatively confined area. The Village setting is used in meditation and dream work to stimulate dreams about what is most affecting you at the moment. The village may be haunted, magical or ordinary. You are

limited only by your imagination.

The Forest of Adventure is not necessarily a forest. It involves a whole series of different and strange settings. These settings stimulate dreams that assist you in seeing long-range patterns in your life.

3. Adversaries

The adversaries are those aspects or qualities you wish to confront and overcome. You must give these abstract, intangibles a tangible form. You may represent them as a beast, a monster, another human antagonist, or any combination of these three. Give it a form you will be able to confront in the mythical tradition.

4. Journey

This archetypal energy will be reflected in the playing out of the entire tale. You may visualize yourself upon a journey to achieve a specific goal through which you pass through the Forest of Adventure; or it may involve the achieving of some goal by straightening out or defending the home in the Village. It is through the activity of the journey that you encounter your adversary, who will hinder and try to prevent your success.

5. Death/Rebirth

These are the changes that you go through in order to achieve your goal. In fashioning your personal myth, this phase is most essential. You must decide what you are willing to sacrifice to achieve success. It also involves escaping from your traditional manner of action to an entirely different expression and response to situations in life.

6. Guide/Teacher

This is someone you encounter on your journey in the Forest, or someone who happens to come upon your Village. This individual will assist you in some way. They do not solve the problems for you, but they guide you in solving your own, in discovering your own inner power to bring about the ultimate success. The effort and energy expended is yours, as is the ensuing reward, if you follow the advice of the teacher.

7. The Achievement of the Goal

This is what you bring back home and share with others in your life, enhancing everyone's existence. The goal of your quest, even if it involves eliminating a negative quality or characteristic, has a tangible reward. Visualize the achievement of the goal as a physical reward, i.e. a golden fleece, a treasure chest, a golden chalice, etc. Let the symbol of your goal reflect it and be personal to you.

Often in this exercise individuals complain that they are not creative. They protest that they do not have an imagination and can't think or write along these lines. For such individuals, I provide the following outline.

Set a goal. Name something you wish to achieve or get rid of in yourself or your life. This gives you a title for your personal myth—for example, "JOURNEY TO PROSPERITY."

Next, *list why you want to achieve it.* What will achieving this do for you? How will it enhance your life and the lives of those around you? If it is a quality you hope to eliminate, how will being free of this aspect help you?

List three things that could hinder you from achieving this goal. There may be more, but list three. Next, imagine these three obstacles to your goal. You can see them as beasts, as geographical barriers, or as some kind of form that must be confronted. These are the adversaries you must overcome in achieving your personal quest.

Some individuals like to list real people as their adversaries. Other people are *never* our true adversaries, and they should be kept out of the personal myth-making process. These people only represent qualities that you must overcome. By using real people, you may manifest energies which hinder your ability to perceive your own personal blocks and hindrances.

Your mythical adversaries may have qualities in common with actual individuals, but you do not want to use them. Create a new beast, one that embodies these aspects primally, so that as you confront and overcome this beast, you develop the ability to overcome those qualities.

Visualize your goal. You may imagine your goal is at the top of a distant mountain. Outside of your home is a path that winds its way to the foot of the mountain. On this path, you must cross and overcome your obstacles and adversaries as you progress toward your goal. These obstacles can be the geographical homes of your adversaries. They can be anything from a raging river to a dark, haunted forest. The mountain should be steep and difficult to climb.

If you are using the Village as your setting, the adversaries will come along the road to your Village setting, entering into it and creating problems and difficulties for you. The more you ignore them, the stronger they become.

Prior to each obstacle, you will meet someone. It can always be the same person, or it can be a different person. An effective way of doing it is to follow a common mythical pattern. The same individual comes to you, but in different disguises. This, of course, will not be realized until the goal is achieved. Each time this individual appears, words of wisdom are given, nourishment and strength for the upcoming obstacle.

This basic premise can be adapted for any goal. It also allows for individual input and adaptation. Writing it out is beneficial. It ingrains the imagery and symbols. It strengthens the emotional impact upon the subconscious mind. You can even use some of the basic archetypal images, discussed earlier in the book, and weave them into the fabric of the story for greater impact.

Once the story is written and its imagery decided upon, *prepare for your immersion into the story, just as you did with the other myths.* Prepare with bath and fragrances. Perform the mythic meditation first, using the personal myth or story. Create the mythic dream doorway. Step through the doorway, immersing yourself in the tale you have created.

At the end of the visualization pause, and holding the gift of your goal (the reward of your quest) step back through the doorway, bringing it with you. *You bring the inner reward of your quest into the outer world of your life.*

Close the mythic dream doorway, and take time to *visualize the gift making your life more fulfilled and wonderful.* If you go directly to sleep after the meditation, leave the door open.

CHAPTER SIXTEEN

The Labyrinth of the Soul

Often there is the assumption that initiation involves success. This is not always so. Sometimes our greatest learning comes through our failures. Failures are also initiations. This process is reflected in myths and tales. In the "Tales of King Arthur and the Knights of the Round Table," Sir Gawain and Sir Parsifal fail before ever achieving the Holy Grail. In the meantime, much growth and maturity has been attained.

In most myths and tales of initiation, there are different stages to pass through. These stages involve separation, which leads to a process of making changes in oneself, and then finally synthesizing what has been experienced. In the course of the adventure, there is separation or loss of the ego. In many myths, this occurs during a descent into an underworld. Mythic heroes have been swallowed by monsters, slid into bodies of water, and fallen into labyrinths. All of these force a transfer of attention in the individual. He or she must focus entirely on something new and pressing.

In mythic dream work and meditation, we are stimulating this separation by entering a new realm where the old rules no longer apply. The individual, having entered into this new realm, must make transitions on all levels. Situations and events must be faced differently. In our dreams, the repercussions are instantaneous. In waking life, there is usually a time delay.

This transitional stage is often symbolized as crossing over thresholds, passing through doorways, or facing obstacles. It is during this stage that the mythic hero and heroine confronts the guardians to those thresholds, the negative forces of the unconscious. It is a time of overcoming the powers of darkness within ourselves. We may succeed or not, but if we use our failures, eventually the success comes. It also creates a transformation of the ego.

In the course of the transition, the labyrinth strips away the ego. We see our fears closely. This is often reflected in our nightmares. In nightmare scenarios, the individual finds that he or she is answerable to no one but the self and can rely on no one but the self. It forces one to draw upon great inner resources. A death process occurs, so that new life must be drawn forth.

In our myths and tales, the individual is assisted by a guardian, a teacher, a spirit, a god or goddess, or even a spirit totem. Guidance is given, and if followed, new power is attained. As often as we may feel alone, there is help if we are willing to look for it. We are never without guidance, but we must draw upon our own resources as well.

During this stage, the characteristics for success are developed. Courage, humility, and purity of heart are essential, but so is the need to be true to your nature. Dream alchemy helps us to discern our true nature and helps us unfold it in the outer life circumstances.

In the third stage of synthesis, the hero or heroine applies what has been learned. It is this application which moves us forward. Being true to ourselves enables us to have what we need. This is why we must apply our dreams to our waking life. They help us to synthesize its circumstances and connect us to our true nature and patterns.

Although the next meditation is long, it follows many of the old patterns of the heroic myths of initiation. Once you become familiar with it, it will not take as long to perform in meditation. It is powerfully effective in stimulating an awareness of old patterns that need to be changed. When used with the mythic dream work process, it will stimulate dreams showing where adversaries need to be met and where outworn patterns still exist in your life.

As you begin to relax, you allow the mythic doorway to form before you. As you step through the doorway, you find yourself at the foot of a tall mountain. The sun is high in the sky. On several large boulders snakes have emerged to sun themselves. You move cautiously around them, giving ample distance. Several raise their heads as if to examine you. You flinch instinctively, as the sight of them touches a primal nerve.

You begin to search for a path that will lead you to the top of the mountain, for this is where you must go. You are not sure why, but you know it is one of those things in life that must be done. As you look for a place to begin your climb, you discover a small opening, half-hidden behind some scrub bushes.

You stick your head in slowly, feeling the darkness with your hand first. You remember the snakes, and you can't help thinking this would be a wonderful home for many more of them. There is barely any light, and you dislike the idea of going where you cannot see. You then remember that other cave—that other opening in which you saw your totem. You relax at the thought. Perhaps this will lead you to yet another companion. Maybe this *is* the way to the top.

Summoning your strength and courage, you squeeze into the narrow opening, as if entering into the womb of the mountain itself. The passage is tight and close, and you are not sure how far you will be able to squeeze through. Still you continue, forcing yourself to move, lest you panic.

Before long, the passage widens and opens into a large cavern. Hanging on the four walls of this internal womb are four torches. Their lights dance, stirred by an air source you cannot locate. The air is moist, and there is the sound of dripping. At the back of the cavern is a small pool that has formed from the eons of moisture that accumulates here. The pool is pitch-black, and even the light of the torches reflects off of it, revealing nothing.

You move to the center of the cavern and slowly turn around, examining the area. There are no other tunnels except that through which you have entered. Occasionally the lights shimmer off of the rock formations, hinting of the wealth of minerals within the veins of the mountain. This is obviously not the way to the top, and with a sigh you move to go back to the tunnel.

Before you can take your first step, the ground beneath your feet gives way. It drops out from beneath you, and with a sharp intake of breath, you feel yourself falling. You tumble downward, rolling, spinning and spiraling down. There is no way to stop. There is nothing to grab on to. You are powerless.

With a thump that knocks the breath from you, you land flat on your back. You gasp for breath, your head still spinning. You close your eyes, trying to shake the dizziness. You slowly open your eyes, moving each part of your body gently, checking for any serious damage. As your breath returns, you sit up. You realize you are a little bruised, but no worse for the wear. You stand slowly, stretching your muscles and planting your feet upon the ground. You stomp the ground, testing its firmness.

Satisfied, you glance upward. Ten feet above you in the rock face is the opening through which you plummeted. Amazed that you are unscathed, you look about you for the first time. Around you are seven openings, three on the right, three on the left and one directly ahead of you.

On the walls between these openings are paintings and scripts that you do not recognize. There are images, symbols and designs that are familiar but which you do not understand. There are designs of spirals, reminding you of the mazes you puzzled over as a child, slowly drawing a line that connects one point to a treasure in the center. The difference now is that you are in the center and must work your way to the outer.

You puzzle over which tunnel to take. It is then that you hear the sound. It seems to roll through all of the tunnels until it pours over you. A chill runs through your spine. You know that you are not alone in whatever labyrinth this is. A bellowing pours forth louder through the tunnels. It is closer. The temperature rises, and you know that whatever it is, it is coming with fire. It seems louder from that tunnel directly ahead.

You jump for a tunnel to your right, running blindly into it. It winds and turns so much that you cannot see what is ten feet ahead. Then you hear the bellows again. They are more distant. You slow your pace, relaxing. You have chosen a path that leads away from it.

Ahead of you is an opening. You jump from the tunnel, and your heart sinks. You are back where you started. You have exited out a tunnel opposite of that which you entered. Then the bellowing comes again, and then it turns into deep laughter, mocking you and your efforts. The sound carries strongly through the front tunnel.

You choose another of the side tunnels. You begin to run its length, as it winds and turns. You pray that you will not exit back where you started. You remember an old dream, one in which you tried to run and your legs would not move. You can feel something gaining on you.

This tunnel feels warm, and there is a smell that is familiar and nauseating. You continue on in spite of it. Around the next turn is a light. You burst from the tunnel to find yourself back where you started. The bellowing continues, jarring every nerve and fiber of your being. You begin to understand. All of the tunnels lead you back to where you started. They are not exits. They only repeat themselves. Running into them leads nowhere. If you want out, you must face the tunnel directly ahead—and whatever is in it.

In response to your thoughts, a mist pours out, blocking your view of its opening. In the midst of that mist, an image appears. It is your totem, your guide. A sense of relief washes over you, and within your mind you hear it speak: "When we do not change old patterns, we repeat them. Same situation, different players. Different tunnels, same results. When we quit running away, we grow. We must make our choices from that which is best for us, not out of fear. You can continue running into the old tunnels, and you will avoid that which you fear. You also lock yourself into that which limits and prevents your dreams from being fulfilled.

"We never face more than we can handle. Our fears are delusions that must be overcome. The longer we avoid them, the more powerful they become. It does not matter which path you choose, as long as you choose from the heart—not from fear."

(At this point some individuals may wish to stop the exercise for the day and continue it the next day. Stopping at this point will stimulate revelations about some old patterns that need to be confronted. It may also stimulate an awareness of when these old worn-out patterns first originated. If you choose to stop at this point, simply visualize the mythic doorway forming as the image of your totem dissipates. Step out through the doorway and close it behind you.)

You stand before the front tunnel. You are tired of running. It seems as if you have been running your entire life. With a deep breath, you step into the tunnel. It winds around and around. It spirals up and down. You can no longer tell which direction you are heading. The further you go, the hotter the air becomes. The tension grows. The beast has grown silent, as if acknowledging the fact that you are answering its invitation.

After a time, the tunnel widens and opens into yet another cavern. It is cathedral-sized. A stream runs through the center of it. Rock formations of all types and colors watch stoically, waiting. There is a hint of fresh air, and as brief as it is, it refreshes the mind and the body.

Across the cavern on the other side of the stream is an opening. Through it you can see the outside world. To get to it you must cross the width of the cavern. As you take your first step, the beast moves out from the shadows.

It is massive, its shape blocking all light, filling the cavern with shadows and forms of darkness. You draw back, flinching at its appearance. The smell is sickening. It notices your reaction, and it bellows out a laugh that shakes the foundation of the cavern.

"I repulse you, do I?" Its voice is deep, grating and hollow. It laughs again, mocking and derisive. "Does a parent find its child repulsive?" You look at it puzzled, not understanding, and it laughs once more.

"Yes. You are my father and my mother. I am your creation. I am your nightmare. I am every fear. I am every hurt. I am every anger. I AM YOU!"

As you look into its face, it changes. You see images, reflections of your past. You see all of the hurts others caused you. You see all of the times someone said or did something to hurt you. You see all of the times you said and did things to hurt others so that you would not be hurt. You remember all of the times others said "NO" and told you could not do or be certain things.

You see how you believed them. You see all of the times you gave into your own fears and the fears of others. You see all of the times you did not follow your own heart. You see all of the anger, jealousy, the pain, and the fears of this lifetime and more. You remember all of the times you were not loved and the times you did not love. You see all of the times you blamed yourself for not being lovable enough. You see all of the times you blamed yourself for that which was the fault of others and for that which was beyond your control. And then you see the beast again before you.

The beast glares at you, its eyes flashing with anger and pain. You do not flinch. You do not even fear. Now you feel sorry. Your heart begins to ache.

"When we do not use our feelings and grow from them, they will grow their own way. This is what you see before you." You turn to the voice, and you see your totem beside you, looking upon you with love and speaking within your mind. "That which we do not transmute and use must go somewhere. Growing and evolving requires that we love ourselves in spite of ourselves and our life conditions. It requires that we take responsibility for that which we have created by commission or omission. We must face it and love it without thought of compensation. We must learn from it, so that we do not repeat it. Only when we can face and love our shadow selves can we cross the threshold."

The totem disappears, and you are left facing the beast. "I am so sorry." It roars its response, "I do not want your pity!" A tear rolls down your cheek as you begin to feel the pain of this beast. It moves threateningly in response.

"You will not hurt me any more, nor I you," you speak firmly. "Together we will change what has occurred and we will create a new you." It bellows again, its force making you step back. "Yes, I am still afraid, but I will never let my fear stop me again. I came to face you, did I not? And I know that each time I face any fear, the heart within you will soften. And each time someone loves me, I will share it with you. You are that part of me that needed the love, and at times found it unavailable. And each time I love someone, it will be our love that is felt. For you are a part of me and I am a part of you. You cannot destroy me and I cannot slay you, but together we can change who we are. When I cross that threshold, you will cross it with me. No longer will your soul be locked within this labyrinth of darkness. No longer will my soul be locked within the maze of life's repetitions. We will share the rainbow promise of our dreams."

A spark of sunlight pierces through the veil from the outside and touches the stream. This bit of sunshine sends a ripple of rainbows throughout the waters. The beast pulls back and cries out from the depth of its soul.

Mist and fog gush forth as the fires of pain are released, filling the cavern and cloaking you. As the fog dissipates, you are outside the cavern, again at the base of the mountain. You are standing at the narrow opening through which you first entered. You step back from it, not even questioning the reality of your experience. You breath deeply and freely. You have touched a part of you that has not been acknowledged in a long time. It is as if your ability to feel fully is being re-awakened.

You step back, climbing around the boulders. There is but one snake left. It raises its head in greeting, and this time you do not pull away. The fear is gone. As the snake lays itself back down, it begins to writhe and wiggle shedding its skin before you, its lidless eyes never leaving yours. You understand that it must see all things at all times, and you begin to realize the significance of the mythical snake wisdom.

As the last of its skin is shed, you watch as the snake moves off the boulder. As your eyes return to the shed skin, it is gone. In its place is a small caduceus wand. It is the wand of healing through wisdom and greater awareness. You gently pick it up, and stroke the snakes that wind to the top.

"We will share the rainbow of promised dreams." The hollow voice of the beast is heard within your mind. It is gentler. You understand that the wand is its gift to you for the gift you have given it. Holding the wand close to your heart, you step from the mountain to the mythic doorway you created. At the doorway is your totem companion, waiting patiently and lovingly as always.

CONCLUSION

The Mythic Dreamer
and the Modern Seer

We are developing a new kind of ability through dream work. We are learning to see our lives while awake and asleep. For this to be most effective, we must breathe new life into our symbols. The traditional religious symbols and their significance must be re-expressed and re-experienced. Carl Jung once said, "They always give man a premonition of the divine while at the same time safe-guarding him from the experience of it." With mythic dream work and meditation we open ourselves to a more immediate experience.

Part of the responsibility of the modern seer and disciple is to recognize the significance of every aspect of life. Take time to review and see the events of the day in an objective manner. Review your day in reverse order before going to bed each night. By examining them in this manner, we force our minds to concentrate, and we are less likely to skip over essential aspects. This kind of evaluation enables us to strengthen the good and eliminate the negative aspects.

This reverse examination has a number of benefits. It is a good cure for insomnia. It improves the faculty of memory. The mind will become more attentive as concentration in all areas of life improves. The inner world experience will become more clear and ordered. It leads to the ability to bridge the gaps between the past and the present. Eventually, this exercise will develop our ability to review events of sleep as easily as the events of our waking time. It ultimately helps us to bridge the gulf of forgetfulness between life and death and new life.

Dreams are part of a subtle dimension and certain precautions are beneficial to keep in mind when dealing with any of the subtler dimensions of life. We may not delve deeply enough into what is being reflected in our dream symbols. We may manipulate the images simply to verify a viewpoint, an aspect of the ego or something that is already known. Discouragement can also occur if we apply preconceptions to the experience. Seeking novelty information for amusement or to impress others will create imbalances.

Initially, your dream stimulation response may be strong, but if you do not use it properly, it will close down. Thus you can expect little if you use it as a form of parlor game or psychic thrillseeking. As you begin to use mythic dream work and meditations for unfoldment, many of your dreams will concern themselves with voicing alarm at the mismanagement of your energies to this point. This is a healing process. It is better that such cleansing be accomplished on the inner planes through dreams, rather than through an outer illness.

Because this process of cleansing is almost certain to occur, you could facilitate it by monitoring your emotions once you start working with your dreams. At the end of the day, list all the fears, angers, greeds, hatreds, etc. that you experienced during the day. (This can be done in conjunction with an end of the day review.) Visualize them as a form, any form or color that seems appropriate to you. In this visualization, see these forms dissipated entirely by a higher emotion or energy expression:

- Fear is eliminated by thoughts of divine love, justice, joy, detachment.
- Anger is eliminated by recognizing the divinity in all.
- Hatred is eliminated by the spirit of love.
- Greed is eliminated by the spirit of generosity.

These negative emotions are barriers to developing lucid dreaming, but they are also part of the cleansing process for the astral. After the visualization and review, go to sleep, using your mythic dream techniques. Doing this process will make your dreams clearer and they will more quickly come under your control. Recognize that the dream alchemy process is a life-long process of transmutation. Some aspects of it will have immediate effects, but the ability to control the dreams and walk within them consciously will take time and practice. With perseverance, you will succeed.

Mythic meditation and dream work teaches us to seek out a dimension, investigate it and take spiritual and conscious possession of it. You do not have to be a dream wanderer. Learn to take stock in every dream. Remember that the physical body is just a tool for the development of consciousness.

As you work with the techniques of this book, your dreams will provide indications of growth. They will become more regular in character. The dreams will be more sensibly connected. The cause and effect relationships between the outer life and the dream life will be more easily detected. The dream scenarios and images will no longer involve just normal surroundings, but they will include new worlds as well.

Part of the adventure of dream alchemy is the adventure of the occult. It is the discovery of hidden energies. It is the discovery that you are not a part of the world, you are the world. It is the discovery that everything affects everything else.

It has been said that gnosis is the ability to be surprised by everything. If we know what the outcome is, we quit striving. Becoming the dream alchemist is a process of opening new adventures, adventures that will change and evolve as we change and evolve—all moving toward an outcome which we cannot even dream at this moment. Stephen Larsen tells us in *The Shaman's Doorway* that "as consciousness changes, so do the myths. And as we work with our mythic patterns, we find that they are the precise catalysts which initiate changes in consciousness. The ultimate dialogue must be between consciousness, the undiluted perception of self and the world, and those patterns to which consciousness has proven most susceptible: the archetypes that underlie the shapeshifting bright world of myth."

Becoming the dream master—the dreamtime alchemist —means recognizing that everything is always shapeshifting, especially ourselves. Our search for the hidden side of things requires we learn the duty of happiness and holding it strong and true within our lives. It requires that we be on guard against unsuspected influences and not yield unquestioningly to spiritual inspiration. It requires systematic training. And most of all, it requires that we recognize we are all part of a greater whole—no matter how insignificant our lives may seem. It demands that we recognize the divine life of everything. When we can do this, we can walk within the dream worlds and we can shapeshift our lives in ways we have not yet begun to imagine.

Mythic Dream Worksheets

Part One: Myths

Name of myth: *Date:*

Reason for using the myth/tale:

Character you will visualize yourself as:

Qualities of this character:

What is confronted or overcome by the character?

How does the character change?

Archetypal energy reflected in this tale: ___Self ___Feminine ___Masculine ___Heroic ___Journey ___Adversary ___Death/Rebirth

Mysteries reflected in this tale: ___Lesser (Personality) ___Greater (Individuality) ___Supreme (Spiritual Soul)

Part Two: Dreams

Dream stimulated (description):

Dream title:

Major feeling or emotion:

Major images, characters and/or symbols:

Correspondences to the mythic images:

How did you act in the dream?

Archetypal energies in dream: ___Self ___ Feminine ___Masculine
___Heroic ___Journey ___ Adversary ___ Death/Rebirth

Mysteries reflected within the dream: ___Lesser (Personality)
___Greater (Individuality) ___Supreme (Spiritual/Soul)

What is the dream telling you to do or not do?

What area of your life does it seem to reflect the most?

Other insights or impressions:

An easy way of using this Mythic Dream Worksheet outline is to take a spiral notebook and divide it into sections that will enable you to record one week of dreams. Label the lefthand pages "Myths" and record the information about the myths or tales there. Label the righthand pages "Dreams." Use those pages for recording the dreams you have after doing the mythic dream immersion techniques. In this manner it becomes easier to discern correspondences between the myths and the dreams.

APPENDIX B

Index To Mythic Images And Tales

This index is by no means all-inclusive. It is merely a reference tool by which the individual can begin the process of stimulating dream activity that will reveal how certain qualities are manifesting in one's life.

In the "Index to Strengths," we deal with positive qualities and characteristics. The tales and mythic images associated with them can be used in the dream stimulation process to reveal how, where, and to what degree these qualities are manifesting within your life—either in you or those around you.

In the "Index to Weaknesses," we deal with aspects and qualities that are not as positive. When used in the dream stimulation process, the tales and mythic images will reveal how, where, and to what degree these qualities are manifesting in your life.

Remember that these tales and myths will stimulate dream images and scenarios that reflect similar kinds of energies present your life. Your subconscious will translate those energies into a dream sequence that you can relate to. When using the mythic dream techniques—as described within this book—you are inviting specific revelations, and the dreams that follow will reflect on some level the same energies associated with the myth and tale. They will simply be re-expressed in a dream scenario that is uniquely your own.

Mythic dream work is a self-examination process. It is a means of putting us in touch with all of those energis, which can be strengthening to us. It shows us how to apply them to our life circumstances. It also reveals those aspects that are limiting and hindering our own growth process. Taking responsibility for our growth process requires that we open ourselves to a greater awareness of life and energy. It is recognizing what is at play within our lives and then learning to mold those energies into that which is more creative and productive on all levels. This is true *shapeshifting!*

Index To Strengths

| QUALITY | DREAM STIMULANTS
Mythic Images, Tales, Legends. |
| --- | --- |
| Abundance | Tale of King Midas.
"The Tinder Box."
Egyptian tale of Sheikh Ramadan and Destiny. |
| Aging | Greek tales of Kronos.
Greek tale of Ganymede.
Greek tales of Medusa.
Nigerian tale of "Nana Miriam."
German tale of "Old Man and the Grandson."
Irish tale "Half a Blanket." |
| Alchemy | French tale of "Master and His Pupil."
"Rumpelstiltskin."
Nigerian tale of "Nana Miriam."
African tale of "Leopard Woman."
African tale "Mirror, Sandals and the Medicine Bag." |
| Ambition | Greek myths of Midas, Minos, Achilles and Tantalus.
African tale "Nyangondhu the Fisherman." |

QUALITY	DREAM STIMULANTS *Mythic Images, Tales, Legends*
Artistic Energies (Creativity)	Greek myths and images of Apollo. Greek tales of Orpheus. Greek images and myths of the Muses. "Snow White and Rose Red."
Charisma	Greek images and tales of Achilles. Greek images and tales of Athena. Egyptian tale of "Hassan the Brave."
Compassion	Greek images and tales of Orpheus. Greek images and tales of Asclepius. Irish tale "Half a Blanket." German tale "Old Man and the Grandson."
Conscientious- ness	Greek tales of Perseusness. African "Great Mwindo Epic."
Consistancy	Greek images and myths of Hades. Greek images and myths of Hestia.
Courage	Greek tales of Hercules. Greek tales of Perseus. Greek tales of Athena. The central African tale "Ki and the Leopard." Nigerian tale "Nana Miriam."
Communication	Greek images and tales of Hermes. African tale "Why There is Death in the World." American Indian tale "How Men and Women Got Together."
Confidence	"Labors of Hercules." German tales of "Tyll Ulenspiegel." Greek tales of Odysseus.

QUALITY	DREAM STIMULANTS
	Mythic Images, Tales, Legends

Cunning
> Greek images and tales of Hermes.
> Vietnamese tale "The Fly."
> French tale "Master and his Pupil."
> Burmese "Tall Tales."

Critical
Judgment
> Greek tales of Zeus.
> Sudanese tale "Old Crone and Iblees the Devil."

Common Sense
> East Indian tale of "Monkey and the Crocodile."

Devotion
> Greek images and tales of Ariadne and Selene.
> African tale "Mirimi Giants Who Ate People."

Discrimination
> Icelandic tale "Father of Eighteen Elves."
> Lewis Carroll's *Alice in Wonderland* and *Through the Looking Glass*.

Discipline and
Determination
> German tale of "Master Thief."
> German tales of Tyll Ulenspiegel.
> Egyptian tale "Sheikh Ramadan and Destiny."

Energy and
Endurance
> Greek tales of "Labors of Hercules."
> Greek images and tales of Artemis.
> Greek images and tales of Ares.
> Egyptian tale "Hassan the Brave."
> African tale "Nana Miriam."
> Sumerian tale of Ishtar's descent and rescue of Tammuz.

Emotional
Control
> Greek images and tales of Artemis and Demeter.
> Greek tale of Orpheus and Eurydice.
> Celtic tale of "Morgan Le Fay."
> Tales of the Mayan goddess Ix Chel.

QUALITY	DREAM STIMULANTS *Mythic Images, Tales, and Legends*
Faith	Biblical tale of David and Goliath. Hassidic tale "Magic Mirror of Rabbi Adam." "Tale of Snowdrop."
Family Insight	Shakespeare's *Romeo and Juliet.* "Tale of Tontlawald." Irish tale of "Half a Blanket." Greek tales of Demeter and Persephone. Celtic tale of "Cerridwen and Gwion."
Fertility	All tales of Mother Goddesses. Mayan tale of Ix Chel. Greek tales of Demeter. Greek tales of Aphrodite and Eros.
Forgiveness	Greek tales of Athene. Italian tale "Jump Into My Sack." Greek images and stories of Hephaestus and Zeus.
Foresight	Hassidic tale "Magic Mirror of Rabbi Adam." "Snow White and Rose Red."
Facility for Learning	French tale "Master and his Pupil." South African tale "Mbega the Kgego."
Generosity	Greek images and tales of Athene, Hades and Zeus. Italian tale "Jump Into My Sack."
Glory	Greek tales of Perseus and Hercules. Greek tales of Achilles.

| QUALITY | DREAM STIMULANTS
Mythic Images, Tales, and Legends |
|---|---|
| Glory
(continued) | African tale "The Great Mwindo Epic."
German tale "The Master Thief."
Kiowa tale "Passowee, the Buffalo Woman." |
| Higher
Understanding | Dicken's *A Christmas Carol.*
Chinese tale "Tseng and the Holy Man."
Apache tale of "Wild Pony." |
| Higher Calling | Egyptian tale "Promises of Three Sisters."
American Indian tales of Changing Woman.
Biblical tale (Old Testament) of Joseph.
Biblical tale (New Testament) of Mary and Joseph. |
| Healing | Greek images and tales of Aquarius.
Greek tales of Chiron and the Centaurs.
Greek tales of Artemis (especially for healing children.)
Celtic tales of Bridget.
Chinese tales of Kwan Yin. |
| Hidden Powers | Greek images and tales of Hecate, Circe and Medea.
Grimm's tale "The Tinder Box."
French tale "Master and His Pupil."
"Rumpelstiltskin."
African tale "Nana Miriam." |
| Honesty | Greek images and tales of Athene and Orion.
"Pinocchio." |
| Independence | Tales of the Greek Amazons.
Greek images and tales of Atlas, Hestia and Artemis. |

QUALITY	DREAM STIMULANTS *Mythic Images, Tales, Legends.*
Independence *(continued)*	West African tale of "Fire Children." Grimm's "The Tinder Box."
Intuition	Greek images and tales of Hecate, Circe and Artemis. African Bushmen tales of "Praying Mantis." Celtic tales of Cerridwen and Morgan Le Fay. Celtic tales of Merlin.
Initiative	Greek tales of Odysseus. Tales of King Arthur and the Round Table. English tale "Two Pickpockets." Images and tales of Ares, Artemis and Hecate.
Insight into Enemies/ Discord	Hassidic tale "Magic Mirror of Rabbi Adam." Celtic tales of Morgan Le Fay. English tales of Arthur and Merlin.
Knowledge of Occult	Greek images and tales of Hecate, Circe, Medea. Hassidic tale "Magic Mirror of Rabbi Adam." Grimm's "The Tinder Box." "Alladin and His Lamp." Celtic tales of Merlin and Morgan Le Fay. Egyptian images and tales of Isis. Celtic tales of Cerridwen. African tale "Nana Miriam." Sumerian images and tales of Lilith. East Indian images and tales of Kali.

QUALITY	DREAM STIMULANTS
	Mythic Images, Tales, Legends

Luck

Greek tale of Perseus.
Hungarian tale "Stroke of Luck."

Music

Greek images and tales of Apollo, Orpheus and Pan.
Greek images and tales of Silenus.

Nature Kingdom

East Indian goddess Sarasvati and Vac.
Greek tales and images of Artemis.
African Bushmen tales of "Praying Mantis."
American Indian tales of Changing Woman.

Optimism

Greek tales of Daedalus.
Greek images and tales of Fates.
Egyptian tale of "Promises of Three Sisters."
"The Sword and the Stone."

Organization and Planning

Greek tale of Prometheus.
South African tale "Mbega the Kgego."
English tales of Arthur and the Round Table.

Purity

Greek tales of Artemis and Orion.
Shakespeare's *Romeo and Juliet*.
"Snow White and Rose Red."

Patience

Egyptian tale "Promises of Three Sisters."
South African Tale "Mbega the Kego."

Relationships

Greek tale of Orpheus and Eurydice:
Shakespeare's *Romeo and Juliet*.
Japanese tale "The Ugly Son."
Chinese tale "The King's Favorite."

QUALITY	DREAM STIMULANTS *Mythic Images, Tales, Legends*
Resourcefulness and Versatility	Greek tale of Hercules outwitting Atlas. Grimm's tale "Old Woman in Forest." "Jason and the Argonauts." The Greek epic of Odysseus. The Celtic tale of Cerridwen and Gwien.
Secretiveness	Greek tale of Daedalus. Biblical story of birth and childhood of Moses. Egyptian tale "Promises of Three Sisters."
Spiritual Awareness	Greek tale of life and death of Orpheus. Greek images and tales of Hecate. Sumerian tale of Ishtar. Egyptian images and tales of Isis. Chinese tales of Kwan Yin. English tales of Merlin and his assistance of Arthur.
Spontaneity	German tale "Master Thief." German tales of "Tyll Ulenspiegel."

Index To Weaknesses

QUALITY	DREAM STIMULANTS *Mythic Images, Tales, Legends.*
Abused/ Abusive	Greek tale of Hippolytus. South African tale "Mbega the Kgego." Irish tale "Half a Blanket." German tale "Old Man and the Grandson."
Addictions	East Indian tale "Monkey and the Croco- dile."

Afraid to Act
   (Inability to see,
   choose, decide)
	Grimm's tale of "The Riddle."
	Greek tales of Hermes.
	Icelandic tale "Father of Eighteen Elves."

Aging	Greek images and tales of Kronos. Greek images and tales of Medusa. German tale "Old Man and the Grandson."
Aggression	"St. George and the Dragon." Greek tale of Hercules and the Lernean Hydra. Scandinavian tales of Loki.
Anger	Greek tales of the Furies. Norse tales of Loki.

241

	Hassidic tales of Lilith.
QUALITY	DREAM STIMULANTS
	Mythic Images, Tales, Legends.

Blocked Vision
Greek images and tales of Orion.
Greek images and tales of Polyphemus.
Japanese tale "The Ugly Son."

Carelessness
Greek images and tales of Helios and Hippolytus.
Grimm's tale "Boy Who Went Forth to Find What Fear Was"

Controlling
"Rumpelstiltskin."
Greek tale of Orestes and Clytemnestra.
"Cinderella."

Cruelty
Greek Tales of Sirens, punishment of Prometheus and Tantalus.
German tale "Old Man and Grandson."

Deceit and Dishonesty
"Rumpelstiltskin"
Central African tale "Ki and the Leopard."
Navajo tale "Coyote the Trickster."
German tale "Helping to Lie."
"Snow White and Rose Red."

Delusions
"Snow White and the Seven Dwarves."
Irish tale "Man Who Had No Stories."
Sudanese tale "Old Crone and Iblees the Devil."

Disbelief
"Peter and the Wolf."
English tale "Lazy Jack."
African tale "The Talking Skull."

Disrespect
Norse tales of Loki.
Greek images and tales of Hephaestus.
German tale "The Goose Girl."

QUALITY	DREAM STIMULANTS *Mythic Images, Tales, Legends*
Dogmatism (stubborness/ rigidity)	Greek tales of Zeus and Ganymede. Greek images and tales of Artemis. African tale "Mirimi Giants Who Ate People."
Egotism (false pride, pettiness)	Chinese tale "One Honest Man." "Snow White and the Seven Dwarves." "Cinderella." Grimm's tale of "Boy Who Went Forth to Find What Fear Was." Greek images and tales of Zeus.
Emotionalism	Mayan tales of Ix Chel. Greek images and tales of Achilles. "Rumpelstiltskin." East Indian tales of Kali.
Envy and Jealousy	"Cinderella." "Snow White and the Seven Dwarves." "Beauty and the Beast." Biblical tale of Joseph and the Coat of Many Colors.
Fear (general)	"Cinderella." Chinese tale of "Li Chi and the Serpent."
Fear of Death	Kalahari Bushmen tale "Moon and the Hare." Kalahari Bushmen tale of "Praying Mantis and the Creation of the Moon." All descent myths. Sumerian tale of Ishtar and the rescue of Tammuz. Italian tale "Jump into my Sack." Turkish tale "Youth Without Age and Life Without Death."

QUALITY	DREAM STIMULANTS *Mythic Images, Tales, Legends*
Fear of Death *(continued)*	African tale "Why There is Death in the World" or "The Tortoise and Dog Messengers of God."
Fear of Failure	"Cinderella." "Rip Van Winkle."
Fear of Future	"Shoemaker and the Elves." English tale "The Three Sillies." Japanese tale "The Ugly Son."
Forgetfulness	Chinese tale "The King's Favorite." Greek tales of the Sirens.
Gossip	Grimm's tale "Fisherman and his Wife." Greek tale of Actaeon.
Greed	Navajo tale of "Coyote the Trickster." Tibetan tale "Prayer that was Answered." Greek tale of King Midas.
Hypocrisy	Norse tale "Loki and the Golden Boar." "Night Journey of Muhammed."
Impulsiveness	Greek tale of "Pandora's Box."
Insensitivity	*Through the Looking Glass.* "Beauty and the Beast." Greek tale of Prometheus and the stealing of Fire. Greek tale of the abduction of Persephone by Pinto.

QUALITY	DREAM STIMULANTS *Mythic Images Tales, Legends.*
Irresponsibility	Greek tale of Phoebus Apollo. "Snow White and Rose Red." Greek tales of Pan and Dionysus.
Lack of Com- munication & expression	Kiowa tale "Pasowee, the Buffalo Woman." "Rip Van Winkle." Greek images and tales of Hermes. Egyptian tales of Thoth.
Lack of Com- passion	"Sleeping Beauty." Greek images and tales of Orpheus. Greek images and tales of Asclepius.
Lack of Discipline	Greek tales of Pan. Greek tale of Pandora's Box Navajo tale of "Coyote the Trickster."
Lack of Love	German tale "The Goose Girl." Mayan tales of Ix Chel. Greek tales of Artemis
Laziness (Idleness)	English tale "Lazy Jack." African tale "Nyangondhu the Fisherman."
Loneliness	"Cinderella." Kiowa tale of "Pasowee, the Buffalo Woman." Greek tale of Artemis and Endymion. Egyptian tales of Isis. Greek tales of Demeter and Ceres. "Rapunzel"
Lust	Greek images and tales of Aphrodite, Dionysus, and Eros. East Indian tales of Kali. Greek tales of Dionysus and the Bacchae.

QUALITY	DREAM STIMULANTS *Mythic Images Tales, Legends.*
Manipulation	German tale "The Goose Girl." Japanese tale "The Ugly Son." Greek epics of Perseus and Theseus.
Martyrdom	Greek tale of Demeter and Persephone. Egyptian tale of Osiris. Greek tale of the death of Orpheus.
Narrowminded	Greek tale of Polyphemus. African tale "Nyangondhu the Fisherman."
Insensitivity	*Through the Looking Glass.* "Beauty and the Beast." Greek tale of Prometheus and the stealing of Fire. Greek tale of the abduction of Persephone by Pinto.
Obsessions	Greek tale of Narcissus. Greek tale of King Midas. Swedish tale "The Swan Maiden."
Overindulgence	Greek images and tales of Achilles. Greek tales of Pan. Greek tale of King Midas.
Resentment	"Beauty and the Beast." Greek tale of King Minos. Greek images and tale of Ariadne.
Selfishness	Shakespeare's *Romeo and Juliet.* Tale of Tontlawald.
Submission	"Rapunzel." German tale "The Goose Girl."

QUALITY	DREAM STIMULANTS *Mythic Images Tales, Legends.*
Superstition	Japanese tale "The Ugly Son."
Thoughtlessness	Greek tale of Theseus. "The Shoemaker and the Elves." Grimm's tale "Seven Ravens."
Unfaithfulness	Greek tales of Aphrodite. Greek images and tales of King Minos.
Unforgiving	Norse tales of Loki. Greek tale "Judgment of Themis." Biblical tale of Elijah and the Prophets of Baal. Tales of Pluto and Hades.
Vulnerability	Greek tales of Achilles. Greek images and tales of Adonis and Medusa. Central African tale "Ki and the Leopard."
Weak-willed	Greek tale of Odysseus and the Sirens. Greek tale of Europa. Greek tale of King Minos. South African tale "Mbega the Kgego." Biblical story of the "Garden of Eden."

Select Bibliography

1. MYTHS

Abrahams, Roger. *African Folktales*. New York: Pantheon Books, 1983.

Bauman, Hans. *The Stolen Fire*. New York: Pantheon Books, 1974.

Bolen, Jean Shinoda. *Goddesses in Everywoman*. New York: Harper and Row, 1984.

Bullfinch, Thomas. *The Age of Fable*. New York: Grolier Inc., 1973.

Burt, Kathleen. *Archetypes of the Zodiac*. St. Paul: Llewellyn, 1988.

Campbell, Joseph. *Hero with a Thousand Faces*. Princeton: Princeton University Press, 1973.

———. *Myths, Dreams and Religion*. Dallas: Spring Pub. 1970.

———. *The Power of Myth*. New York: Doubleday, 1988.

———. *The Masks of God 4: Creative Mythology*. New York: Viking, 1968.

———. *Creative Mythology*. New York: Viking, 1968.

Cooper, J. C. *Symbolism*. Northamptonshire: Aquarian Press, 1984.

Courtlander, Harold. *Heart of Ngoni*. New York: Crown Publishers, 1982.

Feenstein, David; and Krippner, Stanley. *Personal Mythology*. Los Angeles: Jeremy P. Tarcher, 1988.

Frazer, J. G. *The Golden Bough*. London: MacMillan, 1922.

————. *Folklore in the Old Testament*. New York: Avenel Books, 1923.

Gettings, Fred. *Secret Symbolism in Occult Art*. New York: Harmony Books, 1987.

Gooch, Stan. *Guardians of the Ancient Wisdom*. London: Wildewood House, 1979.

Gordon, Greg and Randall, Neal. *Monsters of Myth and Legend*. Chicago: Mayfair Games, 1984.

Graham, Lloyd M. *Deceptions and Myths of the Bible*. New York: Bell Publishers, 1975.

Hamilton, Edith. *Mythology*. New York: Mentor Books, 1942.

Harding, M. Esther. *Woman's Mysteries*. New York: Harper and Row, 1971.

Helfman, Elizabeth. *Bushmen and Their Stories*. New York: Seabury Press, 1971.

Henderson, Joseph L., and Oakes, Maude. *The Wisdom of the Serpent*. New York: George Braziller, 1963.

Hildebrandt, Greg. *Favorite Fairy Tales*. New York: Simon and Schuster, 1984.

Jung, C. J. *Archetypes and the Collective Unconscious*. New York: Pantheon Books, 1959.

————. *Symbols of Transformation*. Princeton: University Press, 1956.

———. *Collective Works: Symbolic Life*. Vol. 18. Princeton: Princeton University Press, 1976.

———. *Psychology and Alchemy*. Princeton: Princeton University Press, 1968.

Jung, Emma, and Von Franz, Marie Louise. *The Grail Legend*. Boston: Sigo Press, 1980.

Knight, Gareth. *The Secret Tradition in Arthurian Legend*. Northhamptonshire: Aquarian Press, 1983.

———. *Treasure House of Images*. New York: Destiny Books, 1986.

Knowles, Sir James. *King Arthur and His Knights*. New York: Longmeadow Press, 1986.

Lehner, Ernst. *Symbols, Signs and Signets*. New York: Dover Publications, 1950.

Lemesurier, Peter. *The Healing of the Gods*. Dorset: Element Books, 1988.

Levin, Meyer. *Classic Hassidic Tales*. New York: Dorset Press, 1959.

Mitchnik, Helen. *Egyptian and Sudanese Folktales*. New York: Oxford University Press, 1978.

Murray, Alexander. *Who's Who in Mythology*. New York: Crescent Books, 1988.

Nunn, Jessie Alford. *African Folk Tales*. New York: Funk and Wag nalls, 1969.

Pearson, Carol. *The Hero Within*. San Francisco: Harper and Row, 1986.

Robinson, Adjai. *Singing Tales of Africa*. New York: Charles Scribner's Sons, 1974.

Rugoff, Milton. *World Folk Tales*. New York: Viking Press, 1969.

Rutherford, Ward. *The Druids*. Northhamptonshire: Aquarian Press, 1978.

Shorter, Alan W. *The Egyptian Gods*. Hollywood: Newcastle Publishing, 1985.

Shuttle, Penelope and Redgrove, Peter. *The Wise Wound*. London: Gollancz, 1978.

Steiner, Rudolph. *Egyptian Myths and Mysteries*. London: Percy Lund and Co., 1933.

Stone, Merlin. *Ancient Mirrors of Womanhood*. Boston: Beacon Press, 1979.

Ward, J. and Kuntz, R. *Legends and Lore*. Lake Geneva: TSR, Inc., 1984.

Yolen, Jane. *Favorite Folktales from Around the World*. New York: Pantheon Books, 1986.

Zipcs, Jack. *The Complete Fairy Tales of Brothers Grimm*. New York: Bantam, 1987.

2. DREAMS AND ALTERED STATES

Boushala, Jo-Jean, and Reidel-Geubtner, Virginia. *The Dream Dictionary*. New York: Pilgrim Press, 1983.

Bro, Harmon H. *Edgar Cayce on Dreams*. New York: Warner Paperbacks, 1968.

Cayce, Hugh Lynn. Dreams: *Language of the Unconscious*. Virginia: A.R.E. Press, 1971.

Court, Simon. *Meditator's Manual*. Northhamptonshire: Aquarian Press, 1984.

Hills, Christopher. *Creative Imagination*. Boulder Creek: University of Trees Press, 1986.

Kaplan-Williams, Strephon. *Jungian-Senoi Dreamwork Manual*. Berkeley: Journey Press, 1985.

Savary, Louis and Berne, Patricia H.; and Kaplan-Williams, Strephon. *Dreams and Spiritual Growth*. New York: Paulist Press, 1984.

Sechrist, Elsie. *Dreams: Your Magic Mirror*. New York: Warner Paperback, 1974.

Thurston, Mark A. *How to Interpret Your Dreams*. Virginia Beach: A.R.E. Press, 1978.

Ullman, Monlague and Zimmerman, Nan. *Working With Dreams*. Los Angeles: Jeremy P. Tarcher, 1979.

West, Katherine Lee. *Neptune's Plummet*. Portland: Amata Graphics, 1977.

3. HERBS, FLOWERS, SCENTS AND STONES

Anon. *Ancient Book of Formulas*. Dallas: Dorene Publishing,   1967.

Adams, George and Whicher, Olive. *The Plant Between Sun and Earth*. London: Steiner Press, 1980.

Beyerl, Paul. *Master Book of Herbalism*. Custer: Phoenix Publishing Co., 1984.

Chancellor, Philip M. *Bach Flower Remedies*. New Canaan: Keats Publishing, 1971.

Cunningham, Scott. *Magical Herbalism*. St. Paul: Llewellyn, 1983.

———. *Cunningham's Encyclopedia of Magical Herbs*. St. Paul: Llewellyn, 1985.

De Claremont, Lewis. *Legends of Incense, Herbs and Oil Magic*. Texas: Dorene Publishing, 1966.

Fernie, William. *Occult and Curative Powers of Precious Stones*. New York: Harper & Row, 1973.

Fettner, Ann Tucker. *Potpourri, Incense and Other Fragrant Concoctions*. New York: Workman Publishing, 1977.

F.E.S. Society. Flower Essence Repertory. Nevada City: Flower Essence Society Publications, 1987.

Gruenberg, Louise. *Potpourri*. Iowa: Frontier Cooperative Herbs, 1984.

Gurudas. *Flower Essences*. Albuquerque: Brotherhood of Life, Inc., 1983.

———. *Gem Elixirs and Vocational Healing*. Boulder: Cassandra Press, 1985.

Harford, Virginia, and Milewski, John. *The Crystal Sourcebook*. Sedona: Mystic Crystal Publications, 1987.

Jackson, Judith. *The Spiritual Touch*. New York: Henry Holt and Comp. 1986.

Jensen, Bernard. *The Chemistry of Man*. California: Jensen Publications, 1983.

Junius, Manfred. *Practical Handbook of Plant Alchemy*. New York: Inner Traditions International, 1985.

Lautie, Raymond and Passebecq, Andre. *Aromatherapy*. Northhamptonshire: Thorsons Publishing, 1985.

Mella, Dorothee. *Stone Power*. New York: Warner Books, 1986.

Price, Shirley. *Practical Aromatherapy*. Northhamptonshire: Thorsons Publishing, 1983.

Raphael, Katrina. *Crystal Enlightenment*. New York: Aurora Press, 1985.

Riva, Anna. *Golden Secrets of Mystic Oils*. Toluca Lake: International Imports, 1978.

Scheffer, Mechthild. *Bach Flower Therapy*. Northhamptonshire: Thorsons Publishing, 1986.

Sturzaker, James. *Aromatics in Ritual and Therapeutics*. London: Metatron Publishing, 1979.

Thompkins, Peter, and Bird, Christopher. *The Secret Life of Plants*. New York: Harper and Row, 1973.

Tisserand, Maggie. *Aromatherapy for Women*. New York: Thorsens, 1985.

Vinci, Leo. *Incense: Its Spiritual Significance, Use & Preparation*. Northhamptonshire: Aquarian Press, 1980.

4. SHAMANISM

Achterberg, Jeanne. *Imagery in Healing: Shamanism In Modern Medicine*. Boston: Shambhala, 1985.

Andrews, Lynn. *Medicine Woman*. San Francisco: Harper and Row, 1981.

Castenada, Carlos. *The Teachings of Don Juan*. New York: Ballantine, 1968.

Freud, Sigmund. *Totem and Taboo*. New York: Random House, 1946.

Harner, Michael. *The Way of the Shaman*. San Francisco: Harper and Row, 1980.

Hausman, Gerald. *Meditations with Animals*. Sante Fe: Bear and Company, 1986.

Larsen, Stephen. *The Shaman's Doorway*. New York: Harper and Row, 1976.

Nicholson, Shirley. *Shamanism*. Wheaton: Theosophical Publishing, 1987.

Nollman, Jim. *Animal Dreaming*. New York: Bantam, 1986.
Stevens, Jose and Stevens, Lena. *Secrets of Shamanism*. New York: Avon Books, 1988.

Wolfe, Amber. *In the Shadow of the Shaman*. St. Paul: Llewellyn, 1988.

5. TOTEMS, TALISMANS AND MANDALAS

Anon. *Sixth And Seventh Books of Moses*. Texas: Dorene Publishing,

Anon. *Sixth And Seventh Books of Moses*. California: Egyptian Publishing, 1972.

Arguelles, Jose and Miriam. *Mandala*. Boulder: Shambhala, 1972.

Buckland, Raymond. *Practical Color Magick*. St. Paul: Llewellyn, 1984.

Budge, E.A. Wallis. *Amulets and Superstitions*. New York: Dover Publication, 1978.

Douglas, Nik and Slinger, Penny. *Sexual Secrets*. New York: Destiny Books, 1979.

Fischle, Willy H. *The Way to the Centre*. London: Robinson and Watkins Ltd., 1982.

Johari, Harish. *Tools for Tantra*. New York: Destiny Books, 1986.

Khanna, Madhu. *Yantra*. London: Thames and Hudson, 1976.

Lawlor, Robert. *Sacred Geometry*. New York: Crossroads, 1982.

Mathers, S.L. MacGregor. *The Book of the Sacred Magic of Abramelin The Mage*. New York: Dover Publications, 1975.

———. *The Key of Solomon The King*. New York: Samuel Weiser, Inc., 1976.

Pelton, Robert W. *Voodoo Charms and Talismans*. New York: Popular Library, 1973.

Regardie, Israel. *How to Make and Use Talismans*. Northhampton-shire: Aquarian Press, 1981.

———. *The Golden Dawn*. St. Paul: Llewellyn, 1982.

———. *The Complete Golden Dawn System of Magic*. Phoenix: Falcon Press, 1984.

Regaud, Milo. *The Secrets of Voodoo*. New York: Pocket Books, 1971.

Sun Bear and Wabun. *The Medicine Wheel*. Englewood Cliffs: Prentice-Hall Inc., 1980.

Vandenbroeck, Andre. *Philosophical Geometry*. New York: Inner Traditions International, 1987.

STAY IN TOUCH

On the following pages you will find listed, with their current prices, some of the books and tapes now available on related subjects. Your book dealer stocks most of these, and will stock new titles in the Llewellyn series as they become available. We urge your patronage.

However, to obtain our full catalog, to keep informed of new titles as they are released and to benefit from informative articles and helpful news, you are invited to write for our bi-monthly news magazine/catalog. A sample copy is free, and it will continue coming to you at no cost as long as you are an active mail customer. Or you may keep it coming for a full year with a donation of just $5.00 in U.S.A. ($20.00 overseas, first class mail). Many bookstores also have *The Llewellyn New Times* available to their customers. Ask for it.

Stay in touch! In *The Llewellyn New Times'* pages you will find news and reviews of new books, tapes and services, announcements of meetiongs and seminars, articles helpful to our readers, news of authors, advertising of products and services, special money-making opportunities, and much more.

The Llewellyn New Times
P.O. Box 64383-Dept. 017, St. Paul, MN 55164-0383, U.S.A.

• • •

TO ORDER BOOKS AND TAPES

If your book dealer does not have the books and tapes described on the following pages readily available, you may order them direct from the publisher by sending full price in U.S. funds, plus $1.50 for postage and handling for orders *under* $10.00; $3.00 for orders *over* $10.00. There are no postage and handling charges for orders over $50. UPS Delivery: We ship UPS whenever possible. Delivery guaranteed. Provide your street address as UPS does not deliver to P.O. Boxes. UPS to Canada requires a $50 minimum order. Allow 4–6 weeks for delivery. Orders outside the U.S.A. and Canada: Airmail—add retail price of book; add $5 for each non-book item (tapes, etc.); add $1 per item for surface mail.

FOR GROUP STUDY AND PURCHASE

Because there is a great deal of interest in group discussion and study of the subject matter of this book, we feel that we should encourage the adoption and use of this particular book by such groups by offering a special "quantity" price to group leaders or "agents."

Our Special Quantity Price for a minimum order of five copies of *DREAM ALCHEMY* is $38.85 cash-with-order. This price includes postage and handling within the United States. Minnesota residents must add 6% sales tax. For additional quantities, please order in multiples of five. For Canadian and foreign orders, add postage and handling charges as above. Credit card (VISA, Master Card, American Express) orders are accepted. Charge card orders only may be phoned free ($15.00 minimum order) within the U.S.A. or Canada by dialing 1-800-THE-MOON. Customer service calls dial 1-612-291-1970. Mail Orders to:

LLEWELLYN PUBLICATIONS
P.O. Box 64383-Dept. 017 / St. Paul, MN 55164-0383, U.S.A.

HOW TO SEE AND READ THE AURA
by Ted Andrews

Everyone has an aura, the three-dimensional, shape- and color-changing energy field that surrounds all matter. And anyone can learn to see and experience the aura more effectively. There is nothing magical about the process. It simply involves a little understanding, time, practice and perseverance.

Do some people make you feel drained? Do you find some rooms more comfortable and enjoyable to be in? Have you ever been able to sense the presence of other people before you actually heard or saw them? If so, you have experienced another person's aura. In this easy-to-read and practical manual, you receive a variety of exercises to practice alone and with partners to build your skills in aura reading and interpretation. Also, you will learn to balance your aura each day to keep it vibrant and strong so others cannot drain your vital force.

Learning to see the aura not only breaks down old barriers—it also increases sensitivity. As we develop the ability to see and feel the more subtle aspects of life, our intuition unfolds and increases, and the childlike joy and wonder of life returns.

0-87542-013-3, 160 pgs., mass market, illus., **$3.95**

THE MAGICAL NAME
by Ted Andrews

Our name makes a direct link to our soul. It is an "energy" signature that can reveal the soul's potentials, abilities and karma. It is our unique talisman of power. Many upon the spiritual path look for a "magical name" that will trigger a specific play of energies in his or her life. *The Magical Name* explores a variety of techniques for tapping into the esoteric significance of the birth name and for assuming a new, more "magical" name.

This book also demonstrates how we can use the ancient names from mythology to stimulate specific energies in our life and open ourselves to new opportunities. It demonstrates how to use the names of plants, trees and flowers to attune to the archetypal forces of nature. It provides techniques for awakening and empowering the human energy field through working with one's name.

The Magical Name fills a gap in Western magic, which has been deficient in exploring the magic of mantras, sounds and names. It has been said that to hear the angels sing, you must first hear the song within your own heart. It is this song that is echoed within your name!

0-87542-014-1, 360 pgs., 6 x 9, illus., softcover **$12.95**

SIMPLIFIED MAGIC
by Ted Andrews

In every person the qualities essential for accelerating his or her growth and spiritual evolution are innate, but even those who recognize such potentials need an effective means of releasing them. The ancient and mystical Qabala is that means.

A person does not need to become a dedicated Qabalist in order to acquire benefits from the Qabala. *Simplified Magic* offers a simple understanding of what the Qabala is and how it operates. It provides practical methods and techniques so that the energies and forces within the system and within ourselves can be experienced in a manner that enhances growth and releases our greater potential. *A reader knowing absolutely nothing about the Qabala could apply the methods in this book with noticeable success!*

The Qabala is more than just some theory for ceremonial magicians. It is a system for personal attainment and magic that anyone can learn and put to use in his or her life. The secret is that the main glyph of the Qabala, the Tree of Life, is *within* you. The Tree of Life is a map to the levels of consciousness, power and magic that are within. By learning the Qabala you will be able to tap into these levels and bring peace, healing, power, love, light and magic into your life.

0-87542-015-X, 210 pgs., illus., softcover $3.95

IMAGICK: THE MAGICK OF IMAGES, PATHS & DANCE
by Ted Andrews

The Qabala is rich in spiritual, mystical and magickal symbols. These symbols are like physical tools, and when you learn to use them correctly, you can construct a bridge to reach the energy of other planes. The secret lies in merging the outer world with inner energies, creating a flow that augments and enhances all aspects of life.

Imagick explains effective techniques of bridging the outer and inner worlds through visualization, gesture, and dance. It is a synthesis of yoga, sacred dance and Qabalistic magick that can enhance creativity, personal power, and mental and physical fitness.

This is one of the most personal magickal books ever published, one that goes far beyond the "canned" advice other books on Pathworking give you. You will learn how the energies reflected in such things as color vibration, names, letters, tarot associations and astrological relationships radiate from the "temple" of each sephiroth.

0-87542-016-8, 6 x 9, 312 pgs., illus. $12.95

IN THE SHADOW OF THE SHAMAN
by Amber Wolfe

Presented in what the author calls a "cookbook shamanism" style, this book shares recipes, ingredients, and methods of preparation for experiencing some very ancient wisdoms—wisdoms of Native American and Wiccan traditions, as well as contributions from other philosophies of Nature, as they are used in the shamanic way. Wolfe encourages us to feel confident and free to use her methods to cook up something new, completely on our own. This blending of ancient formulas and personal methods represents what Ms. Wolfe calls *Aquarian Shamanism.*

In the Shadow of the Shaman is designed to communicate in the most practical, direct ways possible, so that the wisdom and the energy may be shared for the benefits of all. Whatever your system or tradition, you will find this to be a valuable book, a resource, a friend, a gentle guide and support on your journey. Dancing in the shadow of the shaman, you will find new dimensions of Spirit.

0-87542-888-6, 384 pgs., 6 x 9, illus., softcover $12.95

YEAR OF MOONS, SEASON OF TREES
by Pattalee Glass-Koentop

Many people are drawn to Wicca, or the Craft, but do not have teachers, covens or like-minded people around to show them how the religion is practiced. *Year of Moons, Season of Trees* serves as that teacher and as a sourcebook for material and background, providing a full Book of Shadows for the isolated Pagan or Wiccan.

Most of Witchcraft in America comes or has been influenced by that of the British Isles. The Druidic sacred trees native to that culture are the focus of this book, with historical background, tree of information, and symbolism in compact reference form. A meditation or ritual experience to enhance the understanding of the Trees and what they represent on inner planes or spiritual levels is also included.

The essence, imagery and mythology behind the Seasons is vividly portrayed and felt in the Seasonal Tree Rites, giving the reader layers of subtle meanings which will continue to be experienced and understood long after the rite is completed.

0-87542-269-1, 7 x 10, 240 pgs. illus., softbound $14.95

WHAT YOUR DREAMS CAN TEACH YOU
by Alex Lukeman

Dreams are honest and do not llie. They have much to teach us, but the lessons are often difficult to understand. Confusion comes not from the dream but from the outer mind's attempt to understand it.

What Your Dreams Can Teach You is a workbook of self-discovery, with a systematic and proven approach to the understanding of dreams. It does *not* contain lists of meanings for dream symbols. Only you, the dreamer, can discover what the images in your dreams mean for you. The book *does* contain step-by-step information which can lead you to success with your dreams, success that will bear fruit in your waking hours. Learn to tap into the aspect of yourself that truly knows how to interpret dreams, the inner energy of undertstanding called the "Dreamer Within." This aspect of your consciousness will lead you to an accurate understanding of your dreams and even assist you with interpreting dreams of others.

0-87542-475-9, 288 pgs., 6 x 9, illus.   **$12.95**

HOW TO DREAM YOUR LUCKY LOTTO NUMBERS
by Raoul Maltagliati

Until now, there has been no scientific way to predict lotto numbers . . . they come up by chance. But overnight, you may find them through a trip into the dimension of the collective unconscious, where "time" and "chance," as we know them, do not exist. In *How to Dream Your Lucky Lotto Numbers*, you will be introduced to an actual dream interpreter, who will guide you in picking your lucky lotto numbers! Author Raoul Maltagliati explains such things as:

- Why we dream.
- How to isolate the key points in a dream that point out your lotto numbers.
- How to find the numberic equivalents of dream subjects.
- How to keep your lotto numbers within the parameters of your lottery (between 1 and 56, for example).
- How to adjust for the moon's influence on your dreams.
- The importance of the day and the month during which you have your lotto dreams.

An extensive dream dictionary helps you discover what numbers you should pick based on your most recent dreams.

0-87542-483-X, 112 pgs., mass market   **$3.95**

THE BOOK OF GODDESSES & HEROINES
by Patrician Monaghan

The Book of Goddesses & Heroines is an historical landmark, a must for everyone interested in Goddesses and Goddess worship. It is not an effort to trivialize the beliefs of matriarchal cultures. It is not a collection of Goddess descriptions penned by biased male historians throughout the ages. It is the complete, non-biased account of Goddesses of every cultural and geographic area, including African, Japanese, Korean, Persian, Australian, Pacific, Latin American, British, Irish, Scottish, Welsh, Chinese, Greek, Icelandic, Italian, Finnish, German, Scandinavian, Indian, Tibetan, Mesopotamian, North American, Semitic and Slavic Goddesses!

Unlike some of the male historians before her, Patricia Monaghan eliminates as much bias as possible from her Goddess stories. Envisioning herself as a woman who might have revered each of these Goddesses, she has done away with language that referred to the deities in relation to their male counterparts, as well as with culturally relative terms such as "married" or "fertility cult." The beliefs of the cultures and the attributes of the Goddesses have been left intact.

Plus, this book has a new, complete index. If you are more concerned about finding a Goddess of war than you are a Goddess of a given country, this index will lead you to the right page. This is especially useful for anyone seeking to do Goddess rituals. Your work will be twice as efficient and effective with this detailed and easy-to-use book.

0-87542-573-9, 6 × 9, 421 pgs., illus.　　　　　　　　　　　**$17.95**

DREAMS & WHAT THEY MEAN TO YOU
by Migene Gonzalez Wippler

Everyone dreams. Yet dreams are rarely taken seriously—they seem to be only a bizarre series of amusing or disturbing images that the mind creates for no particular purpose. Yet dreams, through a language of their own, contain essential information about ourselves which, if properly analyzed and understood, can change our lives. In this fascinating and well-written book, the author gives you all of the information needed to begin interpreting—even creating—your own dreams.

Dreams and What They Mean To You begins by exploring the nature of the human mind and consciousness, then discusses the results of the most recent scientific research on sleep and dreams. The author analyzes different types of dreams—telepathic, nightmares, sexual and prophetic. In addition, there is an extensive Dream Dictionary which lists the meanings for a wide variety of dream images.

Most importantly, Gonzalez-Wippler tells you how to practice creative dreaming—consciously controlling dreams as you sleep. Once a person learns to control their dreams, their horizons will expand and their chances of success will increase a hundredfold!

0-87542-288-8, 240 pgs., mass market　　　　　　　　　　　**$3.95**

The Rites of Assent